C0-BKF-288

WITHDRAWN

THE LANGUAGE AND THE LAW OF GOD

SOUTH FLORIDA STUDIES IN THE HISTORY OF JUDAISM

Edited by
Jacob Neusner
Bruce D. Chilton, Darrell J. Fasching, William Scott Green,
Sara Mandell, James F. Strange

Studies in Philo of Alexandria and Mediterranean Antiquity
EDITED BY
Robert Berchman, Dowling College, Oakdale, NY
Francesca Calabi, Università di Pavia, Pavia, Italy

EDITORIAL BOARD
Mireille Hadas-Lebel, La Sorbonne, Paris, France
Carlos Lévy, Université de Paris XII, Créteil, France
Tessa Rajak, University of Reading, United Kingdom
Esther Starobinsky-Safran, Université de Genève, Switzerland

The South Florida Studies in Philo of Alexandria and Mediterranean
Antiquity series accepts monographs on Philo. Proposals for books to be
published in the series should be sent to Robert Berchman, Department of
Philosophy, Dowling College, Oakdale, NY 11794, U.S.A., or to
Francesca Calabi, via Marchiondi 7, 20122 Milano, Italy

Number 188
THE LANGUAGE AND THE LAW OF GOD
Intrepretation and Politics in Philo of Alexandria
by
Francesca Calabi

THE LANGUAGE AND THE LAW OF GOD

Interpretation and Politics in Philo of Alexandria

by

Francesca Calabi

Scholars Press
Atlanta, Georgia

HIEBERT LIBRARY
FRESNO PACIFIC UNIV.-M. B. SEMINARY
FRESNO, CA 93702

THE LANGUAGE AND THE LAW OF GOD
Interpretation and Politics in Philo of Alexandria

by
Francesca Calabi

First published in Italian as *Linguaggio e legge di Dio. Interpretazione e politica in Filone di Alessandria,* Ferrara, Corso Editore (1998). Translated by Michael Leone.

Copyright ©1998 by the University of South Florida

All rights reserved. No part of this work may be reproduced or transmitted in any form or by any means, electronic or mechanical, including photocopying and recording, or by means of any information storage or retrieval system, except as may be expressly permitted by the 1976 Copyright Act or in writing from the publisher. Requests for permission should be addressed in writing to the Rights and Permissions Office, Scholars Press, P.O. Box 15399, Atlanta, GA 30333-0399, USA.

Publication of this book was made possible by a grant from the Tisch Family Foundation, New York City. The University of South Florida acknowledges with thanks this important support for its scholarly projects.

Library of Congress Cataloging in Publication Data
Calabi, Francesca, 1948–
    The language and the law of God : interpretation and politics in Philo of Alexandria / by Francesca Calabi.
        p.   cm. — (South Florida studies in the history of Judaism ; no. 188. studies in Philo of Alexandria and Mediterranean Antiquity subseries)
    Includes bibliographical references and indexes.
    ISBN 0-7885-0498-3 (alk. paper)
    1. Philo, of Alexandria. I. Title. II. Series: South Florida studies in the history of Judaism ; 188. III. Series: South Florida studies in the history of Judaism. Studies in Philo of Alexandria and Mediterranean antiquity subseries.
B689.Z7C27   1998
181'.06—dc21   98-30808
                                      CIP

Printed in the United States of America
on acid-free paper

To Gianni and Daniele

CONTENTS

ACKNOWLEDGMENTS

I wish to thank Mario Vegetti for having followed the various phases of my work and Giuseppe Laras for his precious teaching and unstinting advise.

I also wish to thank Piero Donini, Roberto Radice, David T. Runia for having been so willing to discuss and to help me to better understand various aspects of Philo's work.

I am particularly grateful to Jacob Neusner for wanting to publish the English version of this essay, and to Tommaso La Rocca for having encouraged publication of the original Italian version.

ABBREVIATIONS OF PHILONIC WORKS

Abr.	*De Abrahamo*
Aet.	*De Aeternitate Mundi*
Agr.	*De Agricultura*
Alex.	*Alexander*
An.	*De Animalibus*
Cher.	*De Cherubin*
Conf.	*De Confusione Linguarum*
Congr.	*De Congressu Eruditionis Gratia*
Contempl.	*De Vita Contemplativa*
Decal.	*De Decalogo*
Det.	*Quod Deterius Potiori Insidiari solet*
Deus	*Quod Deus sit Immutabilis*
Ebr.	*De Ebrietate*
Flacc.	*In Flaccum*
Fug.	*De Fuga et Inventione*
Gig.	*De Gigantibus*
Her.	*Quis Rerum Divinarum Heres sit*
Hypoth.	*Hypothethica (Apologia pro Iudaeis)*
Ios.	*De Iosepho*
Leg.	*Legatio ad Caium*
Leg.All.I,II,III	*Legum Allegoriae, I, II, III*
Migr.	*De Migratione Abrahami*
Mos.I,II	*De Vita Mosis I, II*
Mut.	*De Mutatione Nominum*
Opif.	*De Opificio Mundi*
Plant.	*De Plantatione*
Poster.	*De Posteritate Caini*
Praem.	*De Praemiis et Poenis. De Exsecrationibus*
Prob.	*Quod Omnis Probus Liber sit*
Prov.	*De Providentia*
Q.G.	*Quaestiones et solutiones in Genesim*
Q.E.	*Quaestiones et solutiones in Exodum*
Sacrif.	*De Sacrificiis*
Sobr.	*De Sobrietate*
Somn.I,II	*De Somniis I,II*
Spec.Leg.I,II	*De Specialibus Legibus I,II*
Virt.	*De Virtutibus*

INTRODUCTION

Philo, a Jewish philosopher who lived in Alexandria of Egypt at the end of the I century B. C. and the beginning of the I century A. D., is deeply imbued with the predominant Hellenistic culture of his day. His mother tongue is Greek, and his philosophical reference points the theorizations of the Greek thinkers. However, his principal and constant point of reference is the Hebrew tradition with which he identifies completely; and the text from which he draws, and which for Philo represents both truth and authority, is the *Bible*.

His work is exegetic, consisting in interpreting and explaining the Holy Book given by God to Moses on Mount Sinai. It is a text the meaning of which is not always immediately evident, and the hidden meanings of which are to be constantly probed and clarified with the awareness that man can never grasp their full understanding. This however does not imply that the search for truth is useless, as it nevertheless constitutes a way to approach the truth, to grasp the word of God, and to listen to and apply it. Hence, the importance of interpreting, translating the language of God into human language, understanding God's dictum, and reading the reality enclosed in the word. The *Bible*, which is the law of God, constitutes a representation of what is real, as it is through the word that God created the world. Therefore, to interpret the *Bible* means to grasp the divine will and, at the same time, achieve the highest form of knowledge available to man. But, if in the text written by Moses every single letter is basic to the expression of reality and cannot be modified, what is the relation between the Hebrew text, the Greek text utilised by Philo, and reality? Has the translation the same sacred character and authority as the original? And can both texts equally constitute a valid basis for interpretation? For Philo even the Greek *Bible* means reality; it too contains the truth. Hence, the need to examine what the author means by interpretation, how it relates to the translation, and, lastly, how interpretation can also signify a reading of the text in terms of its practical application.

As interpreter of divine laws, Moses is not only he who wrote the *Bible*, in direct and constant contact with God, but also he who brought the text to man, he who both explained and applied it. Moreover, the *Torah* is not simply the text that contains the knowledge of Israel; it is, at the same time, God's law, order of the cosmos, the model which God followed when creating the world; the very design and structure of reality. One is the law: law of God, order of creation; but also law for man, who in it will find norms of behaviour. Hence, the correlation between biblical text and human laws, between general order and special norms. Even in those situations in which men fail to follow the law, abandon or transgress it, the Law continues to constitute a point of reference, a focus towards which all human actions should bend. Of course, not all rulers conform to divine laws; nations in fact have often autonomously equipped themselves with norms which are quite foreign, when indeed not contrary, to the Law of God. Evil is widely present in the world. But if the Law pervades of itself all reality; if nature itself follows such a Law, how are special laws to be related to the universal cosmic law? And, if God conceived of universal harmony, how is it that evil came into the world? Is it possible to hypothesise a sort of double level of meaning? On one hand, one relative to an atemporal order, a paradigm related to cosmic order and harmony, in terms of human finiteness, and, on the other, one related to human social arrangements in terms of their specificity? Accordingly, these two levels would proceed in parallel fashion without necessarily intersecting, in as much as their two perspectives are different.

Having posited the premises of an approach to the general order and harmony, and to the forms of disorder and imbalance in the world, it is a matter of seeing how they fit within human societies.

The first two chapters of this essay will examine the relation between interpretation of the law and its application, whereas the third focuses on the type of exegesis conducted by Philo, on its hermeneutic principles, and on the interpretative modes which are also found in the Greek commentaries and/or in Rabbinical literature.

CHAPTER ONE

THE LANGUAGE OF GOD, THE LANGUAGE OF MEN

1.1 Moses, legislator and interpreter of the divine Laws

In *De Vita Mosis* I.1, Moses is called *nomothetes* and *hermeneus nomon ieron*, legislator and interpreter of sacred laws. A comparison with the legislators of other nations, while evidencing the excellence of Mosaic laws and their diffusion throughout the land, also seems to attribute to Moses a legislative role similar to that of a Solon, a Lycurgus, a Carondas, and generally to that of other legislators, be they legendary or otherwise. Such a comparison, that is, seems to shift the focus of discussion to Greek theorizations on the origin of constitutions, the source of the law, on the relation between natural law and conventional norms. However, Moses's characterization as *hermeneus nomon ieron* immediately places our analysis in a different light and elevates Mosaic laws onto a totally different plane. What is meant by saying that Moses is *hermeneus*? Is he an interpreter? a translator? an executor? a mediator? Can it be claimed that the laws spread in his name were formulated by him, or is he simply a sort of spokesman, the laws having been given by God and transmitted to Moses who mediated them to man? And, as concerns this transmission, is Moses simply a vessel of a voice that pervades him or does he have an active role, a reading and explanatory function concerning norms which men would otherwise find unintelligible? Is his role that of the translator who transfers, in language that the people can understand, what is expressed in divine language, that of an interpreter who explains the norms, or that of an executor who applies general guidelines?

In *De Praemiis* 53-55, we find a characterization of Moses which can perhaps help us, if not to answer, at least to reformulate the questions therein posited. As *theologos*, Moses is endowed with *eusebeia*, the brightest of all virtues and the one that holds sway over all the others. From this there flow four attributes, as rewards for his virtue: kingship *(basileia)*, the giving of laws *(nomothesia)*, prophecy *(profeteia)*, the high priesthood *(archierosyne)*. Even if characteristics that blend in the figure of Moses, *nomothesia* and *profeteia* are distinct attributes which are not necessarily interdependent. It is still not clear what activities they designate. The text goes on to characterize kingship: Moses became king not with the strength of armies, as was the custom, but as chosen by God, through the spontaneous will of the

governed. God inspires the subjects how to choose. Unable to
articulate sounds (*anaudos*), lacking possessions and wealth, Moses
alone was assigned to Israel as king. He is not characterized by
rhetorical skills nor riches. His, therefore, is not a power stemming
from speeches or money, but designated from above. Although it is said
that the people choose freely, it is clear that it is an inspired choice
(Philo in fact speaks of ὑπὸ θεοῦ), Moses being designated by God.
The reference to his incapacity to articulate sounds leads to other
aspects. It evokes Aaron as Moses's interpreter, and echoes the concept
of *hermeneia*, which, in the passage, has yet to be mentioned.

Moses is *nomothetes*, "the king in fact has to order and prohibit
and the law is nothing but *logos* (word? enunciation? reason?) which
orders what is to be done and prohibits what is not to be done." Moses's
nomothesia, then, is associated with his kingship. This association is
presented as being obvious, but it is not obvious that the king has to
institute the laws that in turn he will make his subjects respect. It is not
obvious, that is, that he subsumes in his person both legislative and
executive powers, not to mention that of priesthood, which is referred
to a few lines further on.[1] Nevertheless, if as king Moses was chosen by
God, even his laws are willed by God. In fact, the text goes on to
enunciate Moses's third characterization: prophecy, which in this
context is assigned to him so that he will not commit errors in terms of
nomothesia. "The prophet is in fact an *hermeneus*; it is God who tells
him, by resounding within him, what he has to say, and with God
nothing is subject to blame." God resounds within; it is therefore a
divine inspiration, an inner voice that sounds from within and which
will subsequently be expressed. This brings us to Moses's *ermeneia*,
which is closely linked, as we have seen, to his *nomothesia* and to his
profeteia. As *prophetes*, Moses is *hermeneus*. Lastly, it too linked to
profeteia, the high priesthood, whereby Moses organizes the cult.
These four characterizations are combined in the person of Moses, in as
much as they are necessary to the exercise of *heghemonia*; and any lack
or weakness in one of these ambits lead to an insecure direction of
public affairs.

It is not my intent to address the theme of the figure of Moses in
Philo. Much has been written in this connection, and sufficient light has

---

[1] Regarding the controversy surrounding the priest-king issue, and in general
the combining of several functions in one sole person, see H.A. Wolfson,
Foundations of Religious Philosophy in Judaism, Christianity and Islam,
Cambridge Mass. (1962) II, 322-342; F. Parente, 'Il giudaismo alessandrino' in L.
Firpo (ed.), *Storia delle Idee politiche economiche e sociali* II, Torino (1985). See
here, chapter two.

been shed on aspects of his figure in terms of how he was perceived in Alexandria.[2]

Nor shall I address in detail the issue of prophecy. What is of interest to me is to examine what Philo means when he claims that Moses is *hermeneus*. Going back to what I said at the beginning, the issues on which I shall dwell are: What does Philo mean by *hermeneia*? Do Moses's and Joseph's *hermeneus* roles have any traits in common? Does *hermeneia* contain in itself an inextricable link with expressed reality? Does it translate the relation between word and thing? In what way is Moses both *profetes* and *hermeneus*? Is Moses a mediator of the word of God? Is he a prophet in as much as he transmits the word? Is he *hermeneus* in as much as he translates the language of God into human language? In as much as he explains the otherwise incomprehensible word? In as much as he makes it applicable? Can we speak of interpretation as an indicator of behavioural modes? Can we speak of exegesis in interpretative terms ultimately geared to action?

1.2. *Moses, Interpreter or Exegete?*

Moses is not simply he who has received the law and transmits it to the people; he also gives indications as to how to behave. This is so particularly in the flight from Egypt and subsequently during the lengthy wanderings in the desert. Even as far as the special laws are concerned, Moses receives indications from God. In unclear situations he asks for clarification and receives instructions as to how to apply

---

[2]   On the figure of Moses in Alexandria, even with respect to Joseph's characterization, cf., for example, Y. Amir, *Die hellenistische Gestalt des Judentums bei Philon von Alexandrien*, Neukirchen, Vluyn (1983) 91 ff.; J. Daniélou, *Philon d'Alexandrie*, Paris (1958) 88-89; J.J. Collins, *Between Athens and Jerusalem. Jewish Identity in the Hellenistic Diaspora*, New York (1983); P.L. Shuler, 'Philo's Moses and Mattew's Jesus: A comparative Study in Ancient Literature', SPhA 2 (1990) 86-103; AA.VV., *La figure de Moïse. Ecriture et relectures*, Genève (1978), in particular R. Martin-Achard, 'Moïse, figure du médiateur selon l'Ancien Testament', espec. 18-19, and E. Starobinski-Safran, 'La profétie de Moïse et sa portée d'après Philon', 67-80; D.T. Runia, 'God and Man in Philo of Alexandria' in *Exegesis and Philosophy. Studies on Philo of Alexandria*, Aldershot, Hampshire (1990) 48-75; D. Sills, Vicious Rumours: *Mosaic Narratives in First Century Alexandria*, SBLSP 31 (1992), 684-694.

Concerning Moses's kingly and priestly authority, his authorship and authority, his role which can perhaps be linked to that of the scribe as author, cf. B.L. Mack, *Under the Shadow of Moses: Authorship and Authority in Hellenistic Judaism*, SBLSP (1982) 299-318; id., 'Moses on the Mountain Top: A Philonic View' in J.P. Kenney (ed.), *The School of Moses: Studies in Philo and Hellenistic Religion*, Studia Philonica Monograph Series 1, Atlanta (1995) 16-28 in partic. 21-22.

the Law (*Mos*. II.213 ff.).[3] Depending on the answer, he sets down new norms which become cogent, an example of legal constitution after Sinai. Moreover, it has to do with an interpretation of principles which have already been affirmed, and therefore an example of textual exegesis, even if exegesis carried out by God, who transmits it to Moses, and not of an autonomous exegesis.[4] The ambit is always that of prophecy of which *hermeneia* constitutes one type. Is Moses an interpreter or even an exegete? When Moses is seen as exegete, can it be hypothesized that Philo intends to claim an autonomous role for Moses with respect to God? In this case Moses's work must not be conceived of as a simple transcription of words dictated by God, but rather as an interpretation-explanation analogous to that of the *Targum* which does not purport to be an inspired work. This, however, seems not to coincide with Philo's reading of the *Bible* which, repeatedly, is attributed to God in the first person. Therefore, it is necessary to clarify those claims whereby Moses is both intercessor (*Mos*. I.101;105) and interpreter (*Mos*. I.83 ff.). Then it will also be necessary to compare those passages in *Mos*. I.40 where mention is made of the Septuagint, *hierofantes*, sacred translators, and to clarify whether their work as translators was inspired.

1.3. *The Translation of God's Word into human Language*

The word of God is word, essence of reality, structure of the world; word as creation, norm, law for man. The Law, that is, is a whole which concerns all the spheres of the real;[5] but how is the divine word to be translated in a human ambit? How can the word - which is norm - be applied? How can the language of God be understood by means of human categories? How to express it? It is a question of translation. Hence, the need for exegesis as a means of understanding the text, and for translation of the Law of God into laws and norms applicable to man. We can ask whether translation from Hebrew, the language of God and of creation, into Greek, is a form of translation of God's language into a language comprehensible to man, or - at least - to a part of mankind. Is translation already a form of exegesis? In fact, the translation by the *Septuagint*, being characterized as an inspired translation, occupies a special plane and assimilates the Greek to the Hebrew text. From this standpoint, it would seem that, strictly speaking, it cannot be understood as exegesis, as a translation in

---

3 Cf. also *Mos*. II.217; 233 ff.
4 Cf. Y. Amir, *op. cit.* (n.2) 88-89.
5 Cf. V. Nikiprowetzky, *Le commentaire de l'Ecriture chez Philon d'Alexandrie*, Leiden (1977) 117 ff.

human terms of the word of God.   Moreover, the Hebrew text is already "translated" into human language.

Furthermore, God's Law posits itself as law for man in both historical and political terms.   Thus, it is necessary to identify the relation between special laws and universal law.   One could imagine a sort of parallelism between exegesis and execution of precepts, but also between exegesis and politics as application of the law.   Politics, obviously, conducted according to the word of God, as an activity of the shepherd of the flock who follows divine guidelines; the politics of Moses.   The relation between word of God and politics is nevertheless a close one, even when it is a question of rulers who are far from possessing Moses's excellence or his adherence to the divine will.   Even the evil rulers who go against the divine will shall bear the consequences and shall be punished as was Gaius and his followers (*Leg.* 206;293).[6] It is here, then, that the attempt to understand the word, exegesis, finds its practical application.   On an individual plane, it is a matter of obeying precepts; on a general plane, or, even more so, when a ruler is involved, it is a matter of politics.   Therefore, there is a close relation between exegesis and politics.[7] Finding the rules for one helps to identify the rules for the other.

2. *Interpretation as Mediation*

The Law structures all of reality and therefore pervades of itself even the world of men.   But men do not necessarily know nor understand the Law.[8] It is the language of God, and as such it cannot be fully grasped by men who will only be able to glimpse some of its aspects, know only some guidelines.   The Patriarchs, the living law, embody the Law; but the other men, even if virtuous and wise, lack a direct relation with it.   Except Moses.   Moses, as king, legislator, prophet and priest, is also interpreter.   On one hand, it is he who receives the Law from God and transmits it to the people; on the other, in cases of doubtful application, he questions God and receives instructions from him.   Finally, as guide of the people, he identifies the modes and forms wherein the Law expresses itself.   In contact with

---

6   This thesis is also extensively found in other works of the Hellenistic period, for example in 2 *Maccabees*, Antiocus and other Gentiles are punished by God for having refused to carry out a law which empirically is not theirs (the laws and traditions of the Jew), but which, in effect, transcends the singularity of peoples, being the law of God.

7   Cf. D.M. Hay, *Politics and Exegesis in Philo's Treatise on Dreams*, SBLSPS 26 (1987) 429-438.

8   Cf. here, chap. 3.

God and with men, Moses is a mediator figure.[9] He beseeches God on
behalf of the people and even of the Egyptians;[10] he transmits to the
people divine indications and norms, and, lastly, he applies them
himself. Hence, the need for interpretation. Not always are divine
words immediately evident; not all modes of behaviour are
immediately codified. This, for example, occurs in reference to what
punishment is to be meted out to the transgressor of the Shabbath
(Mos. II.217), or in reference to the inheritance law (Mos. II.233 ff.).
Not knowing how to act, Moses explicitly questions God who provides
him with guidelines.

The relation between God and Moses can take on various forms,
but nevertheless hinges upon the exceptionality of Moses who, alone
among men, can speak face to face with God, even if God's
countenance cannot be seen. I shall not address here the complex issue
of the vision of God; that to which I want to draw attention is the
special relation which establishes itself between God and Moses, aside
from the precise nature of their relationship. In particular, speculation
is in order as to Moses's interpretation, his translation of the divine
word, his applied reading.

The first problem that arises is whether it is an inspired work or a
simple explanation achieved by means of human instruments. Often, in
Philo's text, the author speaks of profeteia, hermeneia, dieghesis,
diakrisis. Clearly, these terms refer to different types of reality, to
different types of interpretation. As profetes, Moses is inspired, often
imbued with God of whose word he is the instrument. Not always and
necessarily does Moses know what he will say. The instruments of his
prophecy are not rational, even if they are intellective. What acts is
noetic vision, a going beyond sensorial experience, the pervasion of
God's word of which Moses's mouth and vocal cords become
instruments, possibility of articulation and expression intelligible to
men, whose limited capacity to comprehend calls for empirically
concretized communication. Relationship with God occurs in a state of
wakefulness; one however in which normal cognitive functions are
suspended. It is a condition of ecstasy, of going out of one's habitual
sensorial dimension.[11] It is, nevertheless, a condition of passivity with
regard to divine action which, through Moses, communicates with the

---

[9] Cf. P. Borgen, 'Philo of Alexandria' in M.E. Stone (ed.), Jewish Writings of the
Second Temple Period, Assen Philadelphia (1984) 270-271; D.T. Runia, 'God and
Man' cit. (n.2).
[10] Mos. I.101; 105.
[11] Cf. D. Winston, Two Types of Mosaic Prophecy according to Philo, SBLSPS 27
(1988) 442-455, discussed by J.R. Levinson, 'Two Types of Ecstatic Prophecy
according to Philo', SPhA 6 (1994) 83-89.

people. Moses is God's voice, as Aaron is Moses's.[12] In this light, Moses lacks an independence of his own, his own autonomy of judgement and action, and limits himself to reporting God's orders and instructions. He mediates the word and thus his prophecy is *hermeneia*. *Hermeneia* as translation, transference from one language to another, from one ambit to another. In other situations, Moses's intervention seems rather more active, not a simple translation, but veritable interpretation, comprehension and solution of questions and problems. Moses does not limit himself to being a vehicle of transmission of the divine word, to giving the law which has been established by God, to being, that is, a legislator. He also becomes an interpreter and executor of that law, a hermeneus of formulations which are either complex or too general to be immediately and correctly applied. Naturally, interpretation always derives from the word of God, and is not an autonomous reading by Moses who, at times, questions God directly about specific points and receives an answer, and at times refers to previous indications. But above all, even when Moses's interpretation of divine directives is not rendered explicit, the very decisions he takes for the people, the norms that he institutes, the legislative procedures that he proposes are, *de facto*, a translation into the concrete and quotidian. Thus, as we have seen, Moses *theologos* combines in his person both kingship and the role of legislator, of prophet and of priest, since "the king must order and prohibit, and the law is nothing but the *logos* that orders what has to be done and prohibits what has not to be done [...] But, to avoid errors, Moses was attributed the power of prophecy: the prophet, in fact, is *hermeneus*. It is God who inwardly suggests to him what he has to say".[13] Prophecy and *hermeneia* are geared to the exercise of kingship.

3. *Joseph, the interpreter of Dreams*

Joseph too is an interpreter; an interpreter of dreams. His work, although under God's aegis, is not fully inspired. That is why, in his case, one usually speaks of *dieghesis* [14] and *diakrisis*,[15] and rarely of *diermeneuein*.[16] If, in terms of the biblical account, Joseph interprets dreams, first his own, and later those of his prison mates, then those of Pharaoh, in terms of allegorical interpretation, as a political person Joseph interprets the dreams of the people, and fulfils their

---

12 *Mos.* I.84.
13 *Praem.* 53-54.
14 *Ios.* 28; 96.
15 *Ios.* 93; 98; 110; 116; 125; 269.
16 *Ios.* 95; 189.

aspirations.[17] We are indeed far from the inspired interpretation of Moses who, as legislator and king, translates in concrete terms not the demands of the people, but divine prescriptions. On the other hand, the moment he himself dreams, Joseph is a prophet and his dreams derive from God. The 'vision' of the sun, of the moon and stars and that of the sheaves are an announcement of his future role. As already for Moses interpretation and prophecy have different connotations, also in Joseph at least two types of interpretation can be seen: different is his relation with God, different is his role of explanation. But if dreams are at times sent by God to announce events, and in them therefore is present a divine will, it can be affirmed that also Joseph's explanation is linked to God's will. Thus, we are back to what was previously stated: it is necessary to clarify whether Joseph's interpretation is inspired or is based on human categories, and thus one which proceeds by probable interpretations, by conjecture.

As representative of political man, Joseph interprets the dreams of the collectivity (*Ios.* 125). Given the uncertainty and precariousness of the human condition and of the situation of nations, men wander as if sunk in sleep, and are deceived by what they believe is their capacity to see the nature of things with the power of reasoning (*Ios.* 140-141). In reality men are dragged along by their sensations; life is full of disorder, confusion and uncertainty. Hence, the need for action by the political person who interprets the dreams that are dreamt in a state of wakefulness, and explain with verisimilar conjectures that which is good, that which is evil, that which needs be done, and how to act. Here, naturally, it is not a question of dreams sent by God, but of dreams experienced in a condition of wakefulness by individuals who are subject to both error and trouble. Yet, the interpreter of dreams, the political person, is a moral guide; he who points out the path to follow. In this sense he is analogous to Moses, even if the characteristics of the directions and types of vision are obviously quite different. It is clear moreover that Moses's 'visions' are not dreams, and, in this respect, Philo adheres strictly to the tradition which explicitly repeats how Moses's prophecies never occur in a dream-like state, but are the result of a direct relation with God who speaks only with Moses face to face, and not through enigmas (*Num.* 12.6-8). Also, even in Joseph's case, quite different naturally are the wakeful dreams of the collectivity as interpreted by the political person and the dreams predictively sent by God to Pharaoh, or to Joseph himself.[18]

---

[17] *Ios.* 125-126.
[18] Cf. *Somn.* I.1-2; 190; II.1-7. As for the inspiration of dreams and the different types of dreams with respect to their prophetic character see E. Bréhier, *Les idées philosophiques et religieuses de Philon d'Alexandrie*, Paris (1925) 194 ff.

4. Interpretation and conjectural Explanations

Joseph's entire life is characterized by his relation with dreams and their interpretation. While still in his paternal home, he sparks the ire of his brothers by his ability to read dreams in terms of their deeper meanings. His brothers, in fact, through symbols know how to grasp hidden meanings, to follow traces of what is not evident, to read clues (§ 7). It is a clarification procedure based on conjectures; a cognitive process centred on intellectual acuteness, on a well utilized human capacity which makes it possible to read hidden reality. Moses's procedure διὰ σημείου is quite different (Mos. II.263). Even in De Josepho there is a hidden object (ἀδηλούμενον) which is brought to light through a reading of clues, even if it is a question of σύμβολα, and not of σημεῖα. In Moses however, there is the intervention of divine inspiration, which is totally absent in Ios. 7, and Moses's task does not only consist in reading hidden reality, but also in explaining to others, if not the loftiest realities, at least what is accessible to men. What takes on particular relief is Moses's dimension as mediator. Moreover, to the eyes of his brothers Joseph's vision is false, a ὄναρ which is said to be καταψευσμένη φαντασία(§7). There comes through an allusive ambiguity: on one hand the fallaciousness which the brothers attribute to φαντασία;[19] on the other, the effective truthfulness which assimilates it to true visions, such as that in Mos. II.252, or in De Josepho itself (101-103), to the dreams of the king, interchangeably called φαντασίαι or ὄψεις. Even here, with regards to God-sent visions which become signs (ὑποσημαίνουσαι §100) of future events, interpretation consists in reading such signs. We witness here an opposition between the verisimilar conjectures by the wise men of the kingdom, who are incapable of grasping the deep hidden meaning, and of following the traces of truth (§105), and the real wisdom of Joseph who is able to dispel the shadows of darkness and bring to light that which is hidden (§106).[20] In the case of the head baker and the head cup-bearer, the two eunuchs are beset by anguish over their dreams, precisely because they are aware of the revealing nature of oneiric visions. They are to be interpreted; that is, they are to undergo a process whereby their hidden meaning is disclosed, which is possible when God so wishes. In other words, it is a question of *diakrinein*, of giving an interpretation that is the explanation of what is enshrouded, the very object of a quest by

---

[19] Cf. P. Graffigna, 'Osservazioni sull 'uso del termine φαντασία in Filone d'Alessandria', *Koinonia* 16 (1992) 5-19.
[20] Cf. § 90.

those who pursue truth. It is certainly not the same plane as that of
prophecy or of inspired interpretation attributed to Moses, but there is
nevertheless an attempt to explain the hidden meaning of vision. At
paragraph 95, the interpreters of dreams (*kritai*) interpret
(*diermeneuousi*), the divine (*loghia*) and prophesy: if the explanation of
the dream vision (φαντασία) is a διήγησις, an exposition, where it is a
matter of interpreting divine words, it is a question of *diermeneuein*
and *profetein*, that is of interpreting, translating and explicating.

We find here combined various terms which allude to different
forms of explanation: *diakrisis*, which mostly indicates an explanation
through human categories, more than an interpretation of a prophetic
type;[21] *dieghesis, hermeneia*. This raises the problem of whether it is
possible to postulate a distinction between *hermeneia*, interpretation of
λόγια θεῖα and *diakrisis*, an explanation of dreams, even if sent by God;
diakrisis which, precisely as an explanation conducted with human
instruments is often linked to conjectures (see §116). Actually, precisely
the same passages of §116 clarify in what way Joseph's *diakrisis* is
linked to the presence of the divine spirit, and the dreams sent to
Pharaoh have a clear predictive function willed by God who, through
dreams, signifies a reality.[22] Joseph's interpretation is not truthful
because of some special knowledge of his, but because it is linked to
divine inspiration (§110). God himself, who sends dreams to the king as
a premonition of future events, sends the inspiration to Joseph who
thus becomes an intermediary between a God-sent vision and how it is
interpreted by mankind. He is an interpreter, a translator of the divine
language (now expressed as a vision instead of in words) into human
language, and furthermore suggests remedies whereby to face
preannounced events. In this sense, his role closely resembles that of
Moses who "translates" the word of God and expresses its applicative
forms. In both characters, nevertheless, what is essential is the very
moment of inspiration, which differentiates Moses from the Egyptian
wizards, and Joseph from the false sages. In both cases, knowledge is
given by the relation with God; one which, alone, makes it possible to
make out a reality which is otherwise precluded to mankind. The
presence of the divine spirit, however, does not eliminate the
conjectural nature of interpretation (§116), or, at least, the possibility
that he who listens to the interpretation may consider it στοχαζομένη:
casual, hypothetical, probable; not, however, true.

---

21 See §§ 93, 98.
22 See also §§ 100; 107.

5. Interpretation and Politics

In his name and in the way he is described, Joseph subsumes all the traits of the political man he betokens. He is colorfully clad, thus symbolizing the infinite changes a political man must adapt to in order to cope with the changing situations. Because of his ability to modify his attitudes and decisions depending on circumstance, he recalls the helmsman who readjusts his direction depending on the forces of the sea (*Ios.* 33), or the physician who does not always administer the same remedies. The elasticity underlying the political person's behaviour easily leads him to take on the role of a demagogue who is keener on pleasing the crowds - while at the same time tyrannizing them - than on pursuing a just conduct. It is to this aspect of the political man that the account of the selling off of Joseph alludes:

> "when the would-be popular orator mounts the platform, like a slave in the market, he becomes a bond-servant instead of a free man, and, through the seeming honours which he receives, the captive of a thousand masters. Again, he is also represented as the prey of wild beasts, and indeed the vainglory which lies in ambush and then seizes and destroys those who indulge it is a savage beast."[23]

Here are evidenced the worst aspects of politics, those that approximate the figure of the politician to that of the demagogue.

The ambiguity of the politician's role has been amply treated.[24] What I would recall is that the nature, not only of political man, but also

---

[23] *Ios.* 35-36, trans. by F.N. Colson. All translations of Philo's works are from *Philo in ten volumes (and two supplementary volumes)*, English translation by F.H. Colson, G.H. Whitaker (and R. Marcus), Loeb Classical Library, London 1929-62).

[24] Cf. C. Kraus Reggiani, 'Introduzione' a *De Josepho* in C. Kraus Reggiani (edit. by), *De Opificio, de Abrahamo, De Josepho*, Rome (1979) 267 ff.; E. Hilgert, 'The Dual Image of Joseph in Hebrew and Early Jewish Literature', *Biblical Research* 30 (1985) 5-21.

On Joseph's role, as a figure involved in complex dynamics in his relationship with Israel and with Egypt, in a context of politics allegorically understood, cf. J. Cazeaux, 'Nul n'est prophète en son pays. Contribution à l'étude de Joseph d'après Philon' in J.P. Kenney (ed.), *The School of Moses cit.* (n. 2) 41-81, in part. 61-66. M. Petit, 'L'homme politique: interprète de rêves selon Philon d'Alexandrie (*De Josepho* 125) ὁ πολιτικὸς πάντως ὀνειροκριτικός ἐστιν ' in D. Tollet (ed.), *Politique et religion dans le judaïsme ancien et médiéval*, Paris (1989) 41-45, speaks of Joseph's ambiguity both as a character and as an interpreter of dreams. According to M. Petit, there is a bipolarism in *De Josepho* which would place considerations on Joseph the man in the ambit of literary exegesis, whereas of the figure as a political person in that of allegorical exegesis. This double assessment of Joseph, the literal and the allegorical, is also considered by

of politics qua activity, qua *politeia* of special cities, is expressed in the very name of Joseph. A reading of the account of Joseph, as of many other biblical accounts, implies a transition from a literal explanation τὴν ῥητὴν διήγησιν to an analysis of hidden meaning: "for, broadly speaking, all or most of the law-book is an allegory"(*Ios.* 28),[25] all, therefore, or almost all passages have to be interpreted. Specifically, Joseph's name alludes to the superabundance of laws and special regimes with respect to the only city, the only law, the only regime that follows the *logos* of nature. Special laws are "additions" in terms of the law of nature, just as political man is an "addition" compared to man who lives according to nature (*Ios.* 31). It appears, therefore, that if men lived according to nature there would be no need of other laws, nor of political men. From this standpoint, politics is typical of a post- or meta-natural stage of society. What is postulated is not a wild state preceding civilization, as a natural state preceding useless and superabundant laws.

We could ask ourselves whether such a state, experienced by men who live according to nature, is that of the Patriarchs, *nomoi empsychoi*. The reference could perhaps conduce to a preceding situation: that of Earthly Paradise. However, it is not the quest for special laws that determined expulsion from Eden, at least not in an immediate sense, as that expulsion was the result of behaviour that departed from the Law of God. Before sinning, Adam and Eve followed the Law of nature. In other ways, he who follows nature is Moses, who follows the Law given by God (to which nature conforms) and applies it. Anyone pretending to add norms and modes of behaviour which do not derive from God, instead of being an interpreter, is a political person, precisely in as much as he pretends to add laws. We are here quite afield from the notion of political person qua executor of divine norms in society, qua interpreter who fulfils the word of God in history (Moses and Joseph himself). Thus, in *Leg. All.* I.74, *logos* translates (ἑρμηνεῦσαι) thought, and φρόνησις consists in "a change of mouth"; φρόνησις"is not found in discourse, but in action and in virtuous actions."

T.H. Tobin, *Tradition and Interpretation in Philo's Portrait of the Patriarch Joseph*, SBLSPS 25 (1986) 271-277.

The coherence of Joseph's assessment in Philo's various works, instead, is highlighted by J.M. Bassler, 'Philo on Joseph: The Basic Coherence of De Josepho and De Somniis II', *JSJ* 16 (1985) 240-255. A basically positive image of Joseph is attributed to Philo by M. Niehoff, *The Figure of Joseph in Post-Biblical Jewish Literature*, Leiden (1982) 54-83.
[25] I shall not enter here upon the complex matter of allegorical reading in Philo and of the various types of exegesis. These themes have all been extensively treated, especially in the past decades.

THE LANGUAGE OF GOD

6. Interpretation and Exegesis

Interpretation of the text and of dreams, translation, transfer into a language which is comprehensible to men and in virtuous actions. There are various operations which are all in some way linked to an understanding of the word and to its application. Among the various terms used there are: ἑρμηνεία, διερμηνεία, διήγεσις, διάκρισις, ἐξήγησις. Are they terms that in some way correspond or refer to different operations? Which of these operations is accomplished by Moses, by Joseph, and by some successive exegete? Philo does not always think he is an inspired exegete; certainly he does not consider himself on a par with Moses, nor probably with the Septuagint. How then, in terms of inspiration, are we to consider interpretation by the exegetes subsequent to Moses? Given the Law, whereby here is meant the *Torah* given to Moses on Sinai, can it be thought to be immediately evident? There is a profound hiatus between divine word and human word, and man will never be fully able to grasp God's law, which can only be approached and understood within the bounds of human limitations.[26] Here then lies the problem of what it means to interpret, together with the theme of the relation between understanding of the word and its application. Furthermore, what are the instruments of interpretation: reason, conjecture, inspiration, execution of precepts, political application? Besides his level of excellence, how does Moses *hermeneus* differentiate himself from Philo, or from some other *hermeneus* exegete? It is not my intention to trace the theme of Philonic exegesis, on which much has been written, nor to address the relation between allegorical interpretation and literal interpretation; nor, moreover, to analyze the terms which indicate exegesis. I shall simply recall how, although the term ἐξήγησις and its derivatives seldom recur, Philo mentions it in terms of interpreting the hidden meaning contained in the sacred texts.[27] Thus, for example, are named

> "those who have dedicated their own life and themselves to knowledge and the contemplation of the verities of nature, following the truly sacred instructions of the prophet Moses" (*Contempl.* 64).

> "The exposition of the sacred scriptures treats the inner meaning conveyed in allegory. For to these people the whole law book seems to resemble a living creature with the literal ordinances for its body and for its soul the invisible mind laid up in its wording. It is in this mind especially that the rational soul begins to contemplate the things akin to

---

[26] Cf. here, chap. 3.

[27] Cf. *Leg. All.* III.21; *Spec. Leg.* II. 159.

itself and looking through the words as through a mirror beholds the marvellous beauties of the concepts, unfolds and removes the symbolic coverings and brings forth the thoughts and sets them bare to the light of day for those who need but a little reminding to enable them to discern the inward and hidden through the outward and visible" (*Contempl.* 78).

Much broader is the use of the verb ἑρμηνεύω and related terms. ʹΕρμηνεία indicates diverse modes of interpretation, from simple translation which, while still being a turning into another language of what is said in Hebrew, nevertheless attempts to grasp the deep sense of reality, to inspired translation, to interpretation proper - either inspired or not - , to transmission of the divine word, to an intelligible expression of the word.

7. *Moses as translator, instrument, mediator, exegete, interpreter*

What would seem to be called for here is an analysis of the more frequent and significant uses of the term ἑρμηνεία and other related forms. However, so as not to interrupt the thread of our present analysis, I shall list said uses at the end of this chapter, in paragraph 9, and continue here with a reading of the already quoted text *De Vita Mosis* I.1. It is the text that opens with the characterization of Moses as νομοθέτης and ἑρμηνεύς νόμων ἱερῶν. From the very outset of the work Moses's double role is therefore clarified: he gives the laws but also interprets them. They are sacred laws, given by God, and well known throughout the land. What does Philo mean when he says that Moses is their ἑρμηνεύς? In light of the various meanings of the term, for which the reader is referred to paragraph 9, we can think that Moses is translator, in as much as he writes in human language what is said by God; mediator, between the divine word and the human word; exegete, in as much as he perceives the relation between terms and reality; clarifier, as he grasps the specificity of the laws and transmits special norms; interpreter, in as much as he applies them.

If we consider *Mos.* I.83-84, we see that what is stressed is the first meaning. To God's request that he become an interpreter of his words to the people, that he explain, that is, to the people the way to follow, Moses (according to *Exodus* 4.10 ff.) attempts to shirk the task by reason of his ἀφωνία, his inability to speak, his incapacity to give sound to the word of God. This, in fact, is the problem in the given context: that of materializing the divine word, of giving it voice, of using mouth, tongue, throat and vocal cords to articulate in sensible sounds that which sensible is not. Moses here is ἑρμηνεύς, in as much as he is a vehicle of the word, like Aaron; when Moses is not able to sustain the task by himself he will be ἑρμηνεύς to Moses, voice of his brother's words. Aaron then, in turn, will be ἑρμηνεύς of Moses, not in so far as he interprets his words, as this is not his task, but in so far as he articulates them, he gives them voice. Thus Moses is God's ἑρμηνεύς the moment he repeats His words and announces them to Aaron, who will announce them to the people. Here, then, Moses is an interpreter in the sense that he mediates the word. God's word, in this context, needs a mediator who can repeat it. Too great is the hiatus between divine word and human word: hence the ἀφωνία which can be overcome only through God's will with the help of interpreters. It is not fortuitous that God's word is often said χρησμός, oracle, a term which expresses the mediatory role of he who transmits and interprets the oracle. Parallel - even if opposite - to Moses's role as vocal instrument, articulation of the word of God, is that of Balaam. He too speaks in as much as God articulates his voice, independently of the will of the prophet who becomes organ, ἑρμηνεύς possessed by God who inspires and compels him to utter words according to His will.[28] He speaks saying inspired words, and limits himself to uttering words without necessarily explaining them. Besides, even Moses, more than explaining the word, repeats it to the people and applies it. He is interpreter in as much as repeater and executor of the word. Of course, Balaam's prophecy is different from that of Moses, as different is the spiritual condition of the one, who speaks as if in a dream (*Mos.* I.289), and is unable to say anything personal (*Mos.* I.286), from that of the other who is awake and aware of what he will say; one,[29] the ambiguous prophet, a true prophet the other. Different also is the quality of their visions.[30] Nevertheless, the two have a common characteristic: the role of instrument through which God speaks by articulating their voices. Like Moses, therefore, Balaam is God's spokesman, and therein lies his ἑρμηνεία.

In such contexts, more than explained, the word is uttered, and the interpreter's role, more than that of the exegete, is that of spokesman, mediator. For Balaam it is not so much a question of applying the word, as of pronouncing it, so that it can be actuated.

---

[28] Cf. *Mos.* I. 275-277. See B. Decharneux, 'Mantique et oracles dans l'oeuvre de Philon d'Alexandrie' in A. Motte (ed.), *Oracles et mantique en Grèce ancienne*, Actes du colloque de Liège (Mars 1989)= *Kernos* 3 (1990) 123-133; B. Decharneux, *L'ange, le devin et le prophète: chemins de la parole dans l'oeuvre de Philon d'Alexandrie dit 'le Juif'*, Bruxelles (1994).

[29] Cf. J.T. Greene, *Balaam and his Interpreters: a Hermeneutical History of the Balaam Traditions*, Atlanta Georgia (1992) 145-147; id.; *Balaam: Prophet, Diviner and Priest* in *Selected Ancient Israelite and Hellenistic Jewish Sources*, SBLSPS 28 (1989) 57-106; R.M. Berchman, *Arcana Mundi between Balaam and Hecate: Prophecy, Divination and Magic in Later Platonism*, SBLSPS 28 (1989) 107-185.

[30] Cf. L.H. Feldman, 'Josephus' Portrait of Balaam', *SPhA* 5(1993) 48-83, where is addressed the theme of Balaam as prophet with respect to the Rabbinical tradition and the eschatological prophesies in the days of Rome.

Clearly, prophecy and interpretation can be distinct operations which cannot be assimilated. In this regard Philo is explicit (*Mos.* II.191). Yet, there are χρησμοί which are pronounced "as if by an interpreter":

> "Of the divine utterances, some are spoken by God in his own Person with His prophet for interpreter, in some the revelation comes through question and answer, and others are spoken by Moses in his own person, when possessed by God and carried away out of himself" (*Mos.* II.188).

In all cases, what is decisive is the mediator role of Moses, who acts as interpreter of the word. The first type of prophecy speaks explicitly of the interpreter's mediation; whereas in the second type, the answers given by God to questions posed by Moses lead to further explanations (*Mos.* II.192); an example of norm application which is in itself a sort of interpretation. This is something which I have already mentioned in reference to the inheritance law and to the punishment reserved for those who violate the Shabbath. Finally, the last type of prophecy, that which occurs in a state of ἐνθουσιασμός, when the prophet is as if possessed by God and transported outside of himself. That the words of the prophet are not his, but come from God, is confirmed by God himself who, in *Mos.* II.262, affirms the origin of what Moses has said. Inspired, Moses utters prophecies, and makes clear, through divine revelation that speaks in him, hidden truth, the order of the world, the structure of the universe, the harmony of the law which in the divine word is both contained and signified (*Mos.* II.263). Through his words, for example, Moses renders manifest the sacred character and the special prerogative of the Shabbath. He is an exegete who renders explicit a veiled truth (*Mos.* II.269),[31] and clarifier who translates into norms. After having witnessed the conservation of the Shabbath manna (*Mos.* II.264), Moses, frightened by this extraordinary phenomenon, θεοφορηθείς (inspired by God), announces the seventh day.[32] It is an interpretation given by Moses after having witnessed a phenomenon: it is not a prophecy, but an interpretation given in an inspired state.

---

31 Cf. *Ios.* 7.
32 Here, Moses's action is similar to prophecy, without however being a prophecy (§265). Moreover, at § 191, it was claimed that interpretation and prophecy, even if at times similar, are different realities.

8. *Ermeneia and Inspiration*

A problem here arises: does Moses's interpretation always occur in a direct relationship with God?[33] Moses often questions God before formulating a law.When successive exegetes try to give interpretations, are they too inspired, or, at least, should they be in a state approximating inspiration? Certainly the Septuagint would seem to bear out this hypothesis which, however, would hardly apply *in toto* to the exegetes of Philo's time, and, with only a few exceptions, to Philo himself.[34] It can be hypothesized that, as successive kings and rulers lack Moses's degree of excellence, and as successive kings and prophets fail to reach Moses's level as prophet, similarly not even successive interpreters will attain Moses's level as interpreter. Furthermore, can a comparison be drawn between the interpretation by the exegetes who read the law given by Moses, and Moses himself, who wrote this law, albeit interpreting the words of God? Nevertheless, the problem remains: if interpretation has to be disclosure of the truth, in order to grasp it does the interpreter need some sort of inspiration-relation with God?[35]

Different is the sense of ἑρμηνεία in the case of the Septuagint, translators of the *Bible* into Greek. Book II of *De Vita Mosis* (27 ff.) mentions translation, but the term used is not, as might be expected, μεταγραφειν, but ἑρμηνεύειν.[36] Is it simply an immaterial word choice,

---

[33] Cf. Y. Amir, *Die Hellenistische Gestalt cit* (n. 2) 101 ff.; W.E. Helleman, 'Philo of Alexandria on Deification and Assimilation to God', *SPhA* 2 (1990) 51-71, in partic. 67-70, where the theme of Moses, 'god' for Pharaoh, is addressed; R.D. Hecht, *Scripture and Commentary in Philo*, SBLSP (1981) 129-164.

[34] Cf. A.Terian, 'Inspiration and Originality: Philo's Distinctive Exclamations', *SPhA* 7 (1995) 59-62; H. Burkhardt, *Die Inspiration heiliger Schriften bei Philo von Alexandrien*, Basel (1932); S.-K. Wan, 'Charismatic Exegesis: Philo and Paul compared', *SPhA* 6 (1994) 54-82; D.M. Hay, 'Philo's View of Himself as an Exegete: inspired but not Authoritative', *SPhA* 3(1991) 40-52. For P. Borgen, 'Heavenly Ascent in Philo: an Examination of Selected Passages' in J.H. Charlesworth and C.A. Evans, *The Pseudepigrapha and Early Biblical Interpretation*, Sheffield (1993) 243-268, Philo, in his self-assessment, is both a prophetic and inspired exegete. See, however, D.I. Brewer, *Techniques and Assumptions in Jewish Exegesis before 70 C.E.*, Tübingen (1992) 208-210. See also A. Myre, 'Les caractéristiques de la loi mosaïque selon Philon d'Alexandrie', *Science et ésprit* 27 (1975) 35-69.

[35] See H. Burkhardt, 'Inspiration der Schrift durch weisheitliche Personal-Inspiration: zur Inspirationslehre Philos von Alexandrien', *Theologische Zeitschrift*, 47 (1991) 214-225.

[36] See also the *Letter of Aristeas* 3; 11; 120; 301; etc. That it is not only a question of translating the text, but also of explaining it, is clarified at § 305. See the discussion on σεσήμανται in E. Bickerman, 'The Septuagint as a Translation', *Proceedings of the American Academy for Jewish Research*, 28 (1959) reprint. in

or does the use of this word indicate a translation which is interpretation, or, at any rate, an operation whereby a text is conveyed to those who otherwise would not be able to understand it? The aim of translation is to ensure that all men can avail themselves of the Law and improve their own manner of conduct (*Mos.* II.28). Therefore, translation is geared to application. Again, to translate means to convey norms of behaviour: an interpretation which is ethical and, possibly, also political. There occurs an excitement of the divine spirit; an inspiration which moves the Septuagint to prophesy (*Mos.* II.37).[37] Were it a mere translation, many terms could be used to render the same word; instead, in this case, one term alone corresponds exactly to the thing signified, and this notwithstanding the multiplicity of synonyms that are typical of the Greek language (*Mos.* II.38). It is not simply a matter of translating, but of an exact rendering of meaning: of exegesis. From this standpoint, the work of the Septuagint is more akin to that of Moses, prophet and interpreter.

The moment he follows divine guidelines in constructing the sanctuary, in preparing the habit of the high priest, in determining the candelabrum and the other objects of the Tabernacle (*Mos.* II.101 ff.), Moses receives models (παραδείγματα) and articulates them (*Mos.* II.141). These are symbol-rich objects, wherefore their elaboration, beyond its mere material dimension, takes on profound meanings which allude to the highest truths. Once more, Moses's execution of God's orders is significant in terms of higher realities; it is an interpretation of the divine law, it is a teaching (*Mos.* II.141). Moreover, for Moses transmission of divine guidelines is always also interpretation and application, to the extent that, when anyone follows manners of

---

Studies in Jewish and Christian History, part I, Leiden (1976) 191 n. 62; cf. F. Calabi (ed.), *Lettera di Aristeas a Filocrate*, Milano (1995) 9 n. 8. At § 10 of the *Letter*, reference is instead to μεταγραφεῖν. And it is still of matter of ἑρμηνεία at §§ 308-310, where clearly it is a question of holy and just ἑρμηνεία , to the extent that the translation need not undergo any change. On the other hand, Theopompus προερμηνεύει incorrectly. Clearly, in this context ἑρμηνεύω not only means translation, but also interpretation. Here, obviously, reference is to the Septuagint translation into Greek, not of Moses's work; but it is nevertheless significant that the term used, ἑρμηνεύω , is the same used for Moses, who does not translate into a language different from Hebrew, but transmits, reports the words, refers them, writes them, and, by so doing, translates them, in that he renders them comprehensible to the people.

As regards the ambiguity between μεταγραφή and ἑρμηνεία see A. Pelletier (ed.), *Lettre d'Aristée à Philocrate* , Paris (1962) p. 120n.; F. Calabi (ed.), *Lettera di Aristea*, cit. 62 n. and 8-9.

[37] Cf. L. Canfora's interpretation in *Il viaggio di Aristea*, Bari (1996) X.

conduct which differ from those indicated, they are put to death.[38] The transgressor's conduct is alien to the words of God, whereas that of Moses is always in harmony with divine orders. Moses, then, receives the word and actuates it; he translates it, that is, in human verbal language (from mental, or at any rate, divine language) and translates it into actions. His exegesis becomes application.

9. Appendix: Meanings of Hermeneia

I would now like to examine the most frequent and significant uses of *hermeneia* and its related terms:

a) *Spec. Leg.* I.65: here *hermeneus* appears simply as a receptacle who says nothing that derives immediately from him.[39] Cf. *Her.* 259; *Q.G.* III.10; IV.212.

Spec. Leg. IV.48-49: unlike the false prophets who act autonomously, the prophet refers, he is an interpreter, ἑρμηνεύς of someone else who inspires the words he expresses.

> "Knowing not what he does he is filled with inspiration, as the reason withdraws and surrenders the citadel of the soul to a new visitor and tenant, the Divine Spirit which plays upon the vocal organism and dictates words.[40]

We are here in the ambit wherein are distinguished evil men and those who follow the word of God, of which they become instruments. It is in this sense that they become its interpreters:

> "The wicked may never be the interpreter of God, so that no worthless person is "God-inspired" in the proper sense. The name only befits the wise, since he alone is the vocal instrument of God, smitten and played by His invisible hand".[41]

Still in the sphere of prophecy as ἑρμηνεία regarding the word of God which suggests what needs be said, I would recall the previously analyzed passage in *De Praemiis* 53-56, which also introduces the

---

[38] See Phinheas and the Midianite. Cf. *Leg. All.* III. 242; *Post.* 182; *Mut.* 108; *Mos.* I.301-304; 313. The episode, however, is interpreted symbolically by Philo.

[39] Cf. H. Burkhardt, *Die Inspiration heiliger Schriften*, cit. (n. 34) 152 ff.

[40] Cf. A. Mosès (ed.), *Spec. Leg.* III-IV, Paris (1970) 228 n. 1, who compares the passage in question with *Mos.* II.189-191, where Philo, distinguishing three types of prophecy, speaks of ἑρμηνεία , where the prophet is simply a spokesman for the word of God.

[41] *Her.* 259.

relationship with action: it is a matter of seeing what has to be done and what has not to be done.

b)ἑρμηνεία as translation. It is not a simple linguistic translation: the terms contain meanings linked to the essence of the thing expressed. In this perspective, *hermeneuein* means shedding light on the profound meaning of terms, wherefore translation, transition from Greek to Hebrew - but also from thought to word - indicates the deep meaning of the term. Analysis of a term reveals the reality concealed in the word; translation discloses said reality.[42] Words are interpreters (at times even untruthful ones) of facts.[43] Thus, to translate means to grasp the hidden sense within a term and render it with an expression that contains its concealed reality. Besides the passages cited in the footnote, let us refer back to *Leg. All.* III.175, which speaks of manna, God's *logos*. Here *logos* is the word ῥῆμα which comes from the mouth of God, because the mouth τὸ στόμα is σύμβολον of the λόγος, and the word τὸ δὴ ῥῆμα is a part of the λόγος.

The name's relevance in signifying reality, its connection with what it has to signify, is often stressed by Philo who attributes to Adam the task of naming things:

"that [they be] in no wise incongruous or unsuitable, but bringing out clearly the traits of the creatures who bore them. [...] Adam received the impressions made by bodies and objects in their sheer reality, and the titles he gave were fully apposite, for right well did he divine the character of the creatures he was describing, with the result that their natures were apprehended as soon as their names were uttered" (*Opif.* 149-150).

"Elsewhere the universal practice of men as a body is to give to things names which differ from the things, so that the objects are not the same as what we call them. But with Moses the names assigned are manifest images of the things, so that name and thing are inevitably the same from the first and the name and that to which the name is given differ not a whit" (*Cher.* 56).

That hidden reality is expressed by words is often affirmed, as, for example, in *Leg. All.* III.225: "Moses, moreover, gives intimations of such a conflagration of the mind [...], when he says [...] means [...]." Moses, therefore, speaks using words that contain their deep meaning.[44]

---

[42] Cf. *Leg. All.* I.68; 90; II.89; 96; III.18; 19; 25; 68; 74; 77; 79; 83; 93; 95; 96; 175; 186; 218; 225; 226; 228; 230; 231; 232, etc.

[43] *Spec. Leg.* IV. 60.

[44] Even terms that indicate extremely important realities of both a religious ambit and of tradition, as the 'Shabbath', are to be read in this perspective. Cf.

The relation between name and reality is particularly clear when, instead of a generic term, it is a question of a proper name. This, for example, can be noticed in connection with Dotan.[45] The name is interpreted (*Mut.* 121); it is a symbol which can ἑρμηνεύεσθαι. In the case of Moses, the plurality of his names depends precisely on the personage's richness; a richness which is alluded to by his various names,[46] as when he:

> "interprets and teaches the oracles vouchsafed to him he is called Moses; when he prays and blesses the people, he is a Man of God; and when Egypt is paying the penalties for its impious deeds he is the God of Pharaoh, the king of the country. [...] Because to enact fresh laws [...] is the task of one whose hands are ever in touch with divine things [...] one who has received from Him a great gift, the power of language to express prophet-like the holy laws (ἑρμηνείαν καὶ προφητείαν νόμων ἱερῶν)" (*Mut.* 125-126).

Moses receives the laws from God, he interprets and expresses them prophetically. He pours the benefit of benediction upon the others, and is therefore called man of God (cf. §128). He rules and punishes; he applies the laws.

Also, " 'Abraham' is interpreted ἑρμηνεύεται "elevated father", and 'Abraaham' 'elect father of the sound'"(*Mut.* 66). A name signifies the reality which it represents, wherefore any variation in a name - even one letter - indicates a variation of reality: Abraham has undergone a process of change. Similarly Sarai, who was first 'specific' virtue, becomes Sarah, 'generic' virtue:

> "in the same measure as the genus is greater than the species is the second name greater than the former" (*Mut.* 77).[47]

This explains the great attention that is paid to names.[48] It is a reading that grasps the symbols represented by the terms, or by

---

Cher. 87: "And therefore often in his laws [Moses] calls the shabbath, which means 'rest', God's shabbath, not man's, and thus he lays his finger on an essential fact in the nature of things."

[45] Dotan means sufficient abandon. Cf. *Post.* 32. See also *Post.* 55; 74; 120.

[46] Cf. V. Nikiprowetzky,"Moyses palpans vel liniens": On some Explanations of the Name of Moses in Philo of Alexandria', in F.E. Greenspahn, E. Hilgert, B.L. Mack (edd.), *Nourished with Peace. Studies in Hellenistic Judaism in memory of Samuel Sandmel*, Scholars Press Homage Series 9, Chico, California (1984) 117-142.

[47] Cf. *Cher.* 7.

[48] Similar explanations are provided for many other names: Jacob-Israel (*Mut.* 81), Joseph (*Mut.* 89), Psonthomphanech (*Mut.* 91), Ruben (*Mut.* 98), Efraim (*Mut.* 98), Raguel (*Mut.* 105), Beelfegor (*Mut.* 107), Arfaxad (*Mut.* 189), Emor (*Mut.* 193), Dina (*Mut.* 194), Ishmael (*Mut.* 202), Leah (*Mut.* 254), Eden (*Somn.*

accounts which are also to be interpreted. Ἑρμηνεύειν, thus, in this context, means to interpret, to explain a meaning contained in a given term. Said process is not limited to evidencing the translation of a term, but stresses its interpretation:

> "Haran is [...] rendered sometimes 'dug', sometimes 'holes', one thing being signified by both words" (*Somn.* I.41).[49]

Similarly, in *Cher.* 65, the accent is on the choice of the name Cain, precisely to stress the notion of 'possession'. Allusion to the deeper sense, to the interpretation of language which signifies reality, is clear. In *De Somniis* there is again mention of a Mosaic expression, the singularity of which

> "might well lead even the slowest-witted reader to perceive the presence of something other than the literal meaning of the passage: for the ordinance bears the marks of an explanatory statement rather than of an exhortation".[50]

The text goes on to claim that the passage in question cannot be interpreted in a literal, but rather in an allegorical sense. The cloak, the subject of the account, symbolizes the word. It is an expression the hidden meaning of which is to be identified and expressed, and the term is the translation in words of a reality the verbal expression of which is not necessarily immediately evident.

c) Analogous, but with specific aspects, is the case of names wherein their formulation in Greek is evidenced.[51] What is here particularly noteworthy is that transposition from the Hebrew, in

---

II.242), Haran (*Somn.* I.41). Regarding the Hebrew etymologies of names see L.L. Grabbe, *Etymology in Early Jewish Interpretation: the Hebrew Names in Philo,* Atlanta Georgia (1988) 42 ff.; R. Goulet, *La philosophie de Moïse: essai de reconstruction d'un commentaire philosophique préphilonien du Pentateuque,* Paris (1987) 58-62. For an analysis of the name Israel and of the meaning enclosed in its change cf. G. Delling, "The One who sees God" in Philo' in *Nourished with Peace cit.* (n. 46) 30 ff.

[49] Cf. *Post.* 41: "It is important, then, that we should know that each of the names mentioned [Enoch, Metusael, Lamech] has a meaning that can be taken in two ways."

[50] *Somn.* I. 101.

[51] See, for example, Tare (*Somn.* I.47), Ramesse (*Somn.* I. 77), Shittim, Mohab (*Somn.* I.89). Cf. also *Somn.* I.206; 254; II.33; 35; 36; 47; 89; 173; 192; 211; *Congr.* 20; 25; 40; 41; 48; 51; 56; 61.

constant reference to the idea that names are not casual, corresponds to the essence of the reality indicated. [52]

A special case of correspondence is evidenced in *Mos.* II.39-40. In reference to the Septuagint, translation from Hebrew into Greek is mentioned, and it is claimed that the translators found the right words to express reality. What is stressed is the perfect correspondence to the original (in a way similar to geometry). Aside from the probably inspired nature of the Septuagint translation, what here bears underscoring is the perfect rendition of the original words - and of the things signified - achieved by the translation. It is precisely because of this perfect adherence to the original meaning and the inspired character of their work,[53] that the Septuagint are called ἑρμηνεῖς, but also ἱεροφάντες and προφητεῖς.

d) In *Leg. All.* I.74-77 there appears the expression λόγος ἑρμηνευτικός. Reference here is to the mouth. The mouth as expression of thought? The word that expresses? The word that translates? The word as translation of thought? Aaron, the sacred word, needs Moses, God's friend, to heal Miriam's transformation.

> "Prudence is discerned in "alteration of the mouth", that is in the word of utterance undergoing a transformation. This comes to the same thing as saying that prudence is not seen in speech but in action and earnest doings."

[52] Cf. B. Lévy, *Le logos et la lettre. Philon d'Alexandrie en regard des Pharisiens,* Lagrasse (1988) 52-56. The correspondence between things and words is a theme addressed by D. Dawson, *Allegorical Readers and Cultural Revision in Ancient Alexandria,* Berkeley Los Angeles (1992) 80-89. The author points out how the correspondence, present both in Adam and Moses, is preserved in the transition from Hebrew to Greek. Dawson speaks of a chain which, from the essence of things, returns to the very essence through transition from the names of Adam, to Hebrew, to Moses's inspiration, to the translators of the Septuagint. The language, however, can also present ambiguities. Thus, the words of the serpent do not correspond to the essence of things. The transition from Adam's naming of things to scriptural language is a movement which, starting from individual names, reaches the level of complete formulations. The ambiguity of the serpent's words lies more in syntactic ambiguity than in the names themselves.

Regarding the relationship between name and thing in various Philonic passages and the difficulties which surface in reference to some formulations, cf. D. Wilson, 'Aspects of Philo's Linguistic Theory', *SPhA* 3 (1991) *Heirs of the Septuagint. Philo, Hellenistic Judaism and Early Christianity,* 109-125, in partic. 124-125. See also M.R. Niehoff, 'What's in a Name? Philo's Mystical Philosophy of Language', *Jewish Studies Quarterly* 2 (1995) 220-252. See, also, F. Calabi, 'Lingua di Dio, lingua degli uomini: Filone alessandrino e la tradizione della 'Bibbia'', *I castelli di Yale* 2 (1997) 95-113.

[53] Cf., however, L. Canfora, *op.cit.*(n. 37) X.

Immediate is the reference to the passage in *Mos*. I.84, where
Moses will be God's mouth and Aaron Moses's, even if there, more
than on the word's operative application, stress is placed on the
weakness of Moses's word, on the incapacity of the human word to
express the word of God. To Moses's objections, God has words of
reassurance: I have given man mouth, tongue, throat, the vocal
apparatus enabling him to utter. Given the divine will, everything will
correctly be articulated. Aaron, Moses's ἑρμηνεύς, will be for him the
mouth which enables him to express the will of God, of which Moses is
ἑρμηνεύς. The word of God has need of a vocal instrument to be
understood by man. In *Det*. 39-40, Aaron is said to be mouth,
interpreter, prophet of Moses. Language is the mouth of intelligence.

> "Speech is the expounder of the plans which understanding has formed in
> its own council-chamber. Speech, moreover, is spokesman and prophet of
> the oracles which the understanding never ceases to utter from depths
> unseen and unapproachable."[54]

Moses does not know how to speak, in the sense that he does not
consider it right

> "to find a fitting instrument in the language uttered by the organs of
> speech, and prints and impresses on his understanding the lessons of true
> wisdom" (*Det*. 38).

At this stage, therefore, Moses has yet to translate in empirical
language that which is noetic. Only in his relation with Aaron, his voice
and interpreter, does there occur a transition from thought to
expressed word. Language is the interpreter of what the mind has
intimately decided. Voice is like a light that enlightens thoughts hidden
in the mind, and discourse manifests those thoughts: language as
thought-articulating sound (*Det*. 126-129 ff.). There is joy when

> "Speech [...] sees and fully apprehends the sense of the matter shown to it;
> for then it lays hands upon it, and gets hold of it, and becomes a perfect
> interpreter of it. [...]. But neither must all speech without exception meet

---

[54] On the passage in question see R. Radice's note (Filone di Alessandria, *Tutti i
trattati del commentario allegorico alla Bibbia*, R. Radice (ed.), Milano (1994),
who echoes K. Otte, *Das Sprachverständnis bei Philo von Alexandrien, Sprache
als Mittel der Hermeneutik*, BGBE7 Tübingen(1968) and A.C. Thiselton ('The
"Interpretation" of Tongues: a New Suggestion in the Light of Greek Usage in
Philo and Josephus", *The Journal of Theological Studies* , 30 (1979) 23 ff., and
posits a relation between Philonic theory on language and Paul of Tarsus's
position.

thoughts [...] but the perfect Aaron must meet the thoughts of the most perfect Moses" (*Det.* 129).

All that is said from paragraph 38 to those which I have just quoted establishes a relation between language and thought. Here reference is not so much to Moses as God's interpreter, as to Aaron, discourse, interpreter of Moses, thought.[55] There are in us two rational principles: one, external production προφορικός; the other, internal ἐνδιαθετός. There are also two virtues which provide the outwardly-producing principle with revelation, and that which concerns thought (διάνοια) with truth.

"For it is the duty of the thinking faculty to admit no falsehood, and of the language faculty to give free play to all that helps to shew facts clearly with the utmost exactness" (*Mos.* II.129).

Moses is the intellect (νοῦς), Aaron his word (λόγος). The intellect is trained to apprehend holy things, the word to express them in a holy manner.

In *Leg. All.* III.119, the λόγιον, as expression of divine communication, is ὄργανον φωνητήριον, vocal instrument. The result is fulfilled λόγος.

e) The language-thought link is recalled in *De Migratione*, where ἑρμηνεία is similar to a copy of supersensible natures:

"because mind has speech for its house or living-room, secluded from the rest of the homestead (the body). It is the Mind's living-place, just as the hearthside is man's. It is there that the Mind displays in orderly form itself and all the conceptions to which it gives birth, treating it as a man treats a house. And marvel not at Moses having given to speech the title of Mind's house in man; for indeed he says that God, the Mind of the universe, has for His house His own Word. [...] Who, then, can that House be, save the Word who is antecedent to all that has come into existence? the Word, which the Helmsman of the Universe grasps as a rudder to guide all things on their course? Even as, when He was fashioning the world, He employed it as His instrument, that the fabric of His handiwork might be without reproach". [56]

Here is clearly affirmed the connection between word of God and creation; between word of God, intellect, reality.[57]

---

[55] However, at paragraph 133 reference is made to discourses that interpret divine doctrines. Clearly, when speaking of Moses it is not easy to distinguish the two planes.

[56] *Migr.* 3-6.

[57] Cf. K. Otte, *op.cit.*(n. 54).

As in God, so too in man, the word is the home of the intellect. The relation between intellect and word does not however imply that the two need be identified. Even less so, therefore, can it be thought to assimilate word and noetic realities.

> "Again, quit speech also, "thy father's house", as Moses calls it, for fear thou shouldst be beguiled by beauties of mere phrasing, and be cut off from the real beauty, which lies in the matter expressed. Monstrous it is that shadow should be preferred to substance or a copy to originals. And verbal expression is like a shadow or copy, while the essential bearing of the matters conveyed by words resemble substance and originals".[58]

f) The meaning of ἑρμηνεία as expression, vocal articulation which is possible only through the lips, appears in *Somn.* II.262:[59] if the lips are closed words fail to be emitted.'Ερμηνεία, thus, even as sound expression of words, as word emission.[60]

Verbal expression, translation into words, is present in various passages, for example in *Cherubim.* Here, in paragraphs 101-105, discussion touches on the invisible soul, the earthly home of invisible God.[61] The theme of word translation, of the verbal expression of concepts is also addressed in *Det.* 79, where, unlike the passage cited from *Cherubim,* which concerned human expressions, Philo dwells on words pronounced by God: "Your brother's blood". The problem raised, however, is that of translating concepts into words, of verbalizing what is thought. [62]

The relation between thought expression and form of discourse is also analyzed in *Congr.* 24-33. Here, verbal expression as sound emission is closely connected to expressive modes, to the kind of argumentation used, and to rationality as a thought source to be externalized. The ascetic (Jacob), he who, that is, trains himself and will have virtue as a reward for his actions, shall take two legitimate wives and two concubines, the latter slaves to the former.

---

[58] *Migr.* 12.

[59] Cf. also *Somn.* II. 274.

[60] Cf. A.C. Thiselton, *op.cit.*(n. 54) 15-36.

[61] "And that the house may have both strength and loveliness, let its foundations be laid in natural excellence and good teaching, and let us rear upon them virtues and noble actions, and let its external ornaments be the reception of the learning of the schools. [...] From the study of the introductory learning of the schools come the ornaments of the soul, which are attached to it as to a house. Grammar[...] Geometry[...] Rhetoric seeks out and weighs the materials for shrewd treatment in all the subjects which it handles, and welds them to the language that befits them. Sometimes it raises us to a pitch of strong emotion, at other times the tension is relaxed in a sense of pleasure. With all this it gives fluency and facility in using our tongues and organs of speech."

[62] Cf. *Congr.* 17.

"For since our soul is twofold, with one part reasoning and the other unreasoning, each has its own virtue or excellence, the reasoning Leah, the unreasoning Rachel.[...] Necessarily then Leah will have for handmaid the faculty of expression by means of the vocal organs, and on the side of thought the art of devising clever arguments whose easy persuasiveness is a means of deception, while Rachel has for her's the necessary means of sustenance, eating and drinking. Moses has given us, as the names of these two handmaidens, Zilpah and Bilhah. Zilpah by interpretation is "a walking mouth," which signifies the power of expressing thought in language and directing the course of an exposition (διεξοδικῆς ἑρμηνείας)."63

Zilpah, therefore, represents the capacity to externalize thought in forms of discourse; she is slave to Leah, who represents the faculty of reason.

The relation between concept and word leads to that between reality and word, and therefore to ἑρμηνεία as translation according to point b). Now, some attribute to themselves that which, instead, comes from God: the thoughts of the intellect, the expressions of language and the representations of sensations (τοῦ νοῦ τὰς διανοήσεις, τοῦ λόγου τὰς ἑρμηνείας, τῆς αἰσθήσεως τὰς φαντασίας) 64 But the word cannot express (ἑρμηνεύειν)

"anything [...] did not He Who framed and adjusted to harmony the instrument of the voice beat out the music of its notes, opening the mouth and giving strength to the nerves of the tongue".65

The word, therefore, as ἑρμηνεία of reality, albeit always expressed by the will of God.

g) ἑρμηνεύειν to interpret, to examine. Cf. *Somn.* II. 32:

"Now, the varieties of the sheaves, that is to say of the doings which may be called our nourishment, are so countless [...] It may not, however, be out of place to instance some of these varieties which are introduced in his story of his dreams."

h) ῾Ερμηνεία as transmission. In *Det.* 63 ff. reference is made to the safekeeping of holy things:66 God has given his laws; perfect man,

---

63 *Congr* 26-30.
64 *Her.* 108; 110.
65 *Mut.* 56.
66 "He (Moses) charges him who is but half perfect to set to work and do holy actions, [...] while he charges the perfect one to labour no more, but to keep watch over all that he has acquired as the result of toilsome practice. [...] Watching or

once having succeeded in acquiring them, preserves them; he is both their interpreter and teacher; he teaches them to Jacob. What is evidenced here is the role of transmission by the interpreter, who conveys to others what he himself has received.

Furthermore, in *Spec. Leg.* II.189, the interpreter transmits the special laws. A distinction is made here between words given by God to the people through an interpreter and the words given by God directly to the people. The interpreter, therefore, as intermediary, as a vehicle of communication.[67] In *Praem.* 1-2 it is affirmed that the divine words (λογία) which were mediated by the prophet Moses are of three types: 1) those relative to creation, 2) historic (relative to either virtuous or evil lives throughout various generations, and to their respective rewards and punishments), 3) legislative, which involve both a general introduction and special laws. Ten principles were inspired (κεχρησμῳδῆσθαι), not through a ἑρμηνεύς, but formed in the highest Heavens; and the special laws were established by the prophet. The commandments of a general order, structured and endowed with a rational form in Heaven, were given directly by God without the mediation of an interpreter; the special norms were transmitted by the prophet. Here ἑρμηνεύς, almost coinciding with προφήτης, is the mediator who transmits to man the word of God.[68]

---

guarding is something complete, consisting in entrusting to memory those principles of holy things which were acquired by practice. To do this is to commit a fair deposit of knowledge to a trustworthy guardian, to her who alone makes light of the nets of forgetfulness with all their cunning devices. 'Guardian' is therefore the sound and appropriate name which he gives to the man who remembers what he had learnt. At an earlier stage, when he was in training, this man was a pupil with another to teach him, but when he became capable of watching and guarding, he obtained the power and position of a teacher, and appointed for the subordinate duties under the teacher his own brother, the word of utterance. [...] Accordingly the mind of the truly noble man will be guardian and steward of the teachings of virtue, while his brother, utterance, will minister to those who are seeking education, going over with them the doctrines and principles of wisdom.[...] So he expressly avouches that the fully accomplished man is guardian of the words and covenant of God. Furthermore he has made it clear that he is the best utterer and setter forth of judgements and laws. For utterance is an operation of the organ of speech which is akin to it, and watchful guardianship is found to be the function of the mind, which was created by nature to be a vast storehouse, and has ample room for the conceptions of all substance and all circumstances."

[67] Cf. J.P. Martin, 'El texto y la interpretación: la exégesis según Filón de Alejandría', *Revista Biblica* 39 (1977) 211-222.
[68] Cf. *Decal.* 32-35; *Spec. Leg.* III.7. See also *Leg.* 99. Here ἑρμηνεύς, through divine things, assimilated to προφήτης is Hermes. What is however stressed is the messenger's role as mediator. Cf. A. Pelletier (ed.), *Legatio ad Caium*, Paris (1972) 132 n.

CHAPTER TWO

HARMONY AND DISORDER

1. Harmony and the Loss of Balance

The notion of interpretation linked to practical application as discussed in the preceding chapter could prompt a simplification. The idea, that is, that the word of God, as a creative and ordering force, as cosmic law, is also immediately law for men, who in his city follow the law's directives. If we were thus to understand Philo's reasoning, we would be committing a gross simplification. The plane of divine law is one thing, that of human law is another. Within the sphere of the latter there are similarly two levels: one concerns those who follow, or - at least theoretically - should follow the law of Moses as received by God, and those other cities which have given themselves human laws. The problem of the relation between forms of order is, however, raised, as for Philo, in a given state; order and harmony are not only to be desired, but are to be connected with the order and harmony that exist in the cosmos. That is, with the order and harmony of the law laid down by God, creator and foundation of that order.

In the following pages I shall attempt to reconstruct these connections, and in particular to see whether the interpretation of harmony in one ambit implies consequences for the other; whether the disharmonies and conflicts which trouble order bear in themselves an attempt at re-establishing an equilibrium, even if transgression can be seen as an instance of broken harmony; whether a series of reactions to transgression (the plagues of Egypt, Providence intervening against the wicked) can be seen as an attempt to re-establish order. In particular, and in reference to the social ambit, estrangement from an ideal order raises questions about the coherence and continuity among the various spheres. How do social conflict, political error, the degenerate forms of power relate with a general scheme of harmony and obedience to divine law? How do tyrannical regimes and evil states fit into a general plan willed by God?

Is the negativity present in nations to be considered as a deviation from the positive city-model of which Moses is the ideal ruler, or has it an autonomy of its own? And what is the relation between justice and injustice, equality and inequality, harmony and disorder? Together with these considerations, I shall also explore the transformation that

some notions of Greek political theorizations of the V-IV century
underwent in Philo.

What has changed, however, is the initial perspective: we are no
longer dealing with rules and orders which derive meaning from the
political life of the *polis*, as with order and harmony contained within a
framework wherein social harmony runs parallel to the order of
nature.   Before being political, the norms here in question are
essentially ethical, deriving from a source which is external to the *polis*:
God. A personal God, a God who has revealed his law through words.
The reference to God, as an external source of norms, constitutes one of
the characterizing aspects of Philo's thinking in comparison with that of
other contemporary authors who address similar themes, such as the
Stoics and the Neopythagoreans. Their theorizations, in fact, differ
from those of Philo, whose claims, for example, about the living law
and the figure of the ruler are only apparently similar to
Neopythagorean formulations.

In the same way, a reading of the similarities between the
situation of the soul, that of the city and forms of reasoning, recalls
Platonic and Aristotelian formulations, even though the expression of
these various ambits is specific. The harmony of ordered society,
wherein everyone keeps to his place, for example, brings to mind
analogous Platonic theses. Here, however, the perspective is different,
as it is not a question of an assigned order in the city, but of a pre-
political order: acceptance of roles is acceptance of ethical laws in as
much as they are divine, not in as much as they are given by the city.
Whereas for Plato acceptance of order substantiates itself in the city,
even if it runs parallel to the order existing between the parts of the
soul and is presented in universal terms (the noble lie),[1] for Philo the
foundation of political order is ethical, and draws substance from its
relation with God. Conflict, which is detachment from established
order, is detachment from a law of divine origin. In this sense there is
no difference between imbalance in the city and imbalance in the soul; in
fact, the former stems from the latter, and transgression of the law is
departure from a role of obedience to the word of God.[2]   It is not

---

[1] *Resp.* III. 406c; 417b. Cf. Vegetti, *L'Etica degli antichi*, Bari (1989) 113-125. An
ethical reading of political problems is most evident in the *Letter of Aristeas*
where every theme relative to kingship and government is linked to a relation
with God and virtuous modes of behaviour. Cf. "Introduzione" in F. Calabi
(ed.), *Lettera di Aristea a Filocrate*, Milano (1995) 18-23.
[2] On the other hand, "Having therefore on this wise put a stop to the revolt
within himself and turned clean away from his own pleasure, having thus
shown his zeal for God, the First and Only One, he was honoured and crowned
with the two greatest rewards, peace and priesthood; with peace, because he put
an end to the intestine war of lusts in the soul; with the priesthood, because in

merely a question of knowing how to maintain an order established by rulers or ethically committed individuals, as it is of adhering to an order and to a law that come from God, and which as such are neither questionable nor modifiable. At best, they are unknown and transgressible. However, many are the nations in the world that do not refer to divine law, and instead have given themselves special laws. They follow norms which do not conform to the will of God. It is not a question of deviation or degeneration with respect to an optimal situation, but of two forms of rationality: one, entirely human; the other, which seeks an accord with divine rationality - even though unknowable - and which translates into a taking on of its law. The concept, then, is articulated along two planes: that of the present time and of present empirical conditions, and that of the relationship with the law, with God, with timelessness. In this double frame of reference lies the true hiatus with respect to the theory of the *polis*. Not only is the reference external to the polis itself, but it also has two levels: the present plane being staggered with respect to that of divine rationality. It is not so much an imperfection with respect to a model, of two realities, as it is two levels of discourse. Reality is permeated by only one law, that established by God, and the social order is correlated both to the ethical and cosmic order. There is only one plan according to which God created the universe and established norms in the world.[3]

---

name and in fact it is akin to peace. For the consecrated intelligence, being His minister and attendant, must needs do all those things in which her Master delighteth: He delights in the maintenance of a well-ordered state under good laws, in the abolishing of wars and factions, not only those which occur among cities, but also of those that arise in the soul; and these are greater and more serious than those, for they outrage reason, a more divine faculty than others within us. Weapons of war can go so far as to inflict bodily and monetary loss, but a healthy soul they can never harm. From this it appears that states would have done rightly if before bringing against one another arms and engines of war, with the enslavement and complete overthrow of the enemy in view, they had prevailed on their citizens one by one to put an end to the disorder which abounds within himself, and which is so great and unceasing. For, to be honest, this is the original of all wars. If this be abolished, neither will those occur which still break out in imitation of it, but the human race will attain to the experience and enjoyment of profound peace, taught by the law of nature, namely virtue, to honour God and to be occupied with His service, for this is the source of long life and happiness" (*Post.* 183-186). Cf. also *Sacrif.* 126.

[3] See *Opif.* 17-20; 28; 143; *Spec. Leg.* IV. 187-188; *QG.* III. 42; Cf. R.Barraclough, 'Philo's Politics. Roman Rule and Hellenistic Judaism', in *ANRW* II. 21.1 (1984) 506-508; H.A. Wolfson, *Foundations of Religious Philosophy in Judaism, Christianity and Islam*, Cambridge Mass. (1962) I.189-193; V. Nikiprowetzky, *Le Commentaire de l'Ecriture chez Philon d'Alexandrie*, Leiden (1977) 118-123. On the uniqueness of cosmic and moral laws see A. Myre, 'La loi dans l'ordre

Disorder in one ambit involves disorder in the other. The distance there
is between divine law and human intellect, however, implies that man
cannot aspire to full knowledge of the cosmic harmony established by
God, nor to its full imitation in a human sphere subject to errors and
evil. Thus, there are two aspects to this question; or, perhaps, there are
two planes involved: one relating to a sphere of perfection, to an
atemporal order related to cosmic harmony, relative to human
finiteness in relation to divine perfection, and the other relative to the
human sphere in its finiteness. The two levels of this discourse unfold in
a parallel fashion. My attempt, in this light, is therefore that of
analyzing the notions of law, order, harmony and, correlatively, also at
the terms of political theorization such as, for example, equality,
democracy and monarchy, which, used in an apparently similar
manner, in Philo acquire meanings different from those of the Greek
philosophical tradition.[4] I shall attempt to develop this line of thinking
in the second part of this chapter.

2. Universal Harmony and human Conflicts

In *De Vita Mosis* I.113 some types of punishment meted out to
Pharaoh partly by Aaron, partly by Moses, and in part by God himself
are mentioned. About the punishments inflicted by Moses, we may
wonder "what were the parts of nature which went into their making"?
Nature, therefore, takes part in the punishment, acting as its
instrument. Not stated as a figure of punishment because non
independent, but always moved by God, nature modifies its rhythms
and its norms: water turns into blood (*Mos.* I.99), water animals invade
arid lands (*Mos.* I.103), the air undergoes changes that trigger
unusually harsh weather conditions (*Mos.* I.118), day becomes night
and night day. These extraordinary events are produced by divine
wrath (*Mos.* I.119); there are phenomena that disrupt the harmony of
nature (*Mos.* I.117) and the balance underlying natural phenomena.[5]

---

cosmique et politique selon Philon d'Alexandrie', *Science et Esprit* 24 (1972) 217-
247.
[4] Cf. R. Barraclough, *op.cit.*(n.3) 505-506. Many notions of the preceding
political tradition are reformulated by Philo, thus constituting a point of
reference for successive theories on power, the source of authority and of the
law. This thesis is forcefully maintained by E.R. Goodenough, *The Politics of
Philo Judaeus. Practice and Theory*, Hildesheim (1967) 119; cf. also L. Troiani,
'Giudaismo ellenistico e cristianesimo', in B. Virgilio (ed.),"Aspetti e problemi
dell'ellenismo", *Studi Ellenistici* IV, 1994, in part. 201.
[5] Punishment directly inflicted by God without human mediation, however
always through nature, occurs also when nature is not truly subverted, but only
through a strenghtening of natural activity. An example of this is the gadfly
which attacks with greater ferocity than usual.

Land, water, air and fire, ordered to construct the universe, become, by God's will, sources of destruction and disorder.[6] If God so decides, world order is subverted, and those very elements which God utilized to form the universe are by him used to confound the wicked (*Mos.* I.96).[7] Nature, therefore, participates in acts of punishment, not in that it possesses a will of its own, but as an instrument in the hands of God (*Mos.* I.113). Confronted with Pharaoh's arrogance, God gives warnings to the Egyptians (*Mos.* I.110), to those who hinder divine will and in some way attempt to oppose God's plan. Also in *Mos.* I.156, regarding Moses's lofty virtue and his unique position in creation, Philo states that "each element obeyed him as its master, changed its natural properties and submitted to his command". Also, in reference to manna, what is stressed is the exceptional character of the phenomenon with respect to the natural order (*Mos.* I.200), even if it is possible that some unexplainable phenomena are due not to some extraordinary intervention by God, but to natural possibilities hitherto unknown to us (*Mos.* I.185). Thus, order is disrupted, and cosmic harmony subverted, until God decides to re-establish the foregoing order, only to once again upset it in case punishment proves insufficient (*Mos.* I.120). Nature then has a decisive, even if not autonomous, role in the human sphere; and its regularities are altered in order to punish the wicked. In order, that is, to put an end to the transgressions which occur in the ambit of human order. There is only one rule that governs the cosmos, and it is that established by God.[8] Those which in other words could be termed miracles are here interventions - unprecedented, surely - but somehow implied by the unity of cosmic law, induced by the need to re-establish an order which has been broken in one of the spheres. The latter's harmony can be restored even by interrupting the order in another sphere. It is almost as if nature were taking the situation in hand, by modifying its own patterns of behaviour to re-establish balance. Nature goes beyond its own regularities and prevails upon the harmony of its flux because a greater harmony is at stake, one in which even mankind finds its place in God's plan. Nature works together with God with the aim of restoring a balance among men, and of finding answers to conflicts and injustice. Underlying all this is the notion of a universal harmony, of a cosmic equilibrium which exists in so much as it is founded on the Law. It structures the cosmos (*Opif.* 10;13), the relations between men and animals (*Opif.* 84), the human

---

6 Cf. *Mos.*I .117-119.

7 Cf. J. Mansfeld, 'Heraclitus, Empedocles, and others in a Middle Platonist cento in Philo of Alexandria', *Vigiliae Christianae* 39 (1985) 131-156.

8 [...] "Even the whole world does not move at its own free unshackled will, but is the standing-ground of God who steers and pilots in safety all that is" (*Conf.* 98).

sphere (*Opif.* 69;82) as formed and ordered by God according to a model He himself created(*Opif.* 17-20).

3. Law of nature, Law of God

The Law is transmitted to Moses on Sinai, but is nevertheless also included in the human ambit to the extent that it constitutes a rule for man even before being transmitted to him. The Patriarchs, νόμοι ἔμπψυχοι, embody the Law; they themselves are the living law, a reason-endowed law.[9] They are the demonstration of the accord between human and natural orders. They also indicate that the prescribed norms can be actuated as, even before being transmitted to men and written down, these norms were followed. The Patriarchs did not receive them through tradition nor teaching, but simply followed the laws of nature, deeming the latter the highest institution (*Abr.* 6). [10] With their life, and by impersonating the law, they constituted a pattern of behaviour for those who surrounded them. As guides to the people, they were norm, guideline and source of the law for the others who were thus guided not by force, but by persuasion (*Ios.* 269).[11]

Plato had previously spoken of royal man endowed with φρόνησις, embodiment of the norm, contrasting him with the written laws (*Polit.* 294a; cf. also *Gorgias* 484b), and Aristotle wondered whether, in certain situations, "it is preferable that the best law, or the best man, govern" (*Pol.* 1287b; cf. also 1284a3-14; b26-34).[12] In reference to judges,Aristotle spoke of οἷον δίκαιον ἔμψυχον(*Eth.Nic.* 1132a20).[13]

---

[9] Cf. *Abr.* 5; *Mos.* I.162. See Nikiprowetzky, *op.cit.* (n. 3) 124-126; C. Kraus Reggiani, *Introduzione* in Filone Alessandrino, *De Opificio Mundi. De Abrahamo. De Josepho*, Roma (1979) 173-174.

The relation between human law and divine law, the latter being that of the cosmos, is so interwoven (there is only one law, even if the ambits in which it unfolds are manifold) that it is not even necessary that the law be codified and written, nor even revealed. Surely, after Sinai, Moses represents codification; he is disposer of the law, besides being its interpreter. However, the Patriarchs were *nomoi empsychoi* and, even, Joseph (who embodies political man) precedes written legislation.

[10] Cf. H.A. Wolfson, *op.cit.* (n.3) 182-185.

[11] Cf..L.Tiede, 'The Charismatic figure as miracle worker',*Society of Biblical Literature. Dissertation Series* 1, Missoula (1972).

[12] For Aristotle it is a question of the law's applicability and of the relation between the general and the particular. However, what I would like to underscore is that Aristotle also addresses the relation between the law and superior beings who are not bound by the law. Actually, here too there is a difference with respect to Philo, for whom the Patriarchs, more than not being bound by the law, are themselves the animate law.

[13] According to F. Parente, 'Il giudaismo alessandrino', in L. Firpo (ed.), *Storia delle Idee politiche, economiche e sociali*, II. Torino (1985) 330, in Philo there is

Here the problem lies in the relation between codified laws and superior figures not bound by the laws. Νόμοι ἔμψυχοι are explicitly referred to also by other authors, as aptly clarified by E.R. Goodenough,[14] who recalls a fragment attributed to Archytas :

> "the laws are of two types, animate law, which is the king, and the inanimate, which is the written law."

The king is not subject to the law, he produces it. He is above the laws of the city and conforms not to a written code which binds the other inhabitants of the land, but to the natural law. The norms, that is, are inscribed in the king, who is the animate law; he does not limit himself to imposing respect for the law, he himself is the law, the ordering principle that not only governs lower functions, but structures them.

The king's presentation as animate law is widespread in an extensive body of Neopythagorean literature, of which remain only a few fragments attributed to Diotogenes, Sthenidas, Ecphantus (cited in Stobaeus).[15] What underlies such theorizations is the distinction, which was already present in Aristotle, between νόμος κοινός and νόμος ἴδιος, which is counterposed by the distinction between natural law and law of the city, non-written law and codified law.[16] These notions are present in Philo who, on one hand distinguishes the law written by Moses from the non-codified law νόμος ἔμψυχος, and on the other, a common law, which conforms to nature and was transmitted to Moses, and laws which are peculiar to individual cities.[17] The various nations

---

to be found a Stoic colouring in his idea of inclusion with the universal providential order . See also J. Laporte, *Introduction* in *De Josepho* Paris (1964) 18 ff.

[14] 'The Political Philosophy of Hellenistic Kingship',*Yale Classical Studies* I (1928) 59. Cf. also A. Delatte, *Essai sur la politique pythagoricienne*, Liège (1922) 114. For references to Pythagorean (or Neopythagorean) fragments on kingship cf. E. Bréhier, *Les idées philosophiques et religieuses de Philon d'Alexandrie*, Paris(1925) 18ff.; E.R.Goodenough, *op.cit.*(n.4) 45ff.; G.F. Chesnut, 'The Ruler and the Logos in Neopythagorean, Middle Platonic, and Late Stoic Political Philosophy', *ANRW*. II.16.2 (1978) 1310-1320; G. Giannantoni, 'Il pensiero politico greco dopo Alessandro Magno' in *Storia delle idee politiche economiche e sociali cit.* (n. 13), vol. 1, Torino (1982) 357-362.

[15] Stob. IV, 7. 61-62; 63; 64-66.

[16] Cf. Wolfson, *op.cit.* (n. 3) 174-175.

[17] Cf. *Agr.* 43; *Ios.* 31. See Goodenough, *op.cit.* (n.4) 80; Parente, *op.cit.* (n. 13) 327-328. Concerning the notion that the laws of individual cities are added to correct reasoning see also C. Kraus Reggiani, *op.cit.* (n. 9) 271. As for the Cynic theme of the opposition between civil institutions and "cosmic cities" cf. L. Bertelli, *L'utopia greca*, in *Storia delle Idee politiche, economiche e sociali cit.* (n.13) 549 ff.

have endowed themselves with legislators and man-established laws, which are more or less just, more or less wise and human; but nevertheless, as such, also subject to error and modification. Only Israel, having received the law directly from God, conforms to a stable and eternal order, above the sphere of human vicissitudes (*Mos.* I.87;278; *Decal.* 2; 4; 9), even if, naturally, it does not always conform.[18] Harmony, therefore,and order, in a cosmos where all is willed and ruled by God; harmony of the spheres and order of structured reality according to a numerically identifiable order where monads and hebdomads constitute perfection, and, in some ways, coincide (*Opif.* 100), and where proportion marks the structure of reality. Harmony, therefore, and order, in a cosmos and in a human sphere that conforms to its model, that accepts the law with its hierarchic order (cf. *Leg. All.* III.126; *Decal.* 155).[19] Hierarchy among men and between men and animals:

"On this account too the Father, when he had brought him into existence as a living being naturally adapted for sovereignty, not only in fact but by express mandate appointed him king of all creatures under the moon, those that move on land and swim in the sea and fly in the air. For all things mortal [...] did he make subject to men" (*Opif.* 84).

"So the Creator made man after all things, as a sort of driver and pilot, to drive and steer the things on earth, and charged him with the care of animals and plants, like a governor subordinate to the chief and great King" (*Opif.* 88).

4. *General Law, Special Laws*

The picture is one of an order where every creature has its own place and role, and where acceptance of the Law also implies acceptance of one's own condition in the world. Human paucity before God (*Cher.* 113-121); superiority over the animals and plants, order among men: acceptance of roles and hierarchy implies peace, harmony and balance.[20]

[18] Cf. Wolfson, *op.cit.* (n. 3) 180-181; Parente, *op.cit.* (n.13) 336-337; 344-345.
[19] Cf. D. Farias, *Studi sul pensiero sociale di Filone di Alessandria*, Pubblicazioni degli Istituti di Scienze giuridiche, economiche, politiche e sociali della Facoltà di giurisprudenza dell'Università di Messina 180, Milano (1993).
On this topic I couldn't read P. Borgen's, *Philo of Alexandria. An exegete for his Time*, Leiden (1997), which I received when this book was already in print.
[20] Cf. P.Chambronne, 'Loi et législateur chez Philon d'Alexandrie: remarques sur la formation d'un concept judéo-hellénistique', *Cahiers du Centre George-Radet*, Talence, Université de Bordeaux III, 4 (1984) 45-63.

Before hierarchy is instituted in the cities among the various components of the social body, it is instituted generationally, in a shifting process of decadence from the first man downwards to ever weaker forms (*Opif.* 140). Adam, the forefather, was also the only citizen in the world, which was his home, his city, his homeland.[21]

"Now since every well-ordered State has a constitution, the citizen of the world enjoyed of necessity the same constitution as did the whole world: and this constitution is nature's right relation, more properly called an "ordinance", or "dispensation", seeing it is a divine law, in accordance with which there was duly apportioned to all existences that which rightly falls to them severally. This State and polity must have had citizens before man [...]. And who should these be but spiritual and divine natures, some incorporeal and visible to mind only, some not without bodies, such as are the stars?" (*Opif.* 143-144).[22]

Compared to such a cosmic order, to such a state which comprehends the entire world, the particular cities founded by men to respond to immediate needs are based on particular laws, which are quite different from the great Law of Moses[23] that reiterates the harmony and balance inherent in the Law of God.

"For this world is the Megalopolis or "great city", and it has a single polity and a single law, and this is the word or reason of nature, commanding what should be done and forbidding what should not be done. But the local cities which we see are unlimited in number and subject to diverse polities and laws by no means identical, for different peoples have different customs and regulations which are extra inventions and additions" (*Ios.* 29).

The difference between particular laws is usually explained in terms of objective diversities such as specific territorial or climatic conditions, or different customs (*Ios.* 30), or is attributed to decisions by legislators which vary from time to time. Actually, underlying such particularities there is a spirit of excess, and the fact of making decisions not on the basis of superior universal norms consonant with natural law, but with private interests.[24] To the universal laws that belong to the natural order are preferred the particular laws of

---

[21] Cf. Seneca, *Ep.* 90.42. See Nikiprowetzky, *op.cit.* (n. 3) 143-144 n. 64.

[22] Cf. *Mos.* II. 51; *Opif.* 19.

[23] Cf. H. Koester, 'ΝΟΜΟΣ ΦΥΣΕΩΣ: the Concept of Natural Law in Greek Thought' in *Religions in Antiquity: Essays in memory of E.R. Goodenough*, Studies in the History of Religions. Supplements to Numen 14 (1968) 521-541.

[24] *Decal.* 136. Cf. also *Ios.* 31: "in fact the laws in force in the single cities are additions to the correct reason (ὀρθὸς λόγος) of nature". Cf. Plato, *Gorg.* 483b-c; *Resp.* 338e.

individual cities. Here, the reference to Cynical and Stoic theories is obvious:[25]

> "The Stoics say that the universe is in the proper sense a city, but those here on earth are not- they are called cities, but are not really". [26]

> "That much admired *Republic* of Zeno, who founded the Stoic sect, is aimed at this one main point, that our arrangement for habitation should not be based on cities or peoples, each one distinguished by its own special system of justice, but we should regard all men as citizens and members of the populace, and there should be one of life and one order, like that of a herd grazing together and nurtured by a common law/pasturing. ". [27]

And again, in Cicero, (*De natura deorum* II.62):

> "The world itself was created for the gods and for men, and everything that in it is found was ordained for man's benefit. The world in fact is, as it were, the common abode of gods and men, and the city of both, because they are the only ones to have use of reason and to live according to the law. Thus, as it is to be held that Athenes and Sparta were founded for the Athenians and for the Spartans, and justly it is said that all that is to be found in these cities belongs to these peoples, so does it bear believing that everything that is found in all the world belongs to gods and men."

A cosmic city, therefore, one which goes beyond the barriers between peoples and particular cities, and which is governed by the universal law of nature.

5. *Cities on Earth, Cosmic Cities*

The quoted passages, as others apparently similar,[28] effectively present some substantial differences. In particular, in terms of what is here of interest to us, there emerges the problem of whether the

---

[25] Cf. M. Schofield, *The Stoic Idea of the City*, Cambridge (1991) 64-114. In particular, in reference to Seneca, on p. 93 Schofield speaks of two communities, a larger one containing men and Gods, and another that is only human. There is thus a distinction between human cities and a better cosmic city. The true city is the universe. Schofield relates this theme expressly to Philo (p. 93, cf. also p.143).

[26] Clement of Alexandria, *Strom.*IV, 26 (SVF III. 327), quoted in Schofield, *op.cit.*(n.25)61.

[27] Plutarch, *De Alexandri magni fortuna aut virtute* I.329 (SVF I. 262),quoted in Schofield, *op.cit.*(n.25)104.

[28] Cf. Schofield, *op. cit.* (n.25) 57 ff.

universal law pertains to the city of gods and men, or whether there is a contrast between a cosmic city - and human cities.[29] According to Dyo Chrysostom(XXXVI§21),[30] for example, even if ordered, respectful of the law and led by good rulers, earthly cities will nevertheless be limited and lacking, because there exist not only good elements, save in a cosmic city of gods. Although still speaking in terms of a cosmic city, this concept raises a sharp distinction between earthly cities and heavenly city. There is no unique order which is mirrored throughout the cosmos, even if with differing degrees of perfection. In this sense, Philo's position is different, as for him the law pervades the entire cosmos and its unitary nature is obvious, as it has only one source and foundation: God. Not for this, however, will the order and harmony of heaven be omnipresent.[31] Earthly things are sunk in disorder, and the cities governed by ambition and special interests follow laws which are subject to change and error. We could ask ourselves whether there exist two city models, one positive, the other negative, to which different empirical realities refer; or are we to think of some form of degeneration, or, still, of a relation such as exists between a model and its copy. Hypothesizing two parallel models, even empirical realities would be of two types: one positive (ordered cities), the other negative (cities prey to disorder and error). In this case, however, particular cities, fraught with conflict, upheaval and negativity, would not be so much the products of a degeneration due to human error, selfishness, ambition, etc.; but to the fact of being, from their very origin, related to a negative model. Thus, it would not be so much a case of a paradigmatic city - positive, eternal, ordered - and cities on earth - incomplete, corruptible, prey to disorder - as it would of two city paradigms, one positive and the other negative, and of two types of cities on earth - one positive and the other negative. It is perhaps in this light that D.T. Runia's interpretation[32] of a passage in *De Confusione Linguarum* (107-108) may be read; even if I am not sure this is the right interpretation:

---

[29] See G. Giannantoni, *op.cit.* (n. 14) 353-357.

[30] Cit. in Schofield, *op.cit.* (n. 25) 62.

[31] "The sun and moon and the whole heaven stand out in such clear and plain distinctness because everything there remains the same and regulated by the standards of truth itself and moves in harmonious order and with the grandest of symphonies; while earthy things are brimful of disorder and confusion and in the fullest sense of the words discordant and inharmonious, because in them deep darkness reigns while in heaven all moves in most radiant light, or rather heaven is light itself most pure and unalloyed." (*Ios.* 145). Cf. also *Decal.* 2-4; 5.

[32] *The Idea and the Reality of the City in theThought of Philo of Alexandria*, manuscript p. 11. I wish to thank D. Runia for allowing me to quote from his manuscript, even though it has yet to be published.

"The basic antithesis is between the soul and the city of virtue, equality and justice (which can be called the city of God) and the soul and the city of vice, inequality and injustice, symbolized above all by the tower buildings of Babel. [...] As there are two kinds of soul, there are two kinds of city, the one marked by order and virtue, the other by disorder and vice."

There then are two models, one positive and the other negative; soul models before being city models.

Questions on the coexistence of the two models and on their origin shift to the problem of the origin of the negative soul. The theme is addressed in *De Opificio* 75: the existence of evil in the world, the source of error, the attribution of the origin of negativity. In *De Opificio*, Philo's solution shifts the attribution of evil from God to intermediary figures purposely created. Surely, the introduction of beings that should guarantee perfection and God's good will only shifts the problem. Claiming the absence of evil in the creator is at odds with the creation of beings in charge of negativity. Such problems have to do with the coherence of the divine plan, of providence in the world, of God's uniqueness, and of the presence of evil. This is not the place to address such issues. Nevertheless, where *De Confusione* (107-108) specifically raises the problem of city models, it seems to me that more than an allusion to two models - one positive and one negative - the text introduces a relation between copy and model, along with the notion of degeneration. I shall quote the passage in question in its entirety:

"The law-giver thinks that besides those cities which are built by men's hands upon the earth, of which the materials are stones and timber, there are others, even those which men carry about established in their souls. Naturally these last are models or archetypes, for the workmanship bestowed upon them is of a more divine kind, while the former are copies composed of perishing material. Of the soul-city there are two kinds, one better, the other worse. The better adopts as its constitution democracy, which honours equality and has law and justice for its rulers - such a one is a melody which sings God's praises. The worse, which corrupts and adulterates the better, as the false counterfeit coin corrupts the currency, is mob-rule, which takes inequality for its ideal, and in it injustice and lawlessness are paramount. The good have their names entered on the burgess-roll of the former type of state, but the multitude of the wicked are embraced under the second and baser type, for they love disorder rather than order, confusion rather than fixedness and stability" (*Conf.* 197-109).

It is the dimwit that resorts to the senses (sight and hearing) and to the passions as instruments leading to error. The wicked described in *Gen.* 11.3 bake their bricks in fire, inflame their passions and vices, escaping the control of wisdom (*Conf.* 101). The just man, instead, symbolized by Noah, still unable to contemplate what he truly is, with his soul alone, and without the help of his sensations, will "daub <the arc - that is, his body - with pitch inside and out> to render secure both the representations and the faculties which through his moderation are explicated" (*Conf.* 105).

But, when evil shall have subsided, he will use his incorporeal thoughts to grasp truth.

> "On the other hand the mind called Moses, that goodly plant, given the name of goodly at his very birth, who in virtue of his larger citizenship took the world for his township and country, weeps bitterly in the days when he is imprisoned in the ark of the body bedaubed as with 'asphalt-pitch', which thinks to receive and contain, as with cement, impressions of all that is presented through sense. He weeps for his captivity, pressed sore by his yearning for a nature that knows no body" (*Conf.* 106).

In reference to these passages it seems to me that the comparison between soul and city underscores the presence of elements capable of taking on more or less importance one over the other. Thus, in *Conf.* 111, the presumption is put forward of dividing the faculties of the soul as if they were tribes and peoples, designating some to the rational part, others to the irrational. Again, we have the analogy between the soul and social organization, and, within the two poles of this analogy, what counts is the balance between the various components. Inside the soul, for example, we can choose order, harmony, virtue, or, vice versa, strengthen and fortify vice, the principles of impiety and atheism, disorder (*Conf.* 114). All these are elements which lead back to "that principle of evil that always dies without ever being dead, and whose name is Cain" (*Conf.* 122).

I have introduced this lengthy digression, which regards the soul more than the types of city, to see whether - by analogy - it was possible to hypothesize two models of city - one positive and one negative-; both coexisting and both paradigms of empirical situations; or whether we are to think in terms of a paradigm city and empirical cities, imperfect and transient copies of the former, or, whether the frame of reference need not be that of a degeneration starting from an optimal condition. The uniqueness of Adam, forefather of the world, in one phase of human history, and his role as sole citizen, seem to rule out a plurality - or even a twofoldness - of models. If various are the forms of city today in the world, if at least there are two types - one positive and the other negative - certainly it seems that these cannot refer back to the primordial history of humanity, at least not as far back as to Cain and Abel, and thus even less so to two paradigmatic models.

An analysis of passages from *Conf.* 101-122, by shedding light on the analogy between soul and city, enables us to consider the relation between parts of the soul as a mirror for the relation existing within cities and peoples. And it is clear, as far as the soul is concerned, that there are inside it various parts and various faculties, which can either prevail or be dominated, thus accounting for the different results of human conduct and choices.

6. Source of the Law

Going back to the relation between cosmic order and disorder on earth, between universal law and particular laws, between natural norms and norms of single cities, the hiatus which the Stoics perceived between cosmopolitanism and particular cities, between correct law according to nature and the incorrect laws of the cities, finds parallels in Philo.[33] Also for the Alexandrian, the law's authority source is external to the community; but,whereas the Stoics identified that source in reason, Philo identified it in God. For the former, natural order and rational order are welded; life according to λόγος coincides with life according to nature.

> "*Phronesis* is not only moral science of what is good and what is evil; rather, it is such in as much as it is also theoretical knowledge of nature, whence the moral norm derives. According to Plutarch's testimony, Chrysippus holds that the issue of good and evil, of virtue and happiness, is to be addressed starting "from common nature and from the rule of the cosmos". Physical theory is the basis of moral *phronesis* and of the art of living it proposes (*SVF* 3.68). The ancient science of good and evil then takes on a cosmic content. It is necessary to know and understand the world in order to assent to its providential order, as only in this assent to the norm of nature does virtue reside".[34]

Philo certainly would not subscribe to such an assertion. For him, nature is not the source of the norm, and it is not knowledge of nature that can lead to virtue. Yet, knowledge of individual good welds to that of cosmic good, in as much as there is only one source of good and order: God.[35] Therefore, it is necessary to know the law, which is one. It is not a question of knowing physical law, but that cosmic law which is inscribed in the Law. For Chrysippus, the sage achieves a connection between knowledge and moral action the moment in which, knowing the universal norm, he actuates it.

---

[33] Cf. Schofield, *op.cit.* (n.25) 143.

[34] M. Vegetti, *op.cit.* (n.1) 276 [my transl.].

[35] "When he was minded to found the one great city, He conceived beforehand the models of its parts, and that out of these He constituted and brought to completion a world discernible only by the mind, and then, with that for a pattern, the world which our senses can perceive" (*Opif.* 19).

"In this very nexus between knowledge and moral action, the sage becomes the norm itself, in "shaped" form, or, to use Chrysippus's expression, rendered "visible".[36]

For Philo, on the other hand, the Patriarchs themselves, represent the norm as perfectly compatible, after Sinai, with revealed law written down by Moses. However, as we have seen, universal law is one thing, whereas another are the particular laws of the states. What is necessary is a mediation between Moses's law and concrete situations, be they of Israel or of other countries.[37] Perhaps Joseph, the emblem of political man, in some ways represents the very performer of mediation, he who bears the truth to those who as yet do not know it. In as much as he interprets dreams he

"reveals how the reality of this world is an illusory and transitory larva of a reality which is not subject to sensory perception".[38]

Joseph, however, is not sufficient:

"l'homme politique du *Joseph* vient comme un devin véridique, interpréter le songe commun qu'est la vie de la société et c'est lui qui conduira les hommes vers la vérité. Ce guide pourtant ne saurait être Joseph, et Philon tait son nom à ce moment. C'est Moïse, le vrai chef de l'humanité, parce qu'il est prophète, et par là législateur, prêtre et roi, parce qu'il incarne à la perfection l'idéal de la royauté."[39]

7. Initial Harmony and subsequent Degenerations

Estrangement from a situation of perfection and order, and collapse into the anarchy and disorder of the earth's cities, however constitutes a problem. Transgression and degeneration have made their way into the world and undermined initial harmony and order.[40] The relation between law, nature and man is now different compared

---

[36] Vegetti, *op.cit.* (n.1) 277, [my transl.].

[37] Cf. Nikiprowetzky, *op.cit.* (n. 3) 217-219 n. 161.

[38] C. Kraus Reggiani, *op.cit.* (n. 9) 294, [my transl.]. In *De Somniis* (II. 42-48), Joseph is the emblem of vainglory and of a political power which is seen negatively as a vehicle leading to demagogy and tyranny. See also *Somn.* II. 78-79.

[39] J. Laporte, *op.cit.* (n.13) 38.

[40] Conflict not only in the human world, but also in the universe, clashes with the image of a universe pervaded by harmony and order. Cf. D.H. Hay, 'Philo's Treatise on the Logos-Cutter', *StPh.* 2 (1973) 9-22.

to the situation of Adam, citizen of the world, who lived in harmony with nature. It is also different compared to the condition of Moses, who will be citizen of the world (*Conf.* 105-106) when evil will have abated; when the just man "will be able to go out from the ark to grasp truth with his incorporeal intellect." The cities are presently governed by special laws, dominated by private interests and ambitions, hindered by pride and vice. Perhaps it is not transcendentally impossible to return, if not to Earthly Paradise, which is by now precluded to man, at least to a condition of virtue and harmony. Or perhaps, within Philo's theory, two parallel theses are at play: one relative to an atemporal order, paradigmatic of the order and harmony existing in the cosmos, relative to human finiteness compared with divine perfection; and the other, connected with socio-human organisations in their finiteness. The two levels could proceed in parallel fashion in as much as their perspectives are different.[41]

---

[41] Cf. M. Schofield, *Zeno of Citium's Anti-utopianism*, a review of D. Dawson's book *Cities of the Gods: communist Utopies in Greek Thought*, New York-Oxford (1992). I thank the author for having allowed me to quote from his text even if not yet published. The theme that Schofield addresses is that of utopia in Zeno. He discusses the distinction posited by D. Dawson between 'high' and 'low' political utopianism. On page 186 Dawson speaks of 'high' political utopianism in terms of "a method for articulating an ideal of moral perfection by showing the environment in which virtue can flourish optimally". On page 5 of his review article Schofield quotes, but criticizes, Dawson, where the latter claims that Zeno proposes "a city of the virtuous as a timeless paradigm whose unrealisability was of no importance, since striving for the ideal was everything" (p. 204). Here are put forth hypothetical models to be actuated here and now, and models valid in all places and times; models which link up with Zeno's theme that virtue is obedience to the reason that is in us (aside from, therefore, the notion of here and now). The problem is whether, when referring to Dawson's idea of an atemporal paradigm, we are not in fact shifting into an ambit which differs from that of realisability. Precisely because it is a theoretical model which constitutes a paradigm, it abstracts from problems of realisability, whether relating to the here and now, or to the always and everywhere. This, however, according to Schofield, is at odds with what Zeno himself affirms. "Zeno began his Politeia with a striking assertion of the applicability of his proposal to his own time and place" (p. 7). For Schofield one can speak of anti-utopianism in Zeno. The perspective, then, would be neither of a 'high' unrealisable utopia, nor of a 'low' utopia, but one of different models. The first would be a sort of phenomenology of virtue and virtuous city. In my opinion, it is perhaps better to think in terms of two coexisting planes, the first purely theoretical, detached from whatever intent of realisability in as much as the problem is not even posited; the second, instead, which is practicable. The hypothesis is that in Zeno there could be both levels, but referred to different situations. Obviously, I do not here intend to link these considerations directly to an analysis of Philo, especially as their underlying presuppositions and tenets are different. What is basically different is Philo's reference to the source of cosmic order and harmony.

There is however an hiatus between an order established by God and described - more than prescribed - in the Law, and concrete situations.[42] It is not an hiatus between what should be and what is: Moses's Law is the true being, the description of reality, and not some unattainable goal. The fact that man has estranged himself from it, and transgressed the norm, does not imply - in principle - its unattainability; just as, moreover, conflict, war and strife originate from pride, arrogance,[43] the abandonment of temperance, from stressing special interests, and not from the necessity or ontological impossibility of achieving peace and harmony.[44]

Conflict is generated among countries (*Ios.* 56), between subjects and rulers (*Spec. Leg.* II.92-94), among peers (*Somn.* II.78-79), under the same roof (*Gig.* 51), within the individual soul (*Opif.* 81; *Abr.* 240-244). At the origin of this lies the abandonment of harmony and balance, of temperance and self-control, of an acceptance of the norm, in favour of the unleashed impulses of the passions, of ambition and abuse of power.[45]

"Who does not know the misfortunes which licentiousness brings to nations and countries and whole latitudes of the civilized world on land and sea? For the majority of wars, and those the greatest, have arisen through amours and adulteries and the deceits of women, which have consumed the greatest choicest part of the Greek race and the barbarian also, and destroyed the youth of their cities. And, if the results of licentiousness are civil strife and war, and ill upon ill without number, clearly the results of continence are stability and peace and the acquisition and enjoyment of perfect blessings" (*Ios.* 56-57).

I would simply like to put forth the hypothesis of two coexisting planes of discourse, that are apparently incoherent, and perhaps even irreconcilable, and referring, in fact, to different perspectives.

[42] Cf. *Abr.* 261; *Q.E.* I.21; *Spec. Leg.* II.22.

[43] Cf. Barraclough, *op.cit.* (n. 3) 531-533.

[44] Cf. *Agr.* 75-76; *Conf.* 132-133. There is a city in the world juxtaposed to the intelligible world, the city of perception (*Gig.* 60-61). There are men bound to corporeal pleasure (earth), to the arts and encyclical sciences (heaven), and those who turn to the intelligible (God). Here, the political metaphor upsets the terms of the question: the focus of analysis here is not order in the world, but the types of human life. Cf. J.P. Martin, 'Philo and Augustine. De civitate Dei XIV 28 and XV: Some Preliminary Observations', *StPhA* (1991) 287.

At times, men of the earth are identified with politicians. The politician, then, is the executor of what concerns the body. Hence criticism of Joseph, the political man par excellence. See Goodenough, *op.cit.* (n. 4) 33. On the ambiguity of the figure of Joseph cf. Kraus Reggiani, *op.cit.* (n. 9) 269-282.

[45] Cf. *Decal.* 151-154; *Opif.* 81; *Leg. All.* III. 79.

8. *Error in the World*

If conflict is the fruit of intemperance, vainglory and, in principle, were men capable of controlling themselves and their passions, there should be a situation of harmony, since the world was created by God according to the Law, and human order follows the same norms of cosmic order. Hence, are we to think in terms of an original condition of peace and balance as having been disrupted by degeneration? Are we to hypothesize some sort of primigenial Golden Age?

> "If we call that original forefather of our race not only the first man but also the only citizen of the world we shall be speaking with perfect truth. For the world was his city and dwelling-place. No building made by hand had been wrought out of the material of stones and timber. The world was his mother country where he dwelt far removed from fear, inasmuch as he had been held worthy of all the rule of the denizens of the earth, and all things mortal trembled before him, and had been taught or compelled to obey him as their master. So he lived exposed to no attack amid the comforts of peace unbroken by war" (*Opif.* 142).

And this was the Earthly Paradise.[46] Actually, we have seen that in some ways there is a degeneration from Adam to the successive generations (*Opif.* 140). Evil, however, is already inborn in creation, so much so that God, to whom cannot be attributed the creation of evil, has helpers - intermediary beings - who are responsible for negativity and vice:

> "when man orders his course aright, when his thoughts and deeds are blameless, God the universal Ruler may be owned as their Source; while others from the number of His subordinates are held responsible for

---

[46] Cosmic order established by God is somehow preserved on earth when the Law is followed. True order would be achieved, then, were Israel fully to follow Moses's instructions. We find ourselves here on a meta-historic plane (cf. Wolfson, *op.cit.* (n. 3) 407 ff.), in a sort of ideal city as when reference is made to Abraham, (*nomos empsychos*), or to Joseph. Can we think, in historical terms, of a situation of order? Of a state which somehow recreates the rules of harmony? According to some authors, as for example M. Hadas-Lebel (*Jérusalem contre Rome*, Paris (1990) 345-346), such harmony can perhaps be pursued in a type of cohabitation among peoples as instituted by the Roman Empire. Roman *pietas* re-establishes order, security and freedom (which is essentially religious freedom: cf.*Leg.* 43-56;75;119; 138-151). Certainly it is not a matter of divine order, nor of harmony established by God, but it is nevertheless a settling of conflictual situations. By the same author see also 'Le paganisme à travers les sources rabbiniques des II et III siècles. Contribution à l'étude du syncrétisme dans l'empire romain', in *ANRW* II.19.2 (1979); 'L'évolution de l'image de Rome auprès des Juifs en deux siècles de relations judéo-romains - 164 à +70', in *ANRW* II.20.2 (1987) 846 ff.

thoughts and deeds of a contrary sort: for it could not be that the Father should be the cause of an evil thing to his offspring" (*Opif.* 75).

The fall of man, therefore, is already written in creation and the break of harmony in the Garden of Eden is already present at the moment of its formation. As a *mishnah* (*Avoth* 3.18) will say: "all is foreseen; freedom is given". It is the age-old problem of the existence of evil and of imperfection in a universe created by a perfect being. However, as far as the human world is concerned, conflict is born with the presumption that arises as soon as Adam - the intellect - conjoins with Eve - sensation -, and swells with pride and *philautia*.[47] Error, which is ontologically possible in as much as it is written into creation, realizes itself in the human sphere the moment man swells with pride. Error, therefore, is due to a disproportionate attribution of importance to one's own capacities, to the refusal to recognize one's limits, to see divine greatness and one's own paucity. Precisely the inability to recognize one's proper role is the cause of much strife among men.

9. *Harmony and Disorder*

The desire to go beyond one's limit and pride stand in the way of an harmonious situation of peaceful cohabitation and co-operation. Hence, tyranny and rebellion, discord and chaos. On one hand, it can be that people who do not accept their subordination and rebel, or simply, do not follow the law; on the other, it can be a question of a ruler being a victim of his own arrogance and of a lack of control that prompts discord,[48] or, vice versa, of a weak ruler who gives in to the will of the multitude.[49] Like Jethro, the image of vacuous presumptuousness, who, instead of following his father (= correct reason), follows his mother (= the laws of the cities and of particular nations established more on the basis of opinion than truth,[50] chases after fashion and popular consensus, prescribes laws that run contrary to the norms of nature, and follows appearance instead of truth. He represents the

---

[47] "And the Mind, like one enlightened by the flash of the sun's beam, after night, or as one awakened from deep sleep, or like a blind man who has suddenly received his sight, found thronging on it all things which come into being [...] having acquired the faculty of sense and through its agency laid hold of every form of bodily things, was filled and puffed up with unreasonable pride, and thus thought that all things were its own possessions and none belonged to any other" (*Cher.* 62-64).

[48] Cf. Barraclough, *op.cit.* (n. 3) 532-533; 543.

[49] Cf. *Ios.* 36. Aristotle (*Pol.* 1161a3-9) previously had also linked a situation of anarchy and disorder to a weak master.

[50] Cf. *Ebr.* 34; *Agr.* 43; *Mut.* 104. See Goodenough, *op.cit.*(n.4) 34 and 74; Barraclough, *op.cit.* (n.3) 527.

demagogues who, so as not to displease the multitude, let themselves be overcome by the latter's will and thus pave the way to anarchy. The multitude, more than often allegorically interpreted as the teeming passions, irrational impulses, the sensations and confused opinions of the soul,[51] when not correctly guided are arrogant (*Ios.* 66), intemperant, lacking in self-control and common sense (*Agr.* 44), disordered (*Leg. All.* II.77), prey to passions and pleasures (*Ios.* 60), give themselves over to evil (*Abr.* 22), are inconstant (*Ios.* 36), judge by appearances (*Ios.* 59). They therefore represent the very possibility of error when, instead of being guided, they become guides for others. Compared with wisdom, represented by democracy, mob rule is folly, lack of common sense and self-control, injustice, lack of fortitude (*Virt.* 180).

> "Is it not well to pray that the flock linked to each one of us by a common birth and a common growth may not be left without a ruler and guide? So might mob-rule, the very worst of bad constitutions, the counterfeit of democracy, which is the best of them, infect us, while we spend our days in ceaseless experience of disorders, tumults and intestine broils."[52]

Let us compare what has been claimed with the already cited passage from *Conf.* 108-109. There appear all the basic elements which characterize an ochlocracy: inequality, injustice, absence of laws, chaos, an element of falsification whereby said form of rule attempts to pass itself off as the best mode of government, even though it is merely its worst imitation. It is counterfeit money which, in vain, tries to have currency alongside democracy. As previously for Plato, the lack of a sure guide not only gives rise to conflict, discord and anarchy, but also forebodes injustice and violation, which lead to tyranny:

> "Anarchy, however, the mother of mob-rule, is not our only danger. We have to dread also the uprising of some aspirant to sovereign power, forcibly setting law at naught. For a tyrant is a natural enemy. In cities this enemy is man; to body and soul and all the interests of each of these, it is an utterly savage mind, that has turned our inner citadel into a fortress from which to assail us. Nor is it only from these tyrannies that we derive no benefit. We gain nothing from the rule and governance of men who are too good and gentle. For kindness is a quality open to contempt, and injurious to both sides, both rulers and subjects."[53]

---

[51] *Ebr.* 111-113; *Migr.* 60; 154; 200.

[52] *Agr.* 45.

[53] *Agr.* 46-47. On the upsetting, whereby the tyrant who uses force and violence against the people will be in turn the object of divine judgement, and is at any rate subject to the will of God, since his very power is part of God's plan to punish the people, cf. Barraclough, *op.cit.* (n. 3) 532-533.

Those who command shall be despised by their subjects and, as such, will be unable to conduct public affairs; the underlings will give in to arrogance, convinced of thereby being able to avoid carrying out orders. The result can only be disaster.[54] Free from whatever limitation, the multitude will then attempt to follow their own impulses, to take control, to institute an ochlocracy (cf. *Mos.* I.26), the most ignoble of all forms of government (*Opif.* 171; *Conf.* 108-109), comparable to polytheism which transfers in heaven an image of mob rule, of a disordered situation which lacks a stable and unitary guide, "the order of a legitimate authority such as kingship"(*Fug.* 10).

Revealers of a correct hierarchical relation are the commandments which evidence that the world has only one cause, which is at once its ruler and king, who directs the universe having banned from heaven both oligarchy and ochlocracy, regimes which sprang from disorder and *pleonexia* (cf. *Decal.* 155), which are opposed to harmony and order that derive from acceptance of the divine plan. The preconditions of such a situation are injustice and tyranny, the stifling of whatever form of equality. Even though it founds itself on the multitude, ochlocray - the remotest form of government from democracy (the true form of equality) - shares characteristics in common with tyranny, which in turn is a form of government which can in a way be likened to, and in others is totally foreign to, a kingdom. Closely connected with demagoguery, ochlocracy stems directly from the arrogance of the multitude which no longer perceive any limits to their actions. It also stems from the deceit perpetrated by shrewd rulers, who behave improperly towards the multitude, that are weak, easily manipulated and incapable of grasping their own real interest, which lies in accepting the government of a good ruler. The multitude, in turn, however, "buy" a political person and subject him to a sort of servitude the very moment that, inconstant and for ever seeking new things, they search for a new master (*Ios.* 36).

10. *Inner Harmony and external Harmony*

Having posited the general premises underlying the concepts of order and harmony, and the forms of disorder and the loss of balance in the world, it will now be a matter of seeing how they unfold within human societies. Many scholars[55] have asked themselves, when Philo speaks of ochlocracy, mob rebellion and subversion by the lower strata of society, whether he has in mind the popular anti-Judaic rebellions and movements of the Alexandria of his day. Presumably there are

---

[54] Cf. *Det.* 141; *Somn.* II.287.
[55] Cf., for example, Barraclough, *op.cit.* (n. 3) 524-527.

some references to such events.[56]   However, there is also, in my opinion, a much broader reassessment of Greek political thinking starting with Plato. Formulations whereby mass assemblies are a "mixed crowd of heterogeneous persons [that] says what is right, but [...] thinks and does the opposite [and] prefers the spurious to the genuine" (Ios. 59),[57] echo the boisterous gatherings of shoemakers and tradesmen as depicted by Plato and Aristophanes, or the sundry ochlos in Xenophon's Memorabilia.[58] This is a far cry from the idyllic setting of a people harmoniously and serenely dedicated to virtue and justice, guided by a righteous and virtuous ruler whose major concern is the good of his subjects.[59]   Such as Pinheas, who represents the preservation of order and good government, the abolition of war and factiousness, the pursuit of peace;[60] such as Abraham, who settles quarrels among his shepherds and those of Lot;[61] such as Moses, custodian of the laws and shepherd of the people, as opposed to Jethro;[62] such as Joseph, who brings harmony and peace, who turns discord into concord, tames the most hardened (Ios. 85), thus displaying one of the salient qualities of the political person: self-control whence issue stability and peace, whereas its lack produces civil strife and war.[63] This is why it is fitting that those who personally are not so able, entrust themselves to and obey a ruler who is capable of preaching sophrosyne.[64] Once again we are witnessing conflict within the soul and conflict among men, between inner harmony and external harmony, since there is no difference in terms of the sources of either.

---

[56] See Flacc. 52-53; 65-67; Leg. 132; Cf. Hadas-Lebel, op.cit. (n. 46)   71-72; Goodenough, op.cit. (n.4) 52 ff.   In a similar vein we could perhaps also read Mos. I.138, where, confronting the plague, the Egyptian multitude, terror-striken and doleful, go to the royal palace to request that the Jews be sent away, and upbraid the king.   As yet it is not a revolt, nor a veritable anti-Judaic attack, but in certain periods it could sound as preparatory of successive anti-Jewish attitudes.

[57] The Septuagint call Potiphar a cook, and Philo calls him a cook and a eunuch. He represents the mindless mob that lives in the midst of smoke and neither sees nor generates(virtue) (cf. Ios. 58; Mut. 173). See Goodenough, op.cit. (n. 4) 51.

[58] Cf. Parente, op.cit. (n. 13) 332-333.

[59] Cf. Opif. 144 ; Mos. I.151; Spec. Leg. IV.170. See also Letter of Aristeas 190; 279; 281.

[60] Cf. Barraclough, op.cit. (n. 3) 511, with reference to Post. 182-184.

[61] Abr. 210-219. Cf. Kraus Reggiani, op.cit. (n 9) 164-165.

[62] Ebr. 37; Agr. 43; Sacrif. 50.

[63] Ios. 57. See Goodenough, op.cit. (n. 4) 50-51.

[64] "He judges it most profitable for him who chooses war instead of peace, who by reason of his inward tumult and rebellion is armed as it were with the weapons of war, that he should become a subject and a slave and obey all the orders that the lover of self-control may impose" (Congr. 176). Cf. Q.G. VI. 235-236; Leg. All. 193-194.

Harmony and conflict derive from a right or wrong relation with God and with his laws,[65] a relation which although displayed in various ambits, is nevertheless always one and the same. Thus, he who finds inner harmony is naturally inclined to also outwardly reflect the peace which is in him. This is why just and moderate rulers reverberate their virtue upon their subjects and influence the behaviour of the governed, whether the latter obey out of fear (*Fug.* 98), or are induced to do good by a positive model. This is a theme dear to Hellenistic political philosophy, as often evidenced by Goodenough who, in this connection, establishes a parallel between some passages in Philo and fragments which have come down to us from the Neopythagoreans.[66]   It is a theme to which we shall return further on. What instead I shall dwell on here is the contrast between the wise man, who is also *politikos*, in as much as he is suited to the *polis* and bearer of pacification in the city,[67] and he who loves conflict and is every ready to become embroiled in controversy, and is identified with the Sophists,[68] represented by Ishmael, the wild one: "his hand will be against everyone, and the hand of everyone against him" (*Gen.* 16.12). He utilizes his vast knowledge and sophism to present factious positions and uphold contention.

11. *Harmony and Equality*

In a context of harmony and order, what is obvious is the role of acceptance, awareness of one's own relative place, attention to the performance of one's own tasks in a general framework wherein to each is assigned his role. There should be no political conflicts in such a condition, since its rulers are such because their power is attributed to them by God,[69] and the governed follow the indications of their king in as much as personal power is of no concern to them. Precisely because it comes from God, authority is a responsibility; a duty first and foremost rather than a pleasure, a assumption of tasks and limitations: a king shall be truer to the laws than others, more self-restrained, more

---

[65] *Opif.* 144; *Spec. Leg.* IV. 187; *Conf.* 132-133. See also *Letter of Aristeas* 127; 279; 291.

[66] Cf. also E. Bréhier, *Les Idées philosophiques et religieuses*, cit. (n. 14) 18-23; G.J.D Aalders, *Political Thought in Hellenistic Times*, Amsterdam (1975) 18-27 deals with the so-called *specula principis* starting from Isocrates and Xenophon.

[67] Where there is no harmony and conflict arises (loss of material goods, privation of liberty, cf. *Mos.* I.141-142), however, the Jews behave towards the Egyptians as if in wartime (law of the winner, vengeance under God's protective hand). When conflict explodes, that is, let it - peace at all costs should not be sought.

[68] *Fug.* 209; *QG.* III 33.

[69] *Mos.* I.149; 163; *Praem.* 54; *Mut.* 151-152.   This is a popular theme in Hellenistic literature. See, for example, *Letter of Aristeas* 224.

severe with himself, more virtuous.[70]   Peace, harmony, order and balance should prevail in a situation wherein all are equal while yet being different. All are equal as subjects before their great king, God; they are equal in terms of the providence which watches over them, in terms of their duty to adjust to the divine will; and yet all are different not only because each single individuality possesses a unique value, but also because there exists within the human world - as in the cosmos - a differentiation of aptitudes and functions. Before the just, however, no one is rich or poor, powerful or weak. Virtue is that which distinguishes the individual who rises above the others, he who is superior to his fellow men, and is designated to govern and guide them, not because of an hereditary right,[71] not because of his possessions and wealth, but because of his qualities and virtues. Here, the emblematic figure is that of Moses, who combines in himself all the traits which are proper of a superior being, one endowed with both natural (*Mos.* I.21-22) and acquired qualities (I.22), of great beauty (I.9); one who has received an education suited to a king (I.23) and regal care (I.20), a vast and composite culture: the encyclical sciences taught him by the Greeks, the Assyrian language, Chaldean astrology, the Hebrew tradition (I.32); always has he pursued truth and eschewed falsehood (I.24), and repressed his impulses and let himself be guided by reason (I.26). Able to moderate his desires and to live more according to the dictates of the soul than to those of the body (I.29), he contains within himself so many virtues as to prompt him to ask himself whether his nature be human or divine (I.27). Especially committed to conforming his life to his words (I.29), like a good physician he attempts to alleviate the ills of his people (I.42) and to help the weak (I.50); he puts himself in God's hands in times of difficulty (I.47) and faces all sorts of trials in order to educate himself for both a contemplative and active life (I.48), by following truth instead of appearance, aware of being delegated by God to bring help to the weak. As prophet (I.57), he immediately commands attention and is readily recognizable by the peculiarity of his features(I.59).[72] Subsequent to marrying, he leads his flock, thus acquiring notions which will be useful for his future activity, given the close relation there is

---

[70] *Mos.* I.154; II.8 ff. See *Letter of Aristeas* 207-223.

[71] *Mos.* I.150. Cf. *Letter of Aristeas* 288-290. See L. Troiani, 'Il libro di Aristea ed il giudaismo ellenistico (Premesse per un'interpretazione)', in B. Virgilio (ed.), *Studi Ellenistici* II, Pisa (1987) 55-58.

[72] Cf. *Virt.* 216-218, where Abraham is not really king, but appears to be because of his virtue. Even in *De Josepho*, moreover, Joseph's peculiarity, his loftiness, his virtue, the role which is reserved to him, all appear immediately by his aspect.

between sheep-rearing and the art of governing, as both are[73] geared to the well-being of those governed (I.60-63). Designated by God to look after his people and help them leave Egypt (I.71), he reluctantly accepts the duty and discharges it backed both by the elders and the people (I.73); he fiercely and repeatedly clashes with Pharaoh (I.87 ff.). Hence, he assumes such functions as kingship, priesthood and prophecy.[74]

The combination in one sole person of these three functions appears as quite singular to Philo himself, who purposely explains the underlying reasons; reasons which are linked to providence, and as such directed towards what is good. At any rate, they have to be explained, not being immediately obvious. It is not merely that the functions of king and priest are separate in the Biblical text. Nor is it a question of the distrust Judaic tradition normally manifested towards a fusion of these two roles,[75] What are involved are explicit affirmations by Philo who (as in *De Virtutibus* 54)) sees as dangerous the combination in one sole person of kingship and priesthood. Yet, the two functions are not necessarily separate for Philo; they were not in the days of the first kings (*QE.*II.105), nor are they for Moses. The matter is probably to be viewed in terms of special situations as ascribable to superior figures. Thus, Moses's exceptional qualities can also be seen as placing him in a special condition.[76]

---

[73] Cf. *Agr.* 41-44; 50. The comparison is a classic *topos* of Greek literature. For example, it is frequent in Plato (*Resp.* 416a; 440d; *Polit.* 275b-e). See S. Campese, 'Misthotiké', in M. Vegetti (ed.), Platone, *La Repubblica*, libro I, Pavia (1994) 196 ff. It is, also, a popular image in Greek literature. Cf. Goodenough, *op.cit.* (n. 4) 95 n. 48; Aalders, *op.cit.* (n. 66) 23 ff.

[74] Cf. *Mos.* II.2-6; 66-67; 187; *Praem.* 53-56. Cf. here chap. one .

[75] Cf. however Parente, *op.cit.* (n. 13) 340.

[76] Moreover, it is perhaps possible that these passsages by Philo are to be read more carefully, and that they often bespeak temporary attitudes or situations rather than veritable activities, which are constant and endowed with all the hallmarks of true activity. Thus, in *Mos.* II.66 it is said that Moses has the quality of a high priest, not that he is a high priest, that he has been trained in the acts of cult and divine service (§ 67 and 71), not that he exercises them. At § 75, exercise of the priesthood is proper of Moses ἀληθῶς, a term which could be equivocated: not only in terms of name, but really, in terms of its deepest reality. The hypothesis is, in fact, rather weak.

Regarding an interpretation of *Ps.* 99.6 and Moses's high-priest function during the week of Aaron's investiture (according to most interpretations), but also successively (according to some texts), cf. Wolfson, *op.cit.* (n. 1) 337 ff. In general, it perhaps can be said that before Aaron's election to the priesthood, Moses somehow exercised priestly functions, even if we lack precise biblical reference to any such exercise by Moses. Regarding the line in *Deuteronomy* (33.5) "he was king in Jeshurum", and its relative interpretations, see Wolfson, *op.cit.* (n. 1)326 ff. For a discussion of these passages, see here chap. one.

Moses is often designated as priest, and repeatedly as king, even if such a designation is probably more indicative of a role as governor than of a veritable ruler.[77] Νομοθέτης, νόμος ἔμψυχος, φιλόσοφος, Moses, that is, is also often indicated as βασιλεύς. Furthermore, ἀρχιεροσύνη and προφητεία also pertain to him (Mos. II.2).

12. Moses's Kingship

As we have seen, there are various difficulties associated with Moses' attributions. However, if some problems spring from the combination in one sole figure of various roles, even the designation of King raises questions. This in fact poses the problem of whether Moses's *basileia* can be likened to that of the various kings of the earth and of what is meant by *basileia* (see §I.148; II.3; etc.), also with respect to monarchy. In Aristotle (*Pol.* 1287a), there is already a distinction between the two notions which can at times be superimposed, although this need not occur of necessity. In the case of Moses, it would appear that Philo should speak in terms of his being a guide, head, besides naturally a legislator, interpreter, and much less a king and priest.[78] In *Exodus* 19.6, Israel is referred to as a kingdom of priests and holy people; and in 23.22 there again appears the notion of a kingdom of priests. The reference to kingdom, linked with the idea of election, is nevertheless here a reference to the kingdom of God. In *Ex.*15.18 , as in many other passages, "The Eternal shall reign for ever". The king is God, and Israel a kingdom, in as much as it is governed by such a king. Here, certainly, it is not a matter of a kingdom such as the Davidic or the Maccabean. As we have seen, in the *Bible* Moses is neither king nor priest, despite the passages quoted. Furthermore, neither is he God, in spite of *Ex.* 7. We can probably think of a generic use of the term *basileia*, indicating more a position of pre-eminence than a specific type

---

[77] For Plato, too (*Polit.* 301b), if someone possesses regal science, and alone holds power, he has to be called king in any of the five constitutions he be. See also Aristotle, *Pol.* 1287a.
[78] Cf. Parente, *op.cit.* (n.13) 339.

of rule.[79]   What, however, remains to be seen is the kind of relation which is established between God's rule[80] and that of man.

It is the very notion of kingship which bears analyzing. There arise various meanings of *basileia* that contain changing meanings, and which allude to various forms of government, often considered not in an exclusively political framework, but as related to the divine plan. I have no pretension of presenting an exhaustive picture of the problem, and shall simply offer a few examples of the term, which will enable us to establish a comparison with the Hellenistic notion of kingship as delineated by Goodenough.

13. *Types of Kingship*

a) a meaning of *basileia*, in the sense of sovereignty, dominion and supremacy, is found in *Opif.* 148, where there appear the terms βασιλεία, ἡγεμών, ἀρχή, δεσπόζειν, ὑπάρχειν, δυναστεία. Man is king and rules over the rest of nature, and this is why he has given names to things. There surfaces here the idea of an incontrovertible government which admits of no alternatives; "in as much as men [...] do reign over brut beasts". In *Opif.* 84, man is *basileus* with respect to all other created beings because he is *heghemon*, established as such by God not only *de facto*, but also by verbal designation. God has placed under his command the beings of the sublunary world. Regal power is unquestionable: the animals, in fact, even if they are strong, do not rebel against man's command, and the sheep let themselves be shorn, "accustomed like the cities to paying their annual tribute to he who is their king by natural right" (cf. §85). This, of course, is a secondary government with respect to that of the true ruler, God, who made the first man his lieutenant and head of the rest of creation (*Opif.* 84;88). In this context, *basileus* is always referred to man; never to God.

b) In *Opif.* 17, talking about founding a city, the king turns to the architect.   Here, the king's characterization is constituted by the

---

[79] Even in reference to judges there appear generic terms of regality. Especially in the Orient such terms likely indicate dominion, supremacy, pre-eminence, more than kingdom strictly speaking. Even in the *Bible*, moreover, whether in the Septuagint or the *Massorah*, when the brothers turn to Joseph after his dream of the sheaves, reference is to kingly rule: "will you rule over us? or dominate us?" (*Gen.* 37.8). Goodenough, *op.cit.* (n. 4) 26-27, affirms that in Philo's time the term king immediately evoked a claim to divine rank, which is what sparks his brothers' reaction when they refuse to divinize Joseph. Only to God should προσκύνησις be reserved.

[80] Cf. *Opif.* 71, where the great king is God; *Opif.* 88; 144; *Cher.* 29; 99: God king of kings, Lord of all things; *Deus* 159, and many other passages.

immense ambition of a leader who demands absolute power (*autokratos*), and wants to add luster to his prosperity. Thus, there surfaces the true definition of kingship which we find in *Opif.* 56-57: personal and undivided power. Such aspects are perceived in the alternation between day and night. The sun is like a great king because it alone holds the power for half of the time, while the moon and the stars govern together. Furthermore, when it rises, the sun obscures with its splendour the other stars, like the individual in *Mos.* I.290, who "shall come forth from you one day [...] and he shall rule over many nations". By growing daily, his *basileia* will become immense. Here, possibly, there is an allusion to the Messiah,[81] which however falls outside the purview of our analysis. The image is that of an extended and awe-inspiring dominion that strikes terror in the foe, among whom, clearly, there are many kings.[82]

c) The preceding image contrasts with that of the king sent by God among the people to guide them:

> "But the kingdom of the Sage comes by the gift of God, and the virtuous man who receives it brings no harm to anyone, but the acquisition and enjoyment of good things to all his subjects, to whom he is the herald of peace and order."[83]

Not therefore the king of the Egyptians (*Leg. All.* III.13), metaphorically understood as the impetus of the passions; not Alexander, king of the Macedonians, convinced of possessing complete and absolute power, and who already displays his infantilism and the immaturity of a soul that is incapable of recognizing its own limits and of attributing a proper role to the intellect and to the sensations.[84]

Once again the analogy with the soul and the dominion of the passions makes it possible to identify the proper relation of government wherein the ruler, endowed with absolute power, however limits his dominion and, in some cases, moderates its manifestations. The real

---

[81] Cf. Wolfson, op.cit. (n. 3) 407 ff.

[82] *Mos.* I.252; 258; 263; 267; 275; 277; 285; 287; 292; etc.

[83] *Abr.* 261.

[84] Cf. *Cher.* 63; *Leg. All.* I.41; *Opif.* 139. See also *Sacrif.* 49: "Surely to those who can reason it is a prouder task than kingship to have the strength to rule, as a king in the city or country, over the body and the senses and the belly, and the pleasures whose seat is below the belly, and the other passions and the tongue and in general all our compound being - aye and to rule them with vigour and with a right strong yet ever-gentle hand. For like the charioteeer he must sometimes give the rein to his team, sometimes pull them in and draw them back, when they rush too wildly in unreined career towards the world of external things."

king, aware of his responsibilities and his role, does not play the master, does not yield to tyranny, but wields power with an even hand, restraining himself even before restraining others.[85] A paragon of every virtue, explication of God's words, the ruler becomes guide of the people (Moses), shepherd of the flock he leads far from the shoals of transgression (Egypt) (*Sacrif.* 50), a normative example for the governed;[86] but he is also undoubtedly the very image of divinity on earth,[87] a light for his subjects, example and teacher who, merely by his presence, by his countenance, specifies a line of conduct. In Pharaoh's prison Joseph mollifies the most hardened criminals; teaches modesty and meekness to all. Because of his very countenance, Joseph is a source of learning for those who behold him and a model for his subjects.[88]

> "Since the essence of the *nomos* is that of actuating and producing a certain *ethos*, it is necessary that first of all this *ethos* be realized in the action and figure of the man from whom the law emanates and that he, in a way, "embody" that law. [...] With that Neopythagorean tradition which draws the theme from IV-century Greek thought and which has greatly idealized, in the Hellenistic world, the king figure as "living law" (*nomos empsychos*), Philo repeats that the legislator *par excellence* (*De Vita Mos.* I.162), or the *basileus* (*De Vita Mos.* II.4), must he himself be 'animate law' ".[89]

> "The king is the living law and the law a just king".[90]

That which substantially differentiates Philo from the Hellenistic conceptions of divinized kings is that Moses, and with him any ruler, even if exceptional, is a mediator, an executor with respect to the true King, who is God. Moreover, there is an attempt to liken the good king to God, a sort of *imitatio Dei*,[91] the most open and explicit expression

---

[85] Cf. *Spec. Leg.* IV.187. Cf. *Letter of Aristeas* 147-148; 191; 222-223; 263; 291.

[86] Even for Plato (*Polit.* 294a; 295b), royal man had this normative role. Cf. S. Gastaldi, *Le immagini delle virtù. Le strategie metaforiche nelle 'Etiche' di Aristotele*, Alessandria (1994) 51-52.

[87] Concerning God's kingship as an archetype for kings on earth see N. Unemoto, 'Die Königsherrschaft Gottes bei Philon' in M. Hengel and A.M. Schwemer (ed.),*Königsherrschaaft Gottes und himmlisher Kult in Judentum, Christentum und in der hellenistischen Welt*, Tübingen (1991) 207-256, in partic. 241-250.

[88] *Mos.* I.158-161. Cf. *Letter of Aristeas* 188; 218.

[89] Parente, *op.cit.* (n. 1) 329 [my transl.].

[90] *Mos.* II.4; cfr. *Mos.* I.162; *Abr.* 5; *Det.* 141. For the idea of law as king of the city cf. Plato, *Symp.* 196c; cf. also Aristotle, *Rhet.* III.1406a18, who attributes the expression to Alcidamantes.

[91] Cf. Chesnut, *op.cit.* (n. 14) 1329-1330.

of which can be found in the *Letter of Aristeas,* but which is also present in Plutarch, for whom it is not a matter of divinizing the king in terms of exterior aspects, as of assimilating the king to God on the basis of his virtue.

The Philonic image is that of a king who conforms to the divine will, and who, in conformity with the law, governs a state based on balance and stability.[92]   This does not mean that such a state exists empirically; but is theoretically possible (and perhaps also existed in the past), as it is based on the law of Moses.   Possible deviations and transgressions do not imply that it is impossible that there be a situation which may seem idyllic, and not necessarily utopian nor Messianic.[93] Order, harmony, balance and justice, therefore, are the goals confronting transgression.   The latter not so much as sin, even if in some ways it superimposes itself upon sin, as disorder, as disruption of balance.[94]   Rejection of the Law, in this ambit, does not only mean disobedience to the divine will and transgression of norms, but also disharmony and conflict.   As we have seen in the first part of this chapter, there are order and continuity in the cosmos, and movement is constituted by small imperceptible modifications, which are significant to the eyes of the protagonists in the short term, but not decisive from a long-term, super-vision perspective.   Neither does the hierarchy change, wherefore there is a God who governs all,[95] and there are figures on earth who are his emissaries, mediators, executors *in primis* of his will even with respect to other men.

Thus, there exists a correct hierarchical relation in society, which is a monarchy with respect to God, king and sovereign, and, in some ways, is also a monarchy in the human sphere when there is a Moses who leads the people. However, as we have pointed out, all are equal

---

[92] See *Post.* 184; *Opif.* 144; *Decal.* 40-43. Cf. Wilson, *op.cit.* (n. 3) 381.

[93] Cf. Wolfson, *op.cit.* (n. 3) 425-426.

[94] Heaven is order, the principles of truth are harmony; however the things of this earth throw up disorder (*Ios.* 145). As for transgression as rejection of the Law, see *Ebr.* 95-96.

[95] God too is often referred to as king. There is the distinction between ἡγεμών and βασιλεύς. God's kingly power is then compared with creative power, and can be placed in relation with the nouns κύριος and θεός. On the distinction between these two divine names see here chap. 3. On these themes, which are outside the scope of my analysis, cf. G. Mayer, 'Die herrscherliche Titular Gottes bei Philo von Alexandrien', in D.-A. Koch and H. Lichtenberger (ed.), *Begegnungen zwischen Christentum und Judentum in Antike und Mittelalter: Festschrift für Heinz Schreckenberg,* Schriften des Institutum Judaicum Delitzschianum 1, Göttingen (1993) 293- 302. On the conception of God as king of the world cf. N. Unemoto, *op.cit.* (n.87) 212-223.

and all are equally held to share in virtue and follow the law. It is in this sense that one can speak of democracy.

14. *Democracy as Conformity to the Law*

Democracy is not here intended as meaning *government* of the *demos*, but rather as *participation*, a universal conforming to the law. This means everyone, not the multitude, *demos*, not *ochlos*. Democracy is the opposite of ochlocracy; the latter implying anarchy, disorder, rebellion, the pursuit of desires and passions, rather than virtue and the law.[96] In particular, and in reference to Israel, the accent is on equality with respect to the only true Lord, who is God: "You have all equal rights with us; one race, the same fathers, one house, the same customs" (*Mos.* I.324).

Why should anyone[97] try to be superior to others? The people are seen in their unity; Israel, God's people, holy and rebellious; people, nevertheless, taken collectively, and whose social composition is inessential.The opposition between *ochlos* and *demos* does not so much regard the social arrangement, as how people behave with respect to the law and the duty of obedience, since *ochlos* is a part of *demos*. Naturally, a distinction is made between he who governs and those who are governed, as between the Levites and Israel. However, parallel runs the distinction which intersects both poles of the preceding relation between the holders of virtue and those who lack virtue.

Determination of virtue not only as an attribution of value, but also as entitlement to holding power, is nothing new. What to me seems particularly significant is a comparison, on these very themes, with previous authors who had broadly used - I would almost say "codified" - the notions in question. Even Aristotle distinguished citizens on the basis of virtue and, in certain circumstances, virtue can become the cardinal criterion whereupon to found a constitution (as, for example, an aristocracy), even if for Aristotle, in historic constitutions, there are numerous other evaluation standards (wealth, nobility...) . Thus, social composition plays an important role, and similarly decisive is also the type of activity of the *demos*, which usually does not represent the people in their totality, but rather their more numerous and poorer components.[98] Also for Aristotle, moreover,

---

[96] Cf. *Agr.* 45-46; *Conf.* 108; *Abr.* 242.

[97] Specifically, Core .

[98] In order to indicate a population in its totality, Aristotle generally uses πλῆθος. See, for ex. *Pol.* 1288a 6-15. In 1268a 11-13, Aristotle presents democracy as government of the multitude of have-nots who rule in terms of their own

possession of virtue outstrips, in value terms, the other determinations which constitute entitlements to power.[99] The problem of what is the best constitution is an ever present one. That it be such in absolute terms, or with respect to certain conditions, for Aristotle it is a matter of identifying it and of determining who are its citizens, what are its characterizing criteria (according to virtue, wealth, etc.), what are its public offices and the relation between governors and governed. All this for Philo is inessential. What is important is that the rule of a state be based on virtue. How the population is made up, who accedes to public offices and what are the power relations are not open problems. In the case of Israel, access to the priesthood is determined by whether or not one is born *cohen*; the power of government is determined by God who selects whom to give power to (*Abr.* 261), even if the people's assent has a decisive role.[100] Then, whether such a state is called a democracy, a kingdom, or in some other way, is indifferent. Its real name could be theocracy, as Josephus upholds (*Contra Apionem* II.165). Moreover, if Aristotle seeks the best constitution for most states wherein the greatest number of men can live well; wherein, that is, the greatest number of men can attain their goal (*Pol.* 1295a 25-26), for Philo the best, with respect to virtue, is indicated by God through the law of Moses. The criterion is external to the city. The fact that the laws of political society are the same as those that govern the individual leads to an identification between ethics and politics. It is not a question of Plato's identification, whereby there exists a reciprocal foundation and an inclusion of ethics within the city, nor of the relation of which Aristotle speaks, whereby man outside the city is either beast or God. For Philo the law is divine, and therefore becomes a warrant of proper individual behaviour. Priority is accorded to ethical choices, whence politics derives. In individual terms, each person concerns himself with carrying out the norm, because such behaviour is correct before God; it is correct, that is, both ethically and theologically. The political perspective is secondary, and state sanction is not clearly delineated. As regards justice, even for Aristotle acceptance of the law and prescribed patterns of behaviour is a decisive factor, but the source

---

interests. Entitlement to government participation is afforded by the condition of free men. Cf. 1279 b 8-9; 279b 29; 1280a 6.

[99] Cf. *Pol.* 1284a 3-14; b 26-34,where exceptional individuals in terms of virtue are themselves the law. At 1160b 3-19 are presented various titles displayed by those aspiring to superior rule.

[100] Cf.*Praem.* 54; *Spec. Leg.* IV.157; 170; *Mos.* I. 73; 163; 198; *Ios.* 149. See Wolfson, *op.cit.* (n.3) 329-331. Also in the *Letter of Aristeas* (308-311) the need for consensus by the popular assembly is forcefully stressed, even if here the situation is different. There is nevertheless an implicit reference to consensus by the people gathered in *Exodus* 24.4. Cf. F. Calabi, *op.cit.* (n. 1) 26.

of the law is within the city, and the forms of justice comply with the form of government in force.[101]   Even for Aristotle, as in most of the preceding political literature, beginning with Plato himself, a city's stability is a value criterion, and equality and justice among citizens are founding elements of that stability.   Debate will then focus on the meaning of the term equality, on the distinction between arithmetic and proportional equality, on the value criterion to be adopted as a reference point, and on the parameters which establish a correct relation between governors and governed.[102]

15. *Different Constitutions as Forms of Order and Disorder*

In Philo, the correct relation is established *a priori* by the law of Moses, wherein it is inscribed well before it comes to be this government or that king, which and who are such because so designated by God, independently of power relations or the concrete situations typical of a single state. In this sense - as we have seen - the type of political form is not, after all, important.   There is no real distinction between government by the people and government by one person, between government by the rich and government by the virtuous. The ideal government should be in the hands of the virtuous, the people as a whole, Israel in its complex, since Israel is a holy people, chosen by God so that his law might be made manifest. Thus - as we have seen - *demos* does not indicate a part of the population, and democracy does not indicate government by some in opposition to other forms of government. Democracy and kingdom are compatible, since they both indicate a situation of order and acceptance of the law. All the people follow a specific dispensation; even the king, who may have a special role, but is not consequently totally different from the rest of the population. Democracy, kingdom, ochlocracy and tyranny do not indicate, then, different forms of government, but rather forms of order and disorder, government by law or by anarchy.[103] Thus, two types of constitution can easily live side by side, since, actually, it is merely a

---

[101] "Good man (*agathos*) may no longer identify with the *spoudaios* citizens this quality means above all compliance with the collective needs of the *polis*, and they vary, even radically, depending on the regime in power" (Vegetti, *o p cit.* (n. 1) 199) [my transl.].

[102] Cf. F. Calabi, *La città dell'oikos. La 'politia' di Aristotele*, Lucca (1984).

[103] Even Arius Didymus uses a terminology that is different from the Aristotelian which yet seems to be a model. He speaks of ochlocracy instead of democracy, and democracy stands for polity. Cf. Aalders, *op.cit.* (n.66) 7. On the following page, Aalders, speaking about the pseudo-Aristotelian *Oeconomicus*, claims that in this work what appears to be more important is the way power is exercised than the type of constitution adopted.

On the use of the term democracy in Philo, see Wolfson, *op.cit.* (n.3) 390-395.

matter of a sole model, and the best constitution can alternately be
called democracy or monarchy. In fact, there is no contrast between the
two.[104]   Aristotle (*Pol.* 1287a 3-8), on the other hand, had previously
claimed that "monarchy according to law does not   constitute a special
type of constitution". In Aristotle, however, conditions of possibility
modify the order of reality, and therefore also modify the preferable
solutions. In Philo, Moses guarantees the Law, not single state laws or
single constitutions.[105] The type of constitution chosen, therefore, does
not matter. What count are order, accord with nature that is *logos*,
which is given by God, who is law of the cosmos.   In this sense,
democracy is excellent if it means equality; excellent is kingdom, if it
means acceptance of a hierarchical order.[106]   Going back to the theme
of government forms, with Philo, as compared to preceding authors,
the terms of the question have changed. Monarchy is such with respect
to God, source and guarantor of authority, but also among men,
because the king's function is that of good government with respect to
his subjects.   In this way, the king guarantees monarchy, but also
democracy, as the latter does not mean arithmetic equality among the
governed, but a state of order wherein each person occupies a specific
place, and is included in a hierarchy and in an accepted role, which is
perfectly compatible with monarchy. Its degenerate form, then, will be
that of an ochlocracy; that is, a situation of disorder where those who
should obey try to assume decision-making roles and thus lead to
instability and insurrection.[107] Similarly degenerate is tyranny, where
the monarch fails to fulfil his duty and, with his reckless behaviour,
favours a condition in which the laws are no longer observed and

---

[104] Cf. Wolfson, *op.cit.* (n.3) 384 ff.

[105] Even the re balancing of power, change   in possession of the city, are
sanctioned through an offering to God. Cf. *Mos.* I.254: the moment they take
over the enemy *kingdom*, the cities, the Jews, before dividing the land among
themselves and installing themselves in the cities, offer the early fruits (in this
case, the cities themselves). They are forever mindful that everything is God's
possession, and that man is a foreigner on earth (*Cher.* 77-83; 117-119; cf. *Letter of
Aristeas* 195-196), and therefore return possession to the rightful owner. At the
same time, they make early fruits of the cities, that is, they place them in a
natural - cosmic - order. Not only do they bring the cities back to their rightful
owner, thereby re-establishing the harmony and balance of power, but they also
situate them within nature. Cf. *Mos.*I.259 and 262, where, after the battle won
with God's help, the cities find themselves both empty and full; empty of the
former inhabitants and full of the victors. The same for the countryside. Thus,
God's will pervades the world, not only determining victory, but also the re
balancing of the inhabited world. This parallels what happened with the flood,
or when the giants coupled with the daughters of man.

[106] Cf. *Spec. Leg.* IV.237. Cf. Wolfson, *op.cit.* (n.3) 390-392.

[107] In *De Decalogo*, monarchy represents a heavenly model opposed to oligarchy
and ochlocracy. Thus is presented another negative form of rule: oligarchy.

disorder prevails, whereas a ruler should be like a father to his subjects, one who educates them to observe the laws and order. In some ways, it could be said that the various constitutional forms can be co-present, as they indicate one and the same reality, albeit on different planes; or, two levels of reality: monarchy is in relation to God, democracy to men; monarchy is in relation to government and power, democracy to virtue and acceptance of the law; monarchy in relation to the cosmos in its totality, democracy concerns states in the course of imperial successions, since a kingdom that is triumphant and rich will soon become subject of another kingdom, in an alternating pattern of governor and governed.[108] It, therefore, is a matter of different planes of reality,[109] of

totality	in relation to	the particular:
God (monarch)	"	men (equal amongst themselves. Democracy)
God	"	states (equal amongst themselves. Succession of empires)
overall time	"	particular times in which every single state, which can be ruled as a monarchy, becomes an element of democracy over extended time periods (Succession of empires).

---

[108] Cf. *Deus* 176; *Mos.* I.31; *Ios.* 131-141 See J.Laporte, *op.cit.* (n.13) 34 ff.; Goodenough, *op.cit.* (n.4) 77 ff. As for democracy being radicated in the succession of kingdoms, Barraclough (*op.cit.* (n.3) 521-522) reads the passage quoted from *Deus* and interprets it finalistically in terms of when all the nations acknowledge God's sovereignty. With respect to Colson's interpretation: "the democracy which the world enjoys consists in each getting its turn" (Colson, *Philo with an English Translation*, by F.H. Colson and (vols. I-V) G.H. Whitaker, London (1919-1941) (vols. I-IX), III, p. 489), Barraclough points out that "God's purpose is that no city or nation will be permanently established, except that in the time ahead His nation will be established forever and Israel will attain its ascendancy when all the others have passed their prime [...] so democracy in its ideal form is the submission to God's rule, and when democracy rules in the soul so too does reason the chastener". See also Wolfson, *op.cit.* (n.3) 420-426.
[109] Cf. *Spec. Leg.* IV.237.

Different are the ontological levels and the notion of temporality.

16. V-IV Century political Theorizations and their Rethinking by Philo

Is there a relation between the democracy of which Philo speaks and that of Plato and Aristotle?[110] Is it purely by chance that the term used is the same and that, furthermore, even its corrupted form - ochlocracy - is discussed? In addition, does not the suggestion that order and harmony are positive, and that anarchy and revolt are degenerations, give our analysis a Platonic dimension? Can equality among citizens not evoke the concept of interchangeability according to Aristotle's *politia*? By saying that order is preserved when a sovereign respects justice and follows the Law (indeed, when he himself is the living law), is there not a reference to the Neopythagoreans and, also, to Xenophon, Isocrates and to Plato himself? Has harmony, as conformity to the Law - which is cosmic law - any relation with Stoicism? In fact, in Philo's theorizations there is much that calls to mind the preceding Greek authors. Human political order, which is also cosmic order, reminds us of the Stoics; the *empsychos* law also appears in the Neopythagoreans and recalls regal man in Plato's *Politicus*; harmony-disrupting conflict resulting in ocholocracy and tyranny echoes the degenerate constitutional forms described by Plato and Aristotle. The guiding figures (Moses, Abraham) recall the all-virtuous Neopythagorean king, who applies the law to himself before applying it to others, who is a model for others, who is the living law. The possible co-presence of democracy and monarchy is also found in Aristotle. It seems, therefore, that in Philo there is much of the preceding Greek tradition.[111] The impress, however, has changed from the initial perspective: the source of the law is not within the city, but without. This is so even with respect to the Stoics, who postulate a source which is external to the state, which for them is reason. The difference, therefore, is indeed substantial. The source is not immanent to the cosmos, even if, in some ways, it cannot be said to be totally transcendent, being collocated and rooted in the world and in the cosmos. The Law comes from God, it utterly penetrates and pervades the cosmos, becomes norm for man, and has its own autonomous inscription, even if the relation between Law in God and Law outside of God is not always clear.[112] There is nevertheless an autonomous

---

[110] Cf. Colson and Whitaker, *op.cit.* (n.108) III.489; Goodenough, *op.cit.* (n. 4) 87.

[111] Cf. Goodenough *op.cit.* (n.4) 69 ff.; N.G. Cohen, 'The Greek Virtues and the Mosaic Law in Philo. An Elucidation of 'De Specialibus Legibus' IV 133-135', *StPhA* (1993) 9-19 Parente, *op.cit.* (n.13) 333-336.

[112] See the problem of the thoughts in God's mind in R. Radice, *Platonismo e creazionismo in Filone d'Alessandria*, Milano (1989) 230 ff.. See also J.Dillon, *The*

quality to the law of a type which is quite different from the relation between God - nature - and law in the Stoic sense. Perhaps, in some ways, the notion of providence that runs through Philo's text is more akin to Stoic positions, even if - once again - there is a basic difference: that between a personal God and an impersonal divinity. Even the terms used, which are apparently the same as for Plato and Aristotle, are in fact different. This has been seen in reference to the concepts of democracy and kingdom. Different too is the notion of kingship, which recalls certain aspects of the *specula principis*, without, however, identifying with them. Even the notion of harmony, as acceptance of one's own role, is substantially different from the Platonic meaning of the term, establishing itself as awareness of man's inferiority to God, and consequently shifting to an ethical plane and thus relating to a superior being. The terms used, that is, are often those of the literature of the V-IV century: balance, harmony in the city, justice, etc. What however has changed is the perspective, as the goal of politics is no longer the happiness of the citizen, his positive inclusion in the social sphere. Now, the goal is a harmony which transcends the individual; a cosmic order based on conformity to the divine plan. This does not rule out an individual dimension, that which can be found, for example, in terms of improvement. It is, however, a question of changes which occur more on an ethical than on a political plane. The political dimension can possibly be of value to the governor, but indifferent as regards his subjects. Even for the former, however, the purpose of action is ethical and consonant more with the cosmic than the political order.

17. *The good King and the Law*

A discussion about the various types of constitution draws meaning and strength in situations that are typical of the *polis*, wherein it is still possible - at least in principle - to determine the form of government. Such a discussion falls without Philo's purview,[113] and is similarly unthinkable in the ambit of the *Letter of Aristeas*. This work, in fact, constitutes another interesting term of comparison for Philo's theories. The *Letter* pretends to be addressed to the Ptolemaic king and to his court, a sort of *speculum principis*; it would be meaningless if not in a monarchy, and, especially, in a particular type of monarchy. A series of kingly attributes recall ideals of order and equality, and the

---

Middle Platonists. 80 B.C. to A.D. 220, Ithaca-New York (1977) 91 ff.; D.T. Runia, 'Polis and Megalopolis: Philo and the Founding of Alexandria', in *Exegesis and Philosophy. Studies on Philo of Alexandria*, Aldershot Hampshire (1990) 407-412.
[113] Cf. Wolfson, *op.cit.* (n.3) 383. Philo lives in a period in which mixed constitutions were theorized.

Letter also reproposes themes that are proper to IV-century theorizing. We frequently find terms such as justice and law, even if obviously in reference to a conceptual ambit which is different from that of Plato and Aristotle. The law mentioned in the *Letter* is the law of God and, even when conformity to the law is urged, reference is not so much to the special laws of a city, as to the norms that institute a form of harmony and peace among citizens (§ 291), which is in turn prompted by a divine order (§ 279). The arrangement of a community is established by the king so that everyone may find himself at ease and follow his customs (§ 182), but the model the king follows is always that of a superior arrangement:

> "[...] God rules all things, and [...] in our fairest achievements it is not we ourselves who accomplish our intentions, but God in His sovereignty consummates and guides the actions of us all" (§ 195, transl. by M. Hadas).

God, moreover, is the true king, ruler of the world (§ 19), he who watches over everything (§ 16) and governs with clemency (§ 254), but with justice (§ 131), and whose dominion is everywhere (§ 132), he whom, in every way they behave, all the kings of this earth must strive to resemble (§ 279). The king, therefore, becomes emblematic of every virtue (§§ 26-27; 124; 188; etc.), and of magnificence (§§ 80-81), source of salvation (§ 21) and of justice (§§ 23-25), a guide to correct behaviour (§§ 166-167), a model for his subjects (§ 218), a guarantor of harmony and peace in his kingdom (§ 267). Equality and justice will be ensured by such a ruler, within the ambit of a precise hierarchy:

> "By preserving equality and reminding himself at each turn that he is a man as well as a leader of men. And God humbles the proud, and the gentle and humble he exalts" (§263).

Hence, the king's need to become "everyone's equal" (§257); hence a justice that does not limit itself to distributing material goods, but, much more, which aims at establishing balanced and peaceful relations among subjects (§§267;291), at moderation and self-restraint (§§277-278), at obedience to the laws (§279), at concern over saving inferiors in situations of peril (§§281;292) and providing them with benefits (§§205-207). A king's essential quality, then, will reside in the capacity to

> "keep [himself] incorruptible [...] to be sober the greater part of life, to honour justice and to make friends of men of this character" (§209), and the kingly condition will consist in the ability "to rule oneself well, and not be carried away by wealth and fame into unseemly and extravagant desires" (§211).

The model to follow is that of God's self-sufficiency. Thus, the essence of kingship is interpreted from an ethical standpoint. Power and political relations are not the central issues, which instead are virtue and conformity to the order instituted by God. Even the law, be it the *Law* written by Moses (§§45; 122; 133; 171), or that which exists among men, is nevertheless a means whereby to achieve a happy life (§§127; 279), and to acquire knowledge and justice (§§130-131; 168-169), much more so and sooner than by conforming to an imposed order.

Apparently more a part of historical reality than Philo would appear to be, the *Letter of Aristeas* unfolds on an ideal plane, which however is not the Messianic ideal, but that of an irenic Ptolemaic state. Descriptively, such a perspective is much more utopian than Philo's, presenting as it does a state of cohabitation as historically achieved, whereas it really has the dimension of wishfulness. It is the presentation of an idyllic clime which pretends to be real. It is difficult to know what were the actual relations between the Jewish community and the ruling Gentiles at the time of the *Letter*, given the difficulty involved in dating this work,[114] but not even the rosiest hypotheses can countenance as real the attitudes of patient listening, of respect, and I would even add of veneration, that the king and the Ptolemaic court accord the Jewish sages and the knowledge they impart.

The problem of relations with neighbouring peoples and surrounding communities is, moreover, one which pervades the entire history of Israel and the Diaspora. In particular, as regards the period we are examining, the themes of identity and assimilation, of acquisition of the culture and language of the "Greeks", closely interlace with those of obedience to Mosaic law and of acceptance of the laws laid down by the government under which one lives, when relations are essentially good; and of the degree of acceptance of a foreign yoke and of rebellion to unacceptable impositions, when these relations sour.

18. *Disruption of Harmony and the Action of Providence*

If the *Letter's* universalism tends to present norms and behaviour patterns which can be generalized, and which are not attributable only to one people or to one religion, Philo instead attempts to subsume ideas, situations, forms of thought and of social life under the general concept of Judaism. Yet, how can these themes be connected with the political situation of Philo's time? How can relations proper of the *polis* be transferred to a Jewish ambit? Furthermore, how could the Mosaic

---

[114] On the dating of the *Letter* see F. Calabi, *op.cit.* (n. 1) 27-29.

constitution be defined in terms of Greek categories? In the history of Israel there have been kings, judges and heads. The problem that interests Philo is, above all, ethical and religious: order, acceptance of the laws of God. Even the laws of state are to be accepted, albeit after first accepting God's.[115] Men are equal before God, and it is to God that they are to answer.[116] Government, especially if foreign, is to be accepted in so far as it does not stand in the way of following Mosaic law. [117] As true obedience is due only to God, and what counts, *in primis*, is acceptance of divine law, relation with rulers can only be subordinate to the other more important relationship. In the succession of kingdoms and governments there can be a divine will, a providence, which is not always clear to the eyes of man, wherefore certain regimes, no matter how oppressive and overbearing, can have a specific purpose.[118] It is well, then, to distinguish among governors, lieutenants, wicked officers and kings or emperors - or even among other officers - who instead have often showed themselves to be magnanimous and far-sighted. Thus, it would be a serious mistake to

---

[115] See Bréhier, *op.cit.* (n.14) 13, who clarifies how, whereas the Roman city englobes conquered nations, the Jews adapt to the laws of state when these do not run contrary to their own prescriptions. And so Philo. This of course contrasts which Cicero's position, who would give as universal and natural laws the customs of Rome.

[116] Cf. Barraclough, *op.cit.* (n.3) 522-523.

[117] At least in so far as a part of the community and Philo himself are concerned, an example is that of the Roman Empire under Augustus and Tiberius. Cf. *Leg.* 138-151. For Bréhier, *op.cit.* (n.14) 33, Philo sees realized a strong and peaceful government "dans l'empire romain, qu'il ne serait pas loin de considérer comme le gouvernement idéal, s'il admettait qu'il pût avoir sur la terre, une monarchie véritable et un monarque digne de ce nom".

On Philo's basically positive assessment of the Roman Empire, aside from the vexations and persecutions which he attributes to individual governors or legates, and not necessarily to emperors and certainly not to state structure, Cf. Hadas-Lebel, *op.cit.* (n.46) 62-68; 344-350. In a completely different vein, Goodenough, *op.cit.* (n.4), interprets Philo's analysis from an anti-Roman perspective.

[118] This is a theme which recurs frequently in Judaic literature when analyzing relations between Israel and foreign dominators. Cf. Josephus, *B. J.* V. 412: God himself went over to the Romans and abandoned the holy places. The theme is taken up in later Judaic texts which do not accept the thesis of man's destruction of the temple. If Jerusalem was taken, it the Temple destroyed, certainly this occurred because of the will of God, who entrusted his angels with such a task. Cf. *II Baruch* 77. 8-10; 8.2. Even traditions of Rabbinical source claim said order was imparted to Rome from Heaven. Otherwise, dominion would not be as solid as it is, since it is the Romans who destroyed the city, burned the Temple, and persecuted God's servants (cf. Talmud B., *Avodà Zarà* 18a).

view as equal Gaius[119] and Claudius, Sejanus [120] or Flaccus[121] and Petronius[122], not to mention Augustus [123] and Tiberius,[124] who are presented under the most favourable light.[125] *In Flaccum* 97-103 presents an explicit contrast between Flaccus, characterized by hypocrisy, deceitful intentions, preconceived hostility, and the emperor who immediately reads the dispatches which have been sent to him. It is an example of the traditional distinction between good emperors and wicked governors, lieutenants and officials, and perhaps it is also a defensive attitude on Philo's part so as to avoid accusations of being anti-Roman. But what is of interest here as regards the contrast between good emperors and bad officials is the relation between good and bad actions with respect to the divine plan, and conformity of human actions to the design of justice. Thus, in *In Flaccum* 102 ff.,[126] it is clear that God watches over human events, providence and mercy are omnipresent, and the justice that struggles beside the oppressed is foe to the unpious and the wicked. Here we again find the theme of re balancing and of restoring an order which has been broken; a theme which we have seen at the beginning of this chapter in reference to the operations of nature. There, nature worked together with God to resecure the harmony that had been broken, to punish the wicked and re-establish order and justice among men. Here, instead, divine providence watches directly over human events and, when moderation has been exceeded, it overturns the situation. When faced with an excess of Flaccus's illegality and wickedness, justice, as if a personified entity that acts autonomously, even if obviously guided by the will of God, punishes the wicked and gives new hope to the oppressed. That the wicked be punished, almost by a sort of *contrappasso*, whereby they in turn suffer the same lot they have meted out to others, is an often stressed thesis by Philo who, for example in *In Flaccum* (§116),

---

[119] Cf. *Leg.* 14; 22-59; 90; 104; 342-345; *Flacc.* 182.

[120] Cf. *Leg.* 159-165; *Flacc.* 1.

[121] He is the prefect to whom, in *In Flaccum*, Philo attributes responsibility for the pogrom which took place in Alexandria, which however in *Legatio ad Gaium* is instead attributed to Gaius.

[122] Cf. *Leg.* 209; 243 ff.

[123] Cf. *Leg.* 144-161; 313-317. On the positive quality of Augustus's image in relation to political pacification and concentration of power, see C. Kraus Reggiani, 'I rapporti tra l'impero romano e il mondo ebraico al tempo di Caligola secondo la "Legatio ad Gaium" di Filone alessandrino', in *ANRW* II.21.1 (1984)

[124] Cf. *Leg.* 8 ff.; 141-167; 298-305; *Flacc.* 12.

[125] Cf. Barraclough, *op.cit.* (n.3) 452.

[126] Many other passages, however, could be cited in this connection. The theme is recurrent in Philo in the *Legatio*, and both in *In Flaccum* and *De Josepho*.

attributes the cause of the governor's imprisonment to Flaccus's attitude towards the Jews. His subjects, then, become his accusers (*Flacc.* 126), thus upending the situation, which reveals the fragility of human events while at the same time stressing the sensation of deserved punishment, of the importance of a chastisement which is divine succour to the weak and oppressed. It is precisely the sudden quality of the chastisement (*Flacc.* 124) that enables us to grasp the hand of providence behind this act. Such an intervention is acknowledged by the victim himself, who is convinced that he is suffering a series of misfortunes precisely because of the ills he has wrought upon the Jews (*Flacc.* 170 ff.), and is subsequently mindful of having to continue to suffer adversities until they offset the harm he has done:

> "And I have a clear conviction that this is not the limit of my misfortunes but there are others in reserve to complete the sum and counterbalance all that I did" (*Flacc.* 174).

The Furies evoked by Flaccus are the genii of revenge. However, even more than revenge, the ghosts evoked are those of justice and re balancing. The official's violent death, cut to pieces like a sacrificial animal, is exemplary: Flaccus's mutilations are symmetrical to the wounds inflicted upon the Jews (*Flacc.* 189). Divine intervention manifests itself in a double guise: as *pronoia* (providence) and as *dike* (justice). Also in other passages, providence seems to intervene to modify men's evil projects (*Ios.* 266).

Can it then be hypothesized that providence operates essentially to re-establish a harmony that has been broken? Obviously, it is always wrong to generalize, and it does not seem possible to claim that providence always acts in terms of such an end. At least not explicitly. Thus, for example, in *Ios.* 99, or in *Leg.* 220, or in *Leg.* 336, we witness the action or providence without there being an explicit desire to restore a previous situation of harmony. Moreover, God often acts for reasons unbeknownst to us, and which are well to remain secret (*Ios.* 165; 236). We are unable to grasp the profound reasons for divine action:

> "How long shall we the aged continue to be children grown grey in our bodies through length of years, but infants in our soul through want of sense, holding fortune, the most unstable of things, to be the most unchangeable, nature, the most constant, to be the most secure? For we change our actions about from place to place as on a draught board, and

fortune's gifts seem to us more permanent than nature's, nature's more insecure than fortune's" (*Leg.* 1).

And yet the present time and the many important questions decided in it are strong enough to carry conviction even if some have come to disbelieve that the Deity takes thought for men" (*Leg.* 3).

The intellect cannot reach God, and to us remain incomprehensible even those that are

"God's attendant powers. Such are the creative, the kingly, the providential" (*Leg.* 6).

Here is introduced the relation between chance, nature, providence, God's powers; themes which cannot be addressed in this context.[127] I would simply like to point out that even in these passages the concept of natural order (*Leg.* 1) is present, and is linked to the stability of "nature which of all things is the most unshakeable". There is here also the action of the punitive powers that constitute a part

"of laws and statutes, since no law can be complete unless it includes two provisions - honours for things good and punishment for things evil, but because the punishment of others often admonishes offenders and calls them to wisdom, or, certainly at any rate, their neighbours. For penalties are good for the morals of the multitude, who fear to suffer the like" (*Leg.* 7).

Therefore, punishment not as a self-contained act; not as revenge; but directed to beneficial ends in order to re-establish a situation wherein guilt itself is overcome.

19. *Harmony restored*

Moments of harmony, peace and tranquillity alternate with situations of conflict, anarchy and violence. There is a balancing of sorts, whereby, if the former can be followed by the latter, it happens that, subsequently, extraordinary events will restore a condition of order by punishing the wicked, and thus rehabilitate the oppressed. Thus, at the time of Tiberius's death, there reigned perfect peace and

---

[127] On these themes cf. S. Sandmel, 'Some Comments on Providence in Philo', in J. L. Crenshaw and S.Sandmel (edd.), The divine Helmsman: *Studies on God's Control of Human Events presented to Lou H. Silberman*, New York (1980) 79-85.

tranquillity in the empire; harmony and accord were everywhere (*Leg*.8ff). Promises of happiness, joy and of an end to privilege were rife. Then, such an irenic scenario is suddenly overturned and replaced by a state of disorder and dissension. A simple and wholesome life is forsaken for one marked by excess, vice and dissipation (*Leg*. 14ff.). Such a transition, however, is not voluntary, originating as it does from an illness of Gaius Caligola; an illness which not only extends its effects to Gaius alone, or to the circle of those close to him, but has repercussions throughout the land.

> "For every part of the habitable world shared his sickness, and theirs was a sickness more grievous than that which overcame him. His was of the body only, theirs was felt by all and everywhere, affecting the well-being of the soul, their peace,their hopes and participation and enjoyment of every good thing. Thoughts of the many great evils which spring from anarchy occupied their mind: famine, war, ravaging, devastation of estates, loss of property, abductions, fears of enslavement and death, so deadly that no physician could cure them and the only remedy lay in the recovery of Gaius" (*Leg*. 16-18).

Here, then, it is explicitly stated that his return to health can restore peace and tranquillity. Only the eradication of the sickness, which entails chaos, fear and conflict, can re-establish the foregoing harmony.

> "At this every continent, every island, returned once more to its former happiness, for they felt that they personally shared in his preservation" (*Leg*. 18)

The fact that Gaius's recovery is apparent, that he simulates and is secretly preparing himself for further crimes and plots, does not invalidate the principle, just as the fact that the nations of the earth have deluded themselves about Gaius's recovery does not negate the salvation that would have accrued to them had that recovery been real. The apparent recovery ushers in a new phase in Gaius's life, a sort of interlude which then gives way to a crescendo of falsehood and duplicity, of betrayal and violence, of crimes and cruelty. It is almost a preliminary phase to the final move in the game of bestiality (*Leg*. 22). The effects of Gaius's violence, as previously those of harmony, spread throughout the land. The world is a close-knit unit, and therefore what happens at the centre has immediate repercussions at the periphery. Everywhere ruin, despair, tumult and sadness take root (*Leg*. 89-91). The effects of violence peak with the image of unnatural deaths and wilfully caused diseases. Destruction would be total were it not for justice causing Gaius's death (*Leg*. 108). Whether here it is a question of justice personified, as Pelletier claims (see note *ad loc.*), or of divine justice, the power to which Philo refers in *Legatio* (§7) there is nevertheless an external remedy to an unbearable situation of excess and destruction. A justice figure actively intervenes to put an end to disorder and to re-establish normality.

Returning to what was mentioned at the beginning of this chapter concerning the need to repair the break that has fractured balance, and of re-establishing the harmony which in every sphere can be broken by error and degeneration, it seems to me that even the intervention of providence, in a way, fits just such a perspective. Reference here is not so much to a kind of providence which, watching over the Jews, bestows upon them particular benefits, as to a merciful intervention of *pronoia* aimed at curbing excess and wickedness and at restoring a modicum of equity. Perhaps, as in the case of Pharaoh punished by nature for his excesses which disrupted harmony and the established order, also for Flaccus, even if not a direct instrument of punishment, nature at least is a witness of redress by acting as a benevolent place of welcome for the Jews who have been expelled from their homes and deprived of both shelter and gathering places. The strands become home and dwelling for the Jews who flock to the seashore invoking:

> "Most Mighty King of mortals and immortals, we have come here to call on earth and sea, and air and heaven, into which the universe is partitioned, and on the whole world, to give Thee thanks. They are our only habitation, expelled as we are from all that men have wrought, robbed of our city and the buildings within its walls, public and private, alone of all men under the sun bereft of home and country through the malignancy of a governor. Thou givest also a glimpse of cheering hopes that Thou will amend what remains for amendment, in that Thou hast already begun to assent to our prayers. For the common enemy of the nation, under whose leadership and by whose instruction these misfortunes have befallen it, who in his windy pride thought that they would promote him to honour, Thou hast suddenly brought low [...] to give them a clearer picture of the swift and unhoped-for visitation" (*Flacc.* 123-124).

20. *The Present and the Atemporal: Two Levels of Discourse*

The manner in which relations between Jews and rulers unfold, recognition of the fact that not all dominators are necessarily oppressors, and man's inability at times to clearly perceive the design of providence, all interlace with the description of a government, that of Rome, which in many ways is admired. Many aspects of an empire which, although the wielder of power is not insensitive to his subjects' need for freedom, are presented in a particularly favourable light.

Underlying such considerations is the conviction, which is rather widespread within the Judaism of both that and the successive period, that it is well to follow the local laws and obey the local governors, when this does not entail transgression of the Law. Such positions are variously expressed and become more attenuated in relation to contingent historical conditions, especially in the Diaspora, when relations of subordination are established with Gentile governors.[128] As regards the period being considered, there are times when Ptolemaic kingdoms first, and later the Roman Empire, are inclined towards universalism, which means subsuming diverse nations together with their relative special characteristics, and towards a basic tolerance of specific traits and mores which are not in contrast with their power structure. Other situations, instead, are those in which diversity and particularism are grievously curtailed. Philo sees file before him representatives of both categories, and, if he speaks in enthusiastic terms - idealizing their virtue and broadmindedness - of an Augustus or a Tiberius, God's instruments on earth, pacifiers and civilizers of every town and district, he however fiercely attacks, as we have seen, not only Gaius, but also and especially officials like Flaccus and Sejanus, oppressors and tyrants who stifle all forms of freedom. Philo's perspective is that of a dialogue with invested authority, of relations which can be more or less happy depending on circumstances, but which nevertheless call for confrontation. Even the delegation to Rome and the petitions brought to the emperor fit into this perspective. When confronting dangerous attacks against the community in Alexandria, veritable pogroms, harsh repression, threats of further aggression, Philo seeks alliances and accord with the power structure, not open confrontation or rebellion. More than the semblance of pacification which veils a will to rebel, more than coded messages which more or less deeply countenance an instigation to clash with Rome,[129] what Philo is really looking for - I believe - is whatever possibility of freedom and tolerance. The perspective is not yet one of head-on collision, rebellion or refusal, as will be the case only a few decades further on, at

---

[128] The complexity of relations,the ambiguity of many situations, the difficulty in accepting a foreign government, while at the same time preserving Jewish identity and the alliance with one's fellow people who are struggling against that very government, is a dominant theme in Josephus. Critical of extreme anti-Roman positions, and admirer of the Roman Empire and its administration, he often presents it in a favourable light. An example, among the many, Agrippa's speech in *B.J.*345-401. The empire's grandiosity and its power are, however, in some way undermined by the transitory quality implicit in the idea of succession which characterizes kingdoms. Cf. I. Cervelli, 'Dalla storiografia alla memoria. A proposito di Flavio Giuseppe e Yohanan ben Zakkai', *Studi Storici* 4 (1990) 968 ff.

[129] Cf. Goodenough, *op.cit.* (n.4).

the time of the revolts.[130] Now, a more or less resigned acceptance, an attempt at conquering new spheres of freedom, together with the possibility of cohabitation, find themselves side by side with a feeling of amiration for a great empire.[131] For the Jewish interlocutors it is a matter of finding space within the folds of power, together with an acceptable arrangement which will allow them a plausible existence and the possibility to perform duties incumbent upon men who have above all to answer to God. At the bottom of all this, as I have stated, is the conviction that true obedience concerns the dictates of the law, that the true kingdom is that of God, that regimes and governments are

---

[130] Attitudes of hostility and total refusal will of course intensify in the period of the revolts, when anti-Roman positions take on tones of utter antagonism and instigation to struggle. For a brief outline of the problem cf. F. Calabi, Introduzione a Flavio Giuseppe, *In difesa degli Ebrei. Contro Apione*, Venezia (1993). Even more heated are the attacks during the period following defeat, when hatred for the Romans interlaces with Messianic hopes and exhortations to wait for the end of the IV empire. Cf. Hadas-Lebel, 'A propos des révoltes juives contre Rome', in D. Tollet (ed.), *Politique et religion dans le judaïsme ancien et médiéval*, Paris (1989) 55-57; N. Belayche, 'Les figures politiques des messies en Palestine de la première moitié du premier siècle de notre ère', in *Politique et religion cit.* 58-74. In Philo's time the possibility of living together under a foreign rule still seemed open. Difficult situations are often of a contingent nature. Conflict often appears determined by single individuals destined to be superseded by events. Foreign rule is not necessarily hostile nor a source of profanation.

Even under foreign dominion there still seems to be room to affirm identity and autonomy. Thus, 3 *Maccabees* (a work of early I-century B.C.? Of the time of laography introduced by Augustus), in spite of outraged reaction to forms of assimilation and its clearly polemical tones, stress the distinction between Gentiles who are always hostile towards Jews, and Gentiles who are not really their enemies; underlines the difference between good governors and bad counselors (II.26; VI.23-24) and, on this bases the Jews' obedience to authority (III.4; V.32; VI.25). Loyalty towards a Gentile governor and loyalty to Judaism are not incompatible.

The *Letter of Aristeas* portrays a situation of total syntony with the Ptotemies, actually praised and presented as models. Naturally, the positive nature of Ptolemaic rule and the acceptance of foreign government wanes in relevance in the hypothesis, put forth by Parente, *op.cit.* (n.3) 303 ff., that the *Letter* has as its objective a polemic against the Asmoneans. This however does not rule out, as Parente himself notes (p. 305) that there is "an evident effort to justify [...] subjection to a foreign king."

For the changes in relations between Judaic communities and the central power structure in Alexandria between 280 and 130 B.C., changes which would be echoed in the various needs to translate the *Bible* in Greek in the period under consideration, see G. Dorival, 'A propos de la Septante', in *Politique et religion* (n. 130), 21-28.

[131] Admiration for an empire acknowledged as being grand and efficient, powerful and generous is still present in Josephus.

transitory, being willed and tolerated by God in order to achieve ends known to Him, and that eventually present situations will be overturned.[132] Present government only represents a moment in this process. Its dictates can be empirically and pragmatically [133] accepted, with the awareness that the real reference point lies elsewhere, that the true law has another source, and that the real king is another. The value reference is twofold: the present plane and that of timelessness. As we have seen in paragraph 6 of the initial part of this chapter, two are the standards which govern action, and two are the spheres of discourse. On one hand, there is an ambit characterized by what is finite and transitory; on the other, one where perfection and divine harmony reign supreme. They are not so much two parallel realities, as they are two approaches to a unitary reality, marked by two levels: one related to the present and to human finiteness; the other to atemporality. These two levels coexist in Philo's theory and proceed in parallel fashion, without there necessarily being contrast between them, nor that one prevail upon the other.

---

[132] Cf. *Praem.* 95; 126; 169-171; *QE.* II.76.

[133] Such an attitude will be repeatedly taken up by successive Judaism in various circumstances. Particularly exemplary is the case of Rabbi Yohanan ben Zakkai who, during the siege of Jerusalem, goes to the Roman camp to negotiate with Vespasian the survival of Judaism - its cult, tradition and study - (*A R N* a4; b6; *T.B. Gitt.* 56b). Cf. I. Cervelli, *op.cit.* (n.128) 955-956.

For a presentation of the complex relations at the time of the war of the 70, the *a posteriori* reconstruction of that period by the Rabbis, the establishing of a line of continuity in the pre- and post- 70 period through the figure of Yohanan ben Zakkai, see the works by J. Neusner, in part. *Development of a Legend. Studies on the Tradition concerning Yohanan ben Zakkai*, Leiden (1970);*A Life of Yohanan ben Zakkai. Ca 1-80 C.E.*, Leiden (1970); *The Rabbinic Tradition about the Pharisees before 70; I.The Masters*, Leiden (1971); 'The Formation of Rabbinic Judaism: Yavenh (Jamnia) from A.D. 70 to 100', in *A N R W* II.19.2 (1979).

CHAPTER THREE

EXEGETICAL MODES

1.1 Text's Richness and Exegesis

What I have said so far dealt with Philo's theory and regarded the content of his work and not the nature of his argumentation. The two aspects are strictly related, especially when we consider that Philo's writing is exegetical, his work is an interpretation of the *Bible*, a reading of reality described in the *Bible*. As Nikiprowetzky[1] aptly clarifies - knowledge is of necessity exegesis, the reading of reality emerges from an interpretation of the *Bible*, nature is described and known in the *Torah*, there is a close relationship between law and order of nature and divine law and order incorporated in the *Torah*.[2] The *Torah* is not only a text that encompasses the knowledge of Israel, the revelation given to Moses on Sinai, but, at the same time, the law of God, the order of the cosmos, the model which inspired God's creation of the world, the project and structure of reality. Knowledge comes to

---

[1] Valentin Nikiprowetzky's publication of *Le Commentaire de L'Ecriture chez Philon d'Alexandrie*, Leiden (1977) prompted scholars to refocus on Philo mainly as a commentator of the *Bible*, considering his work primarily as exegetic. Constantly referring to the Biblical text, linking Philonic passages to commented verses, identifying exegetic units in relation to structural lemmata, explaining by *quaestiones et solutiones*, and comparing allegorical treatises with the *Quaestiones in Genesim* and *in Exodum*, all constitute fixed and ascertained tenets. Naturally, this does not entail assimilation among the various interpretative modes which maintain their individuality and positions. If not divergent, said positions are certainly specific, and at times greatly distant one from the other. It would be difficult, for example, to assimilate the unitary theses of Cazeaux to Radice's "exegetic-unit" reading, to the identification of superimpositions of interpretative modes, as in Goulet, to Runia's exegetic analyses, to comparisons with Middle-Platonic literature, as in Dillon, or with Greek rhetoric, as in Mack, to the identification of allegorical meanings, as in Pepin, to considerations of self-perception of Philo as an exegete, as in Hay, to comparisons with Rabbinic exegesis, as in Hamerton-Kelly, or with midrashic modes, as in Belkin. What constitutes a common terrain for rather different readings is a consideration of the inevitable link between Philo's and the Biblical text, the impossibility, by now acknowledged by all scholars, of an autonomous reading aimed at identifying a philosophical discourse which, in some way closed within itself, excludes the exegetic function of Philo's work.
[2] See *Opif.* 3; *Mos.* II.11.

man from God, not only through a direct personal relationship between
individual and God, but in as much as the latter gave the *Torah* to
Israel.[3] God is therefore knowable - albeit limitedly - to the "people
who see God" (according to Philonic etymology)[4] through the
Patriarchs - the living law[5]- and with Moses in the *Torah*. For Israel,
after Sinai, knowledge and wisdom are also achieved through study
and in the practice of the *Torah*. Even "contemplation of the world" is
actuated through exegesis. Every search for knowledge, every
philosophical questioning, and every form of contemplation can only be
exegesis of the sacred text and, conversely, reading the *Bible* entails
knowledge of a profound reality which is not always immediately
evident to those who approach the sacred text superficially, together
with the identification of a deep and hidden meaning above and beyond
the immediate meaning[6]. Exemplary, in this respect, are the
Therapeuts, who devote their lives to contemplation, that is, to
exegesis, and seek the various meanings of Biblical passages.[7]

Keeping in mind these theses, I would like to consider some
aspects of Philo's work which I believe call for deeper investigation:

1) the relationship between Philo's text and the Biblical text and
the meaning of the multiple interpretations often present in Philo's
work; the non-unitary dimension of Philo's text as closely related to a
consideration of the Biblical text's unity;

2) the form and function of quotation;

3) the *Bible* 's authority principle;

4) the form of commentary;

5) modes of interpretation and possible hermeneutic regularities
-if not rules - in some way comparable with exegetic operations and
commentaries of other authors and other research contexts.

A series of considerations which I intend to pursue are, I believe,
applicable to most of Philo's work, and in fact I shall utilize passages
from various treatises. The text, however, which I shall attempt to

---

3   See *Deus* 148.
4   See *Deus* 93; *Praem.* 44; *Somn.* I.171; *Her.* 78 and other passages. Cf. G.
Delling, 'The "One who sees God" in Philo' in F.E. Greenspahn, E. Hilgert, B.L.
Mack (edd.), *Nourished with Peace: Studies in Hellenistic Judaism in Memory of
Samuel Sandmel*, Scholars Press Homage Series 9 (Chico, California 1984) 27-41.
5   *Abr.* 3-6; 275; *Migr.* 130.
6   See *Conf.* 143. Cf. Nikiprowetzky, *op. cit.*(n.1) 102-103; R. Hamerton-Kelly,
'Allegory, Typology and Sacred Violence: Sacrificial Representation and the
Unity of the Bible in Paul and Philo', *SPhA* 3 (1991) 68-69.
7   *Contempl.* 28-30. Ἀσκησις = reading of Scripture and interpretation of the
philosophy of the fathers = contemplation.

analyze more specifically in the second part of this chapter is the *De Mutatione Nominum*.

1.2. *Exegesis as reading reality*

In the words written by Moses - through inspiration,[8] as must be borne in mind - reality is enclosed. The words of the law are the mirror of the intelligible,[9] which can only be grasped and known by reading the *Torah*, by understanding the various meanings encompassed in the Biblical text, by means of textual exegesis. If the *Torah* is truth and reality, and also the law which governs the cosmos, the law of God, its product, exegesis, which is the study of the *Torah*, is also search for divine law and the law of the cosmos.[10] There is a distinction between knowledge that is acquired spontaneously through divine intervention[11] and taught knowledge,[12] which separates the Patriarchs and Moses, who reach a higher, albeit limited, knowledge, from common men who do not reach it.[13]

In the *De Mutatione* (§209) the attempt to know God, Moses' goal, implies a fusion of all human faculties: knowledge , vision, listening to the word of God - listening which also implies following and living his norms (see §200). However, Moses' is a higher state, one not reached by all men. The distinction between the way through teaching and that through exercise is exemplified by Abraham and by Jacob, who both reach virtue and a form of divine knowledge,albeit via different routes (*Mut.83-87*). Being self-taught, Isaac's case is distinct (*Mut. 80*). There is a before and an after with respect to the revelation of the *Torah*.[14] After Sinai, it is possible to aspire to truer knowledge

---

[8]   The Torah's inspired character. Divine inspiration to Moses, cf. *Mos.* II.188 ff.; for the inspired character of the *LXX*, see *Mos.* II.35 ff.

[9]   *Contempl.* 78; 28.

[10]   *Mos.* I.11: 2.48; *Praem.* 46-51; *Migr.* 89; *Post.* 7; *Sacrif.* 13; *Fug.* 66; *Q.E.* II.42. Cf.Nikiprowetzky, *op. cit.* (n.1),102-103; 107-108; 141-142; J. Riaud, 'Quelques réflexions sur les Thérapeuts d'Alexandrie à la lumière de *De vita Mosis* II, 67' *SPhA3* (1991) 186-188.

[11]   See *Praem.* 43-44;*Abr.* 56-62; 70-71; *Plant.* 22. Cf. Delling, *art. cit.* (n.4) 34-35.

[12]   *Conf.* 148; *Gig.* 53-57; *Plant.* 79-84; *Migr.* 40; *Sacrif.* 77-79; *Fug.* 161-174. Cf. B. Lévy, *Le logos et la   lettre.   Philon d'Alexandrie en regard des pharisiens* (Lagrasse (Aude) 1988)

[13]   See *Spec. Leg.* I.38-40; *Praem.* 43, cited in D.T. Runia, 'Redrawing the map of early Middle Platonism: some comments on the philonic evidence' in *Exegesis and Philosophy: studies on Philo of Alexandria* (London 1990) 99.

[14]   *Q.E.* II.38-40; *Decal.* 18; 47; see Nikiprowetzky *op. cit.* (n.1) 124: in the prophet the individual intellect follows the universal intellect "La loi que Moïse promulgue [...]   reproduit les images divines que le prophète porte en son âme".

through exegesis,[15] the way to contemplation,[16] to the search for what is hidden,[17] which in its loftiness can never be completely grasped and mastered by man,[18] but which can nevertheless be approached through textual study.[19] As Nikiprowetzky[20] clarifies,

> "que le vocable désigne d'une façon plus ou moins philosophique Dieu lui-même ou la Nature proprement dite, la φύσις est enfermée dans l'Ecriture. C'est elle qui y parle et s'y exprime, elle dont l'interprétation allégorique permet d'entendre la voix. Et c'est précisément à travers l'interprétation allégorique que les Israélites perviennent à la percevoir."

Reality, therefore, can be investigated through exegesis, by reading a text in its multiple meanings.

1.3. Text's Inexhaustibility

An interpretation, in principle, cannot be unitary: unity is retrievable in the Biblical text of reference; that is, in the text that constitutes the point of departure, the element upon which both explanation and subsequent theorization are constructed. The *Bible*, precisely as it stems from a unique source - it is the *Torah* from Heaven - possesses its own indisputable unity, wherefore there are no passages which are more important than others, no hierarchies nor varying degrees of importance.[21] Drawing together even rather distant passages is not a problem, so long naturally as this exercise is substantiated by interpretative rigor and arbitrary approaches are

---

[15] Cf. D.T. Runia, *Philo of Alexandria and the Timaeus of Plato* (Leiden, 1986), 538-542. See, however, *op. cit.* (n.13) 103, where doubts are raised concerning the possibility, for the exegete, of reaching Moses' level of knowledge and inspiration. True knowledge is acquired through the exercise of reason (*art. cit.* n.13) 125; *op. cit.* 297-300; 391-393; 425-447). Perhaps this does not apply for exceptional men like the prophets.
[16] See Nikiprowetzky, *op. cit.* (n.1) 124-125.
[17] Cf. *Congr.* 172; *Contempl.* 78; *Post.* 18-20; see Nikiprowetzky, *op. cit.* (n.1)124.
[18] Cf. *Det.* 89-91; *Praem.* 40; *Deus.* 55; *Somn.* I.24; 67; Cf. D.M.Hay, 'Philo's View of Himself as an Exegete: Inspired but not Authoritative', *SPhA* 3(1991)49.
[19] See Runia, *art. cit.* (n.13)100: "the epistemic limitations of the exegete in the task of decoding the wisdom contained in the books of the sage Moses". Cf. Nikiprowetzky, *op. cit.* (n.1)190-191.
[20] *op. cit.* (n.1)107-108.
[21] Cf. J. Cazeaux, *La trame et la chaîne, ou les Structures littéraires et l'Exégèse dans cinq des Traités de Philon d'Alexandrie*, Leiden (1983) 505;583.

avoided.[22]   The unitary dimension, that is, cannot be found in commentary or in a theorization which aim at inherent coherence. The depth and complexity of the Biblical text cannot be fully grasped and explained by human interpretation, which is in any case limited. On one hand, we are dealing with an inspired text, a text from heaven, the representation of an unattainable reality in its totality - even if expressed in language comprehensible to man[23] -and on the other, with parallel explanations, with exegeses that are by definition incomplete and which can only grasp aspects of an inexhaustible reading. Hence, the richness of multiple interpretations: not one exegesis rather than another, or one explanation that excludes others, or a univocal reading, but instead all the many valid interpretations[24] which shed

---

[22] The same danger of arbitrariness occurs when approaching parallel interpretations and when presenting allegorical interpretations, according to F. Trisoglio, 'Filone alessandrino e l'esegesi cristiana. Contributo alla conoscenza dell'influsso esercitato da Filone nel IV secolo, specificatamente in Gregorio di Nazianzio' in ANRW. II. 21.2 (592). The utilization of remote passages of the Bible has been studied by J. Cazeaux (n.21), from the standpoint of anticipating a following passage; a sort of attraction of one passage towards another: "une première citation scripturaire, puisqu'il semble toujours partir de là, se projette pour lui dans une autre citation. Il ne le déclare pas immédiatement, mais il la prevoit de loin: elle oriente l'interprétation de la première parole"(p.27). For Cazeaux, there is in Philo's exegesis "une attraction ordonnée qui fait que deux passages de l'Ecriture, deux versets consécutifs surtout, organisent entre eux une séquence d'autres textes, de concepts sous-jacents, d'images, comme les deux pôles d'un aimant organisent les particules de métal" (498-499).
[23] Conf. 135; Deus 52.
[24] For multiple interpretations, see Plant. 113; Agr. 157; Spec. Leg. I.200; 287; Abr. 88; 200; Ios. 125; Migr. 89; 93. Many interpretations of a single verse, for example,in Q.G. III.42, where Philo explains Gen. 17.4. However, he modifies the biblical text adding: "You shall no longer be son, but father; father not of one alone, but of a multitude, multitudinis autem non secundum partes, sed universarum gentium". The LXX says πατὴρ πλήθους ἐθνῶν. Mut. 57-59 skips over the piece in question. On multiple interpretations see P. Borgen, 'Philo of Alexandria' in M.E. Stone (ed.), Jewish Writings of the Second Temple Period: Apocrypha, Pseudepigrapha, Qmran Sectarian Writings, Philo, Josephus (Assen-Philadelphia 1984) 260-263; J. Pepin, 'Remarques sur la théorie de l'exégèse allégorique chez Philon', Colloque du CNRS: Philon d'Alexandrie (Lyon 1966, Paris 1967) 158-159; B.L. Mack, 'Philo Judaeus and Exegetical Traditions in Alexandria' in ANRW II.21.1. 243 n.57, which states: "this phenomenon of multiple interpretation reminds one of a similar capacity in Rabbinic literature; but it occurs also in Hellenistic collections as, for instance, in the multiple etymologies in Cornutus". Conversely, Mack (p.265) sees multiple interpretations as interpretations which are mutually exclusive, and which are referable to various authors or interpretative schools towards which Philo assumes a position, selecting one with respect to the others. See also Runia, art. cit. (n.13) 96-97.

light on some aspects of an inexhaustible reality. Interpretation can
enlighten some of the many facets of truth, without however grasping
its deeper meaning,[25] in that the interpretations of a Biblical passage
are potentially infinite and their apparent contradictions   and
repetitions mark the text's inexhaustibility.[26]

1.4. The Plurality of the Interpretations

The plurality of the interpretations does not mean that some of
them are not to be rejected, nor that some explanations do not appear
inadequate and confutable, while others appear better and endowed
with deeper meaning.[27] In fact, Philo often cites contemporary and past
exegetes who supply erroneous explanations,[28]   whereas in other
passages he ranks, as it were, explanations on the basis of their varying
degree of validity.[29]   However, many are the places in which, more or
less explicitly, the criterion of multiple interpretation is adopted, and
where it is stressed that a plurality of explanations implies richness and
greater depth.   Therefore, it is not a question of a plurality of
explanations due to a sort of "constraint", nor of juxtaposed
interpretations which are impossible to unify, but of a plurality pursued
on the strength of its positiveness, a co-presence which underscores the
diverse facets of too lofty a reality to be grasped with a single
explanation.[30]   On one hand, many possible explanations which
complement, without excluding, one another; on the other, shifts within
an explanation among various aspects and meanings, whereby a text
yields a spectrum of meanings, the various facets of which draw on one
another and are clarified.   It is not, however, a play of reflecting

---

25 *Q.G.* IV.43. See D.T. Runia, 'How to read Philo' in *Exegesis and Philosophy cit.* (n.13) 190.
26 *Migr.* 89-93: grasping the hidden sense. Literal and allegorical meanings. Cf.
V. Nikiprowetzky, 'L'Exégèse de Philon d'Alexandrie dans le De Gigantibus et le
Quod Deus', in D. Winston, J. Dillon (edd.), *Two Treatises of Philo of Alexandria:
A Commentary on De Gigantibus and Quod Deus sit immutabilis*, Brown Judaic
Series 25 (Chico, California 1983) 75n.7.
27 Cf. *Migr.* 89; *Somn.* I.120; *Spec. Leg.* I.59, where it seems that theses of other
commentators are presented, criticized and contrasted by Philo's interpretation.
Cf. Nikiprowetzky, *op.cit*; (n.1), 212 n.122; Mack, *art. cit.* (n.24), 264-265.
28 *Migr.* 89-93; *Spec. Leg.* I.8.
29 Cf. J. Daniélou, *Philon d'Alexandrie* (Paris 1958) 116.
30 One immediately recalls the seventy interpretations of every word of the
Torah postulated in the *Babylonian Talmud* ('Shabbath' 88b) "Every single word
that went forth from the Omnipotent was split up into seventy languages". See
also 'Sanhedrin' 34a.

mirrors, but a series of slight modifications, shifts and semantic enrichment.[31] Hence, the non conclusiveness of interpretations, the differentiated use of quotations and terms. For example, in *De Mutatione* (§125-129) Moses ἀρχιπροφήτες is called θεός with respect to Pharaoh, ἄνθρωπος θεοῦ with respect to the people, *Moses* when interpreting the oracles;[32] or in *De Confusione* (§146) κατ᾽εἰκόνα ἄνθρωπος, generally referred to men,[33] is synonymous with *logos*, which in turn is a qualifier of Israel, of a being not yet worthy of being named υἱὸς θεοῦ, the first of the angels, λόγος πρεσβύτατος which in turn is θεοῦ εἰκών, with a considerable shift with respect to the original κατ᾽ εἰκόνα.

The explanation of verse 17.1 in *Genesis*, where the terms θεός and κύριος appear, can perhaps be considered as an example of interpretative sliding. Starting from the double designation of God, it is a matter of explaining the reason for such a doubling. There is a shift from κύριος as a proper (improper) name, to κύριος for Pharaoh, to κύριος and θεός for Abraham.[34] In *De Mutatione* (§15-24), God is θεός and κύριος, and this double denomination, - beyond all the possible correlations with the the double denomination of God in the Biblical text and the cautionary approach the Tetragrammaton commands, - indicates the diverse aspects of those who establish a relationship with God. Through a reading of the double denomination, different characters and approaches can be grasped. Thus, all the name variations in the *Torah* indicate changes in the nature of the individual in question, or the co-presence of a plurality of aspects in the same person; and two names for one and the same person indicate different aspects.[35]

---

[31] Cf. B.L. Mack, 'Decoding the Scripture: Philo and the Rules of Rhetoric' , in *Nourished with Peace* cit. (n.4) 114.

[32] Cf. D.T. Runia, 'God and Man in Philo of Alexandria' in *Exegesis and Philosophy* cit. (n.13), in particular 56-65; V. Nikiprowetzky, " 'Moyses palpans vel liniens': on some Explanations of the Name of Moses in Philo of Alexandria" in *Nourished with Peace* cit. (n.7), 12-142.

[33] Cf. for example *Opif. 69*.

[34] See D.T. Runia, 'Naming and knowing: themes in philonic theology with special reference to the *De Mutatione Nominum* ' in *Exegesis and Philosophy* cit. (n.13), 76; Runia, *God and Man* cit. (n.32), 53; 73; cf. Cazeaux, *op. cit.* (n.21) 483-491.

[35] Parallels with Rabbinic exegesis. This discourse holds true for the names, but could also hold true for different terms. For a more in-depth discussion of these themes, see the second part of this chapter.

1.5. *Philo's Text   Fragmented Character*

The Philonic text, as we have seen, lacks both the granitic quality which can be found in systematic philosophical works, and a unitary theorization as that postulated, for example, by H.A. Wolfson.[36] Instead, it presents a fragmented character, owing not to extrinsic reasons such as differences between youthful writings and those of old age, or to influences of different philosophical currents, or to different approaches depending on the subject matter under investigation, but to readings based on the unity of the Biblical text, rather than on an inner unity of the commentary. In this connection, explanation shifts acquire a fundamental importance; by emphasizing, alternately, one shade of meaning or another of a term or phrase, thus achieving a union of different meanings and interpretations (varying and distant to the greatest possible extent), it is possible to shed light on a Biblical passage to which reference is made.   However, the latter can never be penetrated in its totality; even though continuously examined, it will nevertheless retain an unexplored identity and an unfathomable silence. That the *Bible* can contain banalities, errors and contradictions is unthinkable.[37]   The search for textual coherence[38] uncovers new aspects which cannot be reduced to a single level of importance. Therefore, fragmentariness is not only a consequence of Biblical reference.   In some ways, fragmentariness is pursued because it stems from the richness of the many varying interpretations, and derives from successive in-depth readings which build one upon the other, and which link together so as to yield new explanations and new assumptions, and to elaborate other forms of interpretation.[39] Then, if the shifts between various meanings are considered, if the phases of these shifts are drawn together, it is possible to obtain a more comprehensive thematic

---

[36] *Philo, Foundations of religious Philosophy in Judaism, Christianity and Islam*, (Cambridge Mass. 1947, reprint. 1968).

[37] *Conf.* 143; *Det.* 13.

[38] For example, when in *Conf.* 146 he inquires after the sons of the men who built the tower, he seeks coherence saying that the sons of the men -polytheistic- are those who listen, and vision is greater than listening.

[39] Nikiprowetzky, *op. cit.* 180-181 explains that the apparent contradictions are due to the form of the commentary. Unity is in the biblical text, not in Philo's, and at p.191, he speaks of multiple exegeses as a mark of the text's richness, but also of human mind's incapacity to grasp the entire truth. On the choice of the reading of one passage rather than another, see Borgen, *art. cit.* (n.24) 263 n.176 who cites *Det.*47. Borgen also refers to other exegetic schools and to other possible interpretations which are co-present in Philo and which reciprocally clarify one another. Cf. also Nikiprowetzky, *art. cit.* (n.26) 75.

image. Furthermore, given its continuous reference to the Biblical text, a treatise may not have a unity of its own, even if it certainly presents elements of cohesion which can be found in the very form of the treatise. At best, cohesion can however derive only from the Biblical text followed in its unfolding, or be found only in a single passage, or in a group of passages, referring to a text on which an interpretation is built.[40] It is not accidental, when studying treatises, that it is often necessary to take them apart in order to analyze their structure and constitutive elements. Philo, however, always presents a unitary interpretative approach;[41] therefore it makes sense to draw together various passages on a same theme, not so much to find unity of thesis, as to identify recurrent themes and to grasp the diverse facets of a single theme. Nikiprowetzky[42] moves in this direction, when claiming that, despite the "exegetic constraint" and constant reference to the Biblical text, it cannot be denied that Philo's discourse is organized around a core. Yet, for Nikiprowetzky, Philonic discourse presents an exegetic constraint prompting the author to constantly rethink and re-elaborate the same passage or group of passages. Hence, the advisability of studying an exegetic motive in Philo, rather than a philosophical theme. However, must the plurality of interpretations and multiple explanations be then considered, negatively, as an exegetic constraint, or rather as a search for the richness of multiple interpretations, the unwillingness to reduce to a single explanation a text which is in itself inexhaustible? In my opinion, as I have already stated, if the coherent and intrinsically unitary element is the Biblical text, inaccessible in its totality to human exegesis, and Philo's discourse constructs itself as commentary, and the basis of each and every proposition is always the *Bible*, then fragmentariness and incoherence are only apparent; they are purposely sought, they constitute an intentional richness, a grouping of explanations around a text, a wealth of readings abutting one upon the other, each clarifying some individual facet. The Biblical text's unity, then, is to be constantly explored and reconstructed without one definite conclusion being a point of arrival, thus considering the interpretation as conclusive. That is, there is the awareness of referring to something concluded -the Biblical text- that Philo's discourse, as that of any exegete, in fact, can

---

[40] Cf. R. Radice, 'Introduzione' in Filone, *Le origini del male* (Milano 1984) who speaks of semantic units.
[41] Cf. D.T. Runia, 'The Structure of Philo's allegorical Treatises' in *Exegesis and Philosophy* cit. (n.13) 126-129.
[42] *op. cit.* (n.1) 239.

never exhaust. Therefore, it is neither a question of conclusiveness nor of fixity, but neither of pure exegetic eclecticism.

1.6. *Exegetic Tradition*

An open textual approach does not exhaust itself in the exegesis of a sole author. Philo feels that he fits into a tradition in which every exegete can have his own coherence and an interpretation of his own; but in which, both within the interpretation of an author, and within the tradition as a whole, all the visions are read, re listened to, and constantly re-elaborated.[43] In the various commentaries upon individual passages there are constant approaches to textual interpretation. Thus, Philo identifies exegetes who are principally literalists or principally allegorists; while interpretative unity, however, is offered only by the Biblical text. The text's coherence, that is, is undeniable[44] and is always to be identified, clarified and stressed even where it seems to be lacking. The *Bible'* s apparent oddities and contradictions are to be explained, and the basic function of exegesis lies precisely in surmounting difficulties and in clarifying elements which at first sight appear incomprehensible. If the *Torah* is infallible and does not entail errors, rethinking, or contradictions, what appears as such has to be explained by exegesis.[45] Thus, for example, if a same form has more than one meaning, consistency is to be sought; if a passage does not appear comprehensible, another will be sought to explain the first; if an account seems implausible, it will be given an allegorical reading. Where a meaning appears unsatisfactory for a term or passage, another is introduced to explain the first, and therefore there will be many parallel explanations. Or, and this is yet another strategy which is pursued at times, multiple meanings are made to accrue to the same term; not so many parallel threads, but the unfolding of a sole thread up to the central nucleus, as with a spiral,

---

[43] *Abr.* 99; *Sacrif.* 77-79; *Spec. Leg.* I.8; Runia, *Redrawing the map cit.* (n.13) 100 states that for Philo one progresses more by studying οἱ παλαιοὶ καὶ θεῖοι ἄνδρες than through independent philosophical speculation. Mack, *art. cit.* (n.24) 242-243; 262-268 refers to Philo's exegetic predecessors . Cf. Hay, *art. cit.* (n.18) 40; B.L. Mack, 'Exegetical Traditions in Alexandrian Judaism; a Program for the Analysis of the Philonic Corpus' in *SPh*3(1974-75) 75 ff.; R. Radice, *Platonismo e creazionismo in Filone di Alessandria*, Metafisica del Platonismo nel suo sviluppo storico e nella filosofia patristica 7 (Milano 1989) 187 ff.; S. Belkin, *Philo and the Oral Law; the Philonic Interpretation of Biblical Law in Relation to the Palestinian Halakah* (Cambridge Mass. 1940) 11 ff.
[44] Cf. Runia, *Redrawing cit* (n.13) 73.
[45] Cf. Runia, *art. cit.* (n.41) 125; see *Det.* 15; *Conf.* 143.

with slight meaning shifts within the same argumentation.[46] Furthermore, there can be various parallel meanings, cosmological, moral and allegorical interpretations, where explanations, while not excluding one another, are not necessarily interrelated: at best, but not necessarily, there can be successive levels of depth.[47] Of greater complexity is the explanation in *Conf.* 146 with regard to the children of men and to the children of the gods, where there appears to be a gradual shift within the explanation itself. Rather than parallel routes, here the same interpretation undergoes a process of successive enrichment.[48]

---

[46] Many interpretations, for example, are put forth regarding the tree of life (*Q.G.* I.10), seen as a symbol of the earth, of the seven celestial circles, of the sun, of the hegemonic part of the soul, of piety, where cosmological, anthropological and moral readings parallel one another. Cf. J. Pepin, *art. cit.* (n.24) 156.

[47] See, for example, the interpretation of the cherubim and of the flaming sword (*Cher.* 21-34). On the theme of the simultaneous presence of various meanings, not necessarily on different depth levels, but, at times, parallel, cf. D. Daube, 'Alexandrian Methods of Interpretation and the Rabbis' in *Festschrift Hans Lewald* (Basel 1953) 39.

[48] At least four coexistent readings are given also for Jacob's ladder (*Somn.* I 133-156). The linking together of topics, parallel to that of the quotations, is presented by Philo as a proper operative method in *Virt.* 16, where he uses the term συνείρω = I link together, I tie, I string together, I interweave (στίχους verses). Συνείρω is a term used in rhetoric and in logic (Aristotle's *Topica*, but also Isocrates, Philodemus, and others) with the meaning of stringing together logical connections and words. Εἱρω is used by Homer (*Od.* 18.295), who refers to a necklace which is linked or strung with amber beads. Post Homeric literature refers to discourses and words. Εἱρω = I thread, I intertwine, I tie, I establish, I arrange, I narrate. The term recalls the Hebrew חרז (*haraz*) = to thread through a hole, to string (pearls), but also to draw parallels between Biblical passages, to explain one passage with another, in order to indicate the linking together of Biblical quotations and passages in an argumentation. The חרז procedure is widespread in Rabbinic literature and is probably also very ancient. In passing from one Biblical passage to another, from the *Torah* to the Prophets, from the Prophets to the Hagiographers, the text takes on new depth, often bringing out aspects which were previously not evident. As, for example, is found in a passage of the *Babylonian Talmud* ('Megillah' 31a), as well as in many other passages. See M. Jastrow, *A Dictionary of the Targumim, the Talmud Babli and Yerushalmi, and the Midrashic Literature* (Jerushalaim 1903) 500, with textual references.

With regard to the concatenation of texts, cf. R. Hamerton-Kelly, 'Some Techniques of Composition in Philo's Allegorical Commentary with special Reference to *De Agricultura*: a Study in the Hellenistic Midrash' in R. Hamerton-Kelly, R. Scroggs, *Jews, Greeks and Christians: Religious Cultures in Late Antiquity, Essays in honour of W.D.Davies* (Leiden 1976) 56; S. Lieberman, *Hellenism in Jewish Palestine: Studies in the Literary Transmission Beliefs and*

In Philo, there is a plethora of meanings to be considered, as well as readings, in order to get to the deepest nucleus of explanation, not only as regards general explanations, but also as regard individual terms. This necessitates a series of operations aimed at elucidating both individual terms and entire biblical passages. On one hand, attempts at reaching univocity;[49] on the other, attempts at broadening the value of individual terms which, in this way, will come to take on more meanings, in that their semantic range has been extended.[50] In this light, explanations bearing on the proper names of characters, and on their modifications, are particularly significant.[51] On one hand, a word represents reality and mirrors it;[52] on the other, language cannot be an

---

Manners of Palestine in the I Century B.C.E.-IV Century C.E. (New York 1950) 48-49.

Speaking of his method at *Virt.* 16, in the quoted passage, Philo clarifies that, like all methods, it can also be used in an excessive or inappropriate way. See *Congr.* 178: λόγον ἐκ λόγου συνείροντος μηκύνειν where the negative effect of dwelling unnecessarily upon a subject recalls Plato, *Resp.* 437A, Aristophanes, *Lys.* 1132. See, however, Herodotus III.60 and Thucydides IV.17. On the way of proceeding we are speaking about, see D. T. Runia, 'Further Observations on the Structure of Philo's allegorical Treatises' in *Exegesis and Philosophy cit.*(n.13)130 cites the procedure stressing the method of explaining Moses via Moses on one hand, and references to rhetorical practice, on the other.

[49] In Rabbinic Literature, the expression כל מקום (*col maqom*) marks the presence of a term or an expression, which is always interpreted in the same way. An analogous procedure is found also in Philo: see *Mut.* 267. Cf. Runia, *Naming and Knowing cit.* (n.34) 80. Other problems are raised by the repetition of a term within a text. D. Gooding, V. Nikiprowetzky, 'Philo's Bible in the *De Gigantibus* and the *Quod Deus sit immutabilis* ' in D. Winston, J.Dillon, *op. cit.* (n.26) 124-125, give an example of an interpretation of Philo regarding the repetition of a term, claiming that it is a question of idiomatic Hebrew expressions inaccurately translated into Greek. Philo would ignore this fact and seek profound meanings to explain what were simply incorrect translations. The same authors, however, also cite parallels that appear in the *Midrash Rabbah*, where the sense of repetition is explained in exegetic terms. Cf. also Lieberman, *op. cit.* (n.48) 45-46.

[50] For the multiple meanings of a term, see *Fug.* 143-165; 177-201 with regard to "source". Cf.Cazeaux, *op. cit.* (n.21) 249 n.50 cited by Runia, *art. cit.* (n.41) 212 and 216.

[51] *Contempl.* 78 can be read in the sense that, before the meaning, it is the language itself (the sacred letters) which gives the first level of literality. Not the literal meaning, but language as a sign from which it is necessary to pass to reach the allegorical meaning. See *Congr.* 172. Cf. Nikiprowetzky,*op. cit.* (n.1) 124: the profound meaning which is mirrored in the mirror of the words (names of the *Torah*).

[52] With regard to the translation of the LXX, Philo claims that each term selected was the one apt to signify reality (*Mos.* II.39); this applies even more so to the original Hebrew text. Cf. Bernard Lévy, *op. cit.* (n.12) 54-55.

identical representation of reality.[53] To a great extent, comprehension difficulties are probably ascribable to the impossibility of translating, in term comprehensible to man, a truth which, by definition, is beyond him.[54] The search for figurative and allegorical meanings, then, stems from the difficulty of understanding, literally, words that lie outside the human ambit, even if they are written in human language. Even the classic distinction between a literal and an allegorical reading (the latter replacing the former when the former cannot sufficiently explain contradictions, anthropomorphisms, or aspects which appear unworthy or incongruous),[55] takes on a much greater complexity.[56] On one hand, we have literal readings, in the plural, many explanations of a grammatical, etymological and historical nature, of a text which appears to be read in its immediacy; on the other, allegorical,[57] psychological, symbolic, ethical, and other readings, which can all coexist and which, at times, -but not always- take on characters of greater depth. Surely, in some passages, Philo explains that an allegorical reading is deeper than a literal one,[58] but this is not always

---

[53] Cf. D. Winston, 'Aspects of Philo's Linguistic Theory', *SPhA*3 (1991) 110 ff.. Concerning the theory of names and the correspondence between names and realia, see the analysis of κύριος in the *De Mutatione*.

[54] Moses and Aaron. Cf. M. Alexandre, 'Rhetorical Argumentation as an exegetical Technique in Philo of Alexandria' in A. Caquot, M. Hadas-Lebel, J. Riaud (edd.), *Hellenica et Judaica: Hommage à V. Nikiprowetzky* ל'י (Paris 1986) 19. Cf. also Hamerton-Kelly, *art. cit.* (n.6) 49.

[55] See *Det.* 167; *Agr.* 131;157; *Fug.* 106; *Plant.* 113; *Leg. All.* II.19. Cf. Pepin, *art. cit.* (n.24) 145-150; 162-167. In relation with an use of allegory against 'improper' readings , use conducted by Judaic- Hellenistic texts as *The Letter of Aristeas* and Aristobulus works, cf. D. Dawson, *Allegorical Readers and Cultural Revision in Ancient Alexandria*, Berkeley-Los Angeles- Oxford (1992) 77.

[56] Nikiprowetzky, *art. cit.* (n.26) 54-55 claims that allegory has an apologetic function opposed to myth and anthropomorphisms; therefore it makes it possible to praise the letter of the *Torah* and to stress the truth hidden in the text. Quotations of *Deus* 125 and 127 on the conformity between Scripture, nature, truth, reason; *Deus* 133, where Philo asks himself if his allegorical interpretation is in conformity with the literal meaning. Concerning the discussion on literal and allegorical interpretation, cf. Daniélou, *op. cit.* (n.29) 11ff.

[57] See *Abr.* 99; *Migr.* 89-93; Cf. Runia, *op. cit.* (n.13) 408; Daniélou, *op. cit.* (n.29) 105-142; Hay, *art. cit.* (n.18) 43; Hamerton-Kelly, *art. cit.* (n.1) 57-58; Mack, *art. cit.* (n.43) 80ff.; Pepin, *art. cit.* (n.24) 158ff.

[58] *Contempl.* 78; *Deus* 133; *Det.* 15; *Q.G.* V.89; VI.241; *Somn.* I.164; Cf. Pepin, *art. cit.* (n.24) 136-137; 143ff.; Daube, *art. cit.* (n.47) 38-39; Th. M. Conley, Philo's Rhetoric Argumentation and Style' in *A N R W* II.21.1.343-371.

the case. In many instances, various interpretations are valid in as much as they are together with others that are equally valid.[59]

2. The Form of Quotation

If Philo's work represents an attempt within a tradition, at explaining and reading a text, which is also a reading of reality, the exegesis of a book the complexity of which exceeds by definition man's capacity to comprehend, it can, however, and must be examined continuously. This should occur with neither the claim nor the presumption of exhausting its richness, but with the desire and task of grasping some of its aspects and hidden meanings: the text is explained in terms of how it is approached. Basic, therefore, in this process is the relationship with the text which finds expression through its utilization. Appropriately, therefore, both the form of the commentary and the mode of quotation warrant investigation. An hypothesis which I find suggestive, but which I have not been able either to substantiate or, to confute, is that the relationship between Philo's text and the *Bible*, and Philo's text and other philosophical texts is different. There is not doubt that, within Philo's thinking, the *Pentateuch* has a different statute from that of the rest of the *Bible* [60] Different is the type of utilization and commentary of the first five books, which are more frequently read and commented upon than the other books, and are certainly endowed with a character of greater authority, often commented upon word by word as a basic reference text, unlike the other books which are often used to support quotations or exegesis more than as objects of direct exegesis.[61] If such is the difference between the first five books and the following,

---

[59] See *Spec. Leg.* I.200; 287; *Agr.* 157; *Plant.* 113; *Abr.* 68; 88; 119; 200; 217; 236; *Ios.* 125; *Migr.* 89-93; cf. Pepin, *art. cit.* (n.24) 139-142.

[60] Specific, for Mack, *art. cit.* (n.31) 113, could be considered the statute of *Leviticus* and *Deuteronomy*. With regard with Moses' authority, cf. B.L. Mack, 'Under the Shadow of Moses: authorship and authority in Hellenistic Judaism' *Society of Biblical Literature. Seminar Papers Series* 21 (1982) 299- 318.

[61] This unique and pre-eminent role of the first five books of the *Bible* with respect to the others, permeates, in fact, a major part of the Hebrew reading of the Scripture. From the more rigorist readings, such as those of the Sadducees, to the broader ones of the Pharisaic tradition, the different statute of the first five books, with respect to the others, is constant, as pre-eminent is the role of Moses. Against this thesis see J. Genot-Bismuth, *Le Scenario de Damas. Jérusalem Hellenisée et les origines de l'Essénisme*, Paris (1992) 382: "A l'époque d'Onias, et par extrapolation, on peut remonter au moins jusqu'à Simon le Juste II, les trois composantes constituant les Livres Saints («*Sefarim*») étaient traitées à égalité et la règle de hiérarchie de sainteté n'apparaît pas encore comme effective."

said difference being noticeable also in the mode of commentary and quotation, can the same be said also for the non-Biblical texts to which Philo refers? For example, can it be hypothesized that, whereas in the Biblical text quotations are often explicit (even if the text is crammed with implicit references), in reference to passages by Greek philosophers the author's name is purposely not made explicit?[62] Is it imaginable, that is, that respect for the sacred text, "to which and from which nothing can be added or eliminated", at times prompts Philo to indulge in quotations between "inverted commas"; quotations, that is, which are exact (or almost),[63] but not inglobed within his discourse, as happens with passages that he uses with greater self-assurance, in that they lack the quality of sacredness? As I have already pointed out, I have not succeeded in demonstrating this thesis which, nevertheless, appears open, especially if we take into account the double type of quotation present in Philo's text: on one hand, explicit, "quoted" quotations, even drawn closely one to the other in a flow of passages referring one to the other; on the other, quotations, at times not easily identifiable, which are inglobed in his discourse, and which are deprived of their autonomy and of a meaning within the departure text. Utilizing A. Compagnon's distinction[64] between *haraz*-type[65] quotations, and quotations elaborated within the text itself, two are the models of quotation;

1) the drawing together of texts which are presented one next to the other, in sequence, without losing the original form;

2) that of quotations inserted in the exegetic text so as to no longer retain the form of explicit quotations. There are no longer, that is, so many passages drawn together and distinct in their individuality. The text itself inglobes the quotation which is not clearly identifiable as such.[66]

---

[62] Many, however, are the Greeks authors who are cited. Cf. Borgen, *art. cit.* (n.24) 256 n.121. See, for example, *Q.G.* IV.1.

[63] See, however, what Nikiprowetzky maintains, *art. cit.* (n.26) 26-27. See also Gooding, Nikiprowetzky, *art. cit.* (n.48) 105; Mack, *art. cit.*(n.43) 92.

[64] *La seconde main ou le travail de la citation* (Paris 1979) 167. I owe the reference to Compagnon's book to F. Spagnolo Acht with whom I discussed these themes. I thank him for all the help he gave me.

[65] Cf. here 7.5.

[66] Quotation implicit in Philo as a technical procedure, cf. Nikiprowetzky, *op. cit.* (n.1) 7. Similarly, also in other authors as for example in Plutarch, occult quotations can be found (cf. A. Mariani, 'Citazioni e strategia argomentativa nel *Maxime cum principibus philosopho esse disserendum'* in G. D'Ippolito, I. Gallo (edd.), *Stutture formali dei 'Moralia' di Plutarco, Atti del 3 Convegno Plutarcheo* (Palermo 1989, Napoli 1991) 143-245, quotation integrated in the context (cf. F.

Regarding the two quotation models which, in my opinion, are both present in Philo,[67] it would be suggestive to claim that the first type is used especially for the Biblical text, the second for non-biblical texts, be they by Plato, Aristotle, and the Stoics, but also by Judaic authors which have not come down to us, and which, precisely because they are inserted in the text, are not easily identifiable.[68] As I have already stated, all this needs to be corroborated. If, in practical terms, it is not possible to postulate such a distinction, it is however indubitable that there are reference texts which in a way constitute the skeleton of the argumentation, and others which merely supply textual backing. It is to this that Runia's distinction[69] between primary and secondary exegesis refers. In Philo's commentary there are the basic text and other Biblical quotations that make up another inter text, which however remains within the Biblical text. Then, there appear other quotations, which are mostly implicit; other Biblical passages, but especially philosophical references, be they to Plato, the Stoics, or to other authors. At times, they refer to generic theories which were sufficiently widespread in Alexandria, as they constituted a sort of common knowledge and accepted theses; at times, however, they are veritable, even if not always explicit, quotations.

Beside the two types of quotations I have referred to, and which in Philo apply essentially to the Biblical text, there is then a third form, the main function of which is that of presenting the positions of others with respect to one's own, so that the latter can emerge. Quotations, therefore, which maintain their reference to the departure text, as on it depends its degree of truth and authority. From quotations cited to substantiate the author's theses, by drawing support and authority from an external text, a phrase can be extrapolated for demonstrative and affirmative reasons, and to support a given thesis.[70] Such quotations are rather infrequent in Philo, for whom the reference text

---

Pordamingo Pardo, 'Las citas de Carmina Popularia en Plutarco, in *Strutture formali dei 'Moralia' di Plutarco cit.* 224) and a "mosaico di citazioni" (G. Casadio, 'Strategia delle citazioni nel *De Iside et Osiride* : un platonico greco di fronte a una cultura religiosa 'altra' in *Strutture formali dei 'Moralia' di Plutarco cit.* 257.

[67] Against Compagnon, *op. cit.* (n.68) which seems to attribute only one type of quotation to Philo.

[68] see R. Goulet, *La philosophie de Moïse: Essai de reconstitution d'un commentaire philosophique préphilonien du Pentateuque* (Paris 1987), who, however, moves along lines considerably divergent from mine.

[69] 'How to read Philo' in *Exegesis and Philosophy* cit. (n.14) 191; 'Further Observations' cit. (n.50) 130-131.

[70] A procedure which is abundantly present, for example, in Plutarch. Cf. Mariani, *art. cit.* (n.66) 243.

constitutes, mainly, a continuous basis also supporting quotations of sporadic passages, which, however, are generally always biblical, and therefore provided with authority, and which always make up the basis of both the text and the argumentation. Usually, these are not simple juxtapositions in support of a thesis or to embellish a discourse.

3. The Principle of Authority

The problem of the different ways various quotations can be utilized arises once again: does an indeterminate reference to so-and-so, to one of the ancients, for example, have specificity? Often it is a reference to a Greek author.[71] Elsewhere, however, reference is to allegorists of the Hebrew culture.[72] In many cases, they are quotations of theses or authors to be confuted, or positions to be discussed. It is possible to think of a different presentation of the quoted texts; a sort of hierarchy:

1) the *Bible*, between "inverted commas", as a sacred and unmodifiable text,[73]

2) other Biblical passages or passages by Rabbinic authors seen as the truth and presented in absolute terms. These are much less traceable than the former, for which it is not necessary to claim paternity, given the character of truth - even if not sacred - of the quoted theses,

3) Greek authors, not necessarily endowed with authority and with a character of undisputed truth, presented usually as positions or examples in support of an argumentation. They are autonomous as regards their quotations, and are characterized precisely for what they are; theses which can either be accepted or rejected; examples.

Thus, we are dealing not so much with a different attitude towards philosophical themes compared with scriptural themes, or with allegorical works compared with the *Quaestiones*,[74] as with the function - in terms of truth and authority - of the quoted text. Examples of the different authority levels of quotations and references are to be found in the *De Mutatione* (§166-167), where the trust owed to God is

---

[71] See *Gig.* 34; *Deus* 134.
[72] *Abr.* 99; *Somn.* I.116-119.
[73] See, however, Ch. Mercier, *Introduction à Q.G* I.II (Paris 1979) 31.
[74] Cf. Mack, *art. cit.* (n.43) 79 ff.

contrasted with that which is attributed to the philosophers.[75] Paragraph 169, then, contains a quotation from *Isaiah*, presented as oracular word. Here there is not a reference to the *Pentateuch*, but, obviously, even the other biblical works, although less quoted and endowed with lesser authority, always have a level of truth and are even the "oracular word of God".

4.1. The Form of Commentary. Analogy with other Commentary Forms

In *Redrawing the Map of early Middle Platonism*,[76] Runia claims that, in presenting various interpretations of a given passage, Philo often cites opposing theses, between which a sage (Philo himself) chooses the more correct. It may be claimed that the same style, that of seeing many interpretations, is applicable to Greek philosophy as well as to the reading of the *Torah*. However - as Runia clarifies - while comprehension of the *Torah* is inexhaustible and all interpretations are valid, in the ambit of philosophy one truth tends to exclude another. The philosophers - in Philo's reading - reached inferior levels of knowledge with respect to Moses, who is a kind of super philosopher, and with respect to the Torah, which contains all truth. On the strength of these considerations, Runia finds Philonic analogies with the anonymous commentary on the *Theaetetus*, in which the νεώτεροι are referred to anonymously (this is how even Philo calls the exegetes), where however the final opinion is that of the author. That is, there is a choice among opinions, not their co-presence. A similar attitude is to be found when confronting authoritative texts: the commentary on the *Theaetetus* suggests that, in the Platonic text are hidden truths which are to be discovered through interpretation and exegesis. The *quaestio* method, wherein ἀπορίαι are educed, reference to other commentators, the multiple-exegesis form consisting in presenting the opinion of two anonymous exegetes first, then a third opinion - usually supported by the author himself - make up all the exegetic characteristics of the anonymous commentary on the *Theaetetus* which, for Runia, are also present in Philo. For the author, comparisons are therefore possible between Philo's method and the method of commentary on Plato and Homer. He notices, for example, other affinities with Porphyrius' *D e*

---

[75] Cf. Radice in Filone di Alessandria, *L'uomo e Dio: Il connubio con gli studi preliminari, La fuga e il ritrovamento, Il mutamento dei nomi, I sogni sono mandati da Dio* (Milano 1986) 364 n.110. Actually, there are many quotations, some explicit, other implicit, from Greek philosophers. Neither are the Biblical quotations consistently presented.

[76] *art. cit.* (n.13) 96-117.

antro nympharum, where the intent to allegorize, the *quaestio* method, the etymological attention to terms and names, and exegetic polyvalence all recall Philo's manner of proceeding. In the same pages, however, Runia also clarifies some basic differences between the quoted commentaries and Philo; differences which caution against too close an assimilation of one commentary to another. A comparison is then established between "the chief hermeneutic assumption, namely that the scriptural *logos* forms a united, rational whole" and the Middle-Platonic method of explaining Plato via Plato on the assumption that their master had produced a coherent body of doctrine"[77] Runia's studies on quoted analogies fall within a research ambit explored also by other scholars who, each in a specific ambit and with references to particular authors, attempt to place Plato's exegesis within a broader mode of commentary. In this way, it is possible to establish comparisons with classical rhetoric, with Middle-Platonic texts, with Neoplatonic commentaries, with Stoic exegeses, and with Rabbinic interpretations. For example, a series of questions relative to a passage's many meanings, to critical marks, to annotations added to a text, are typical of the Alexandrian grammarians' research, and are to be found also in Rabbinic literature.[78] This is clarified by Hamerton-Kelly,[79] who draws Philonic allegory within the ambit of Greek rhetoric, recalling works of the Stoics and the Neoplatonists. He traces the origin of allegorical technique back to Plato himself; in fact, however, he perceives analogies with Rabbinic interpretation. The latter, in turn, could have been influenced by the Hellenistic technique of commentary.

Various studies identify analogies with different research ambits. For Dillon,[80] the form is the same as in Proclus' commentary; for E. Stein,[81] there are Judaic-Hellenistic antecedents; for I. Christiansen,[82] there are present both the Platonic *diairesis* and Aristotelian categories; for H. Leisegang,[83] Stoicism.

---

[77] Runia, *art. cit.* (n.41) 246, 256 n.153.

[78] See Lieberman, *op. cit.* (n.48) 44 ff.

[79] *art. cit.* (n.48) 51-53.

[80] 'The Formal Structure of Philo's Allegorical Exegesis' in D. Winston, J. Dillon, *op. cit.* (n.26) 78-84.

[81] 'Die Allegorische Exegese des Philo aus Alexandreia', *Beihefte zur Zeitschrift für die altest. Wissenschaft* 51 (1929).

[82] *Die Technik der allegorischen Auslegungswissenschaft bei Philon von Alexandrien* (Tübingen 1969).

[83] 'Philon' in *RE* (Vol. 20.1 cols.36-9).

4.2. Comparison with Neoplatonic Commentaries

Let us focus on Dillon's analysis which examines the Neoplatonic commentaries where Plato must be interpreted καὶ φυσικῶς καὶ ἠθικῶς καὶ θεολογικῶς καὶ ἁπλῶς πολλακῶς (Olimpiodorus). Neoplatonic are the use of preceding commentators and the procedure by position and solution of problems.[84] In the comparison with Proclus, there appear many forms of commentary which recall Philo: division of the text in *lemmata*, procedure by position and solution of problems (ἀπορίαι), criticism of either named or anonymous previous commentators, transition from a literal interpretation "which may include historical or philosophical comment, to the "ethical" (ἠθική), which constitutes the moral lessons to be derived from the passage - this level of commentary may be either literal or allegorical - and then to the "physical"(φυσική) or allegorical proper, in which the subject matter of the lemma is taken to represent metaphysical truths" (p. 79). At any rate, according to Dillon, Philo and the Neoplatonists could be traced back to a common source: the tradition of Stoic commentaries of the last two centuries B.C.[85]

Conversely, a series of Philonic procedures are lacking in Neoplatonic commentaries, and can be compared with the Judaic tradition; namely, the etymological study of names and the use of parallel passages typical of the *midrash*, which, in fact, appear also in Neoplatonism.[86] The principle of interpreting a text via the text itself, or, at least, of an author via himself, reappears also in other commentators. For example, it is widespread among the commentators of Homer, in regard to the analysis of both language and content.[87]

4.3. A Text via the Text itself

The theme of a text's unified interpretation, and of the attempt to resolve contradictions and difficulties of a commented work, is dealt

---

[84] A *quaestio* form comparable to Didymus' method is also in the Rabbis: cf. Lieberman, *op. cit.* (n.48) 48. J.J. Collins, *Between Athens and Jerusalem: Jewish Identity in the Hellenistic Diaspora* (New York 1983) 28 identifies parallels with Eratosthenes in the procedure by ἀπορίαι καὶ λύσεις which he examines in Demetrius, the Cronographer.

[85] *The Middle Platonists* (London 1977) 142.

[86] Dillon, *art. cit.* (n.80) 85-86.

[87] Cf. F. Montanari, 'L'erudizione, la filologia, la grammatica' in *Lo spazio letterario della Grecia antica*, 1.II (Roma 1993) 271 ff.

with by P. Donini in reference to Alexander of Aphrodisia. Donini[88] stresses the systematic character of the approach and the attempt at interpreting *Aristotelem ex Aristotele*:

> "Even Neoplatonic commentators shared the systematic approach and saw both Plato's philosophy and that of Aristotle as closed systems even though their interpretations differ markedly from Alexander's Aristotelian reading ."[89]

A method similar to that of the Aristotelian commentators can for Donini be found in Plutarch, who attempts to understand *Platonem ex Platone*, and to remain as faithfully close as possible to the Platonic text,

> "merely taking the liberty of combining a written text with another text of the *Dialogues*, even if some quotations are not extremely precise." (p.82) [my transl.]

In fact, according to Donini, traces of another method are to be found in Plutarch. In the *De Iside*

> "Aristotle shouldn't simply be interpreted *ex Aristotele*; instead, it is necessary to go beyond the letter of the text,of whatever Aristotelian text, presuming to evince from some Aristotelian text what perhaps Aristotle intended, even if he did not say it explicitly."(p. 89) [my transl.]

This is a method which will be theorized and utilized by subsequent commentators. Thus, according to Syrianus,

> "our task will be that of saying what he does not say directly, but which follows of necessity from his premises."[90]

But, according to an hypothesis taken up by J. Mansfeld, paternity of the Aristotelian interpretation, which is presupposed in the *De Iside*, should be attributed to Eudorus. In this perspective,

> "the 'hyper-interpretative' method followed by Syrianus already existed in the first Century B.C., and Plutarch is the first to have used it to our knowledge, but not its inventor" (p.93) [my transl.].

---

[88] Plutarco e i metodi dell'esegesi filosofica' in I. Gallo, R. Laurenti (edd.), *I Moralia di Plutarco tra Filologia e Filosofia* (Napoli 1992) 80-96.

[89] P. Donini, 'Alessandro di Afrodisia e i metodi dell'esegesi filosofica' in C. Moreschini (ed.), *Esegesi, parafrasi e compilazione in età tardo antica*, Napoli (1995) 108 [my transl].

[90] Cited by Donini, *art. cit.* (n.88) 90 [my transl.].

The assumption behind such an interpretation is that, in the thought of an author commented upon, there are either implicit or hidden principles, truths that are to be brought out, and that the commentator's task is that of bringing to light all that is implicit in the basic text.[91]

Doubtless there are parallels between the procedures followed by the authors mentioned and Philo, and some contemporary critics are actively exploring the possibility of identifying common sources of Philonic exegesis and of subsequent commentaries. In particular, there are those who perceive a fundamental hinge-role in authors such as Eudorus. I do not know if a common derivation, a sole interpretative approach, can be demonstrated. It is however certain that some of the themes cited by such authors echo Philo: reading the *Bible* via the *Bible*, the comparison of even distant passages of a text unitarily considered in a systematic perspective, the concept of a hidden meaning which is to be identified behind words grasped in their immediacy. However, I believe there is a basic difference which cannot be ignored. For Philo, the deep meaning and hidden reality of words can be concealed by the verses which, at a first reading, may not immediately appear evident, but are nevertheless present in the words themselves. It is not a question of identifying *id quod non scriptum est*, following the author's intentions,[92] but what *scriptum est*, even if, at first sight, the reader cannot read it.[93] Once again, the text's authoritative character, its absolute completeness and richness are not placed in the slightest doubt; in the *Torah* words can neither be added not eliminated.

4.4. *Exchange between Commentary and Commented Text*

Let us now take another look at some basic aspects in Philo's work:

the plurality of interpretations and term or interpretative shifts where there seem to be contradictions or biblical passages of difficult interpretation; the continuous utilization of the biblical text not only as

---

[91] Cf. P. Hadot, 'Théologie, exégèse, révélation, écriture dans la philosophie grecque' in M. Tardieu (ed.) *Les règles de l'interpretation* (Paris 1987) 19-22.

[92] Cf. Ch. Schäublin, 'Homerum ex Homero' in Museum Helveticum (34, 1977) 224-227; J. Mansfeld, *Heresiography in Context. Hippolytus' Elenchos as a Source for Greek Philosophy* (Leiden 1992) 163-164.

[93] Therefore, in some respects, an exegesis, such as that by Alexander of Afrodisia (as read by Donini, *art. cit.* (n.88) 114) appears closer to Philo's approach.

an object of investigation, but also as an instrument,[94] as a reserve-container of supporting passages and of texts capable of clarifying other obscure texts, as a source of authority and truth.

the exegesis inherent in the Biblical text and the *Bible* itself as an explicative source;

the search for the deep meaning to be extrapolated, not however drawing from the text what is not there (even if implicit), but what is there even if it is hidden.

The *Bible*, therefore, which explains the *Bible*, or, better yet, the *Pentateuch* which explains the *Pentateuch* and all other questions that may arise, and that are always in some way relateable to the *Torah*, as the latter contains and includes every form of knowledge.[95]

Given that the *Bible* is the reference text, but also the truth, revelation on Sinai, both the construction and foundation of the world, Philo's work does not come through as a simple commentary, or, at least, not as commentary in a restricted sense. It is not commentary in the strict sense of the term because it does not claim to be such, presenting itself as an exposition (of the laws and life of Moses)[96] which refers to the *Bible*, which is directed at explaining its hidden meanings, which is a continuous quotation, but which in some ways, structurally presents itself as an autonomous discourse. There is a continuous exchange between commentary and commented text, and a coming together of the two to form an intermediate space, almost an inter text. In other ways, a series of references and attitudes are proper to commentary: the authority of the reference text, the following of the text step by step.[97] The *Bible* is no ordinary text, it is the word of God, and in it there is neither a before nor an after, nor a text that is more important than another:[98] every verse can explain another, and the very order of the basic text is broken up for explicative purposes. Scripture contains a deep truth which has to be examined thoroughly; it

[94] There are also argumentations taken from examples of daily life, or from Greek authors, but surely lacking the extension and authority of textual biblical support.

[95] It is not that there are no other encyclical sciences or knowledge, but they are precisely encyclical; that is, in a way auxiliary and of an inferior level with respect to true wisdom, which is knowledge of Moses' wisdom.

[96] This obviously applies essentially to the treatises, and less to the so called works of the 'allegorical commentary'.

[97] The *De Mutatione*, for example, except for the omission of a few passages which had probably been treated in some other work which has not come down to us, and for some digressions (see, for example §58, to which one returns from §155), follows the order of the text.

[98] Cf. Cazeaux, *op. cit.* (n.21) 583.

is not simply a question of explaining the work word by word, nor of only providing a literal interpretation, but of supplying exegesis in a broader sense, of clarifying hidden meanings, of reconstructing truth. This can be grasped in a text - such as Philo's - which starts from the *Bible* and explains it; then, however, it departs from it in order to provide an explanatory picture which comprises all the truth contained in the entire *Bible*. It does not simply explain individual passages, but reconstructs the entire picture of God's word. This is why, on one hand there is a breaking into pieces, and many are the "digressions", the explanations, the references to other passages; on the other, there is a broadened reconstruction of the word that "manifests" itself in the *Bible*, but which also has to be reconstructed in its hidden meanings, in its apparent repetitions, redundancies, and contradictions, via the many interpretative systems which are all valid in that they are all partial. Hence, the non-systematic course of the commentary.[99] Significant are the many shifts within the cited biblical passages, the rearrangements of words handed down, instances in which a term is anticipated or referred both to the phrase that precedes and to the one that follows. Such procedures are adopted by Philo, examples of which will be seen in the analysis of the *De Mutatione* in the second part of this chapter, and are to be found also in other commentators.[100] Besides the explanatory objective, is there also a different interpretation which is thus given to the text? In Philo, change in word order has an exegetic purpose. In Rabbinic literature, this kind of inversion, with an exegetic finality, has been amply examined:[101] to say Abraham, Isaac, Jacob, or to invert said order, means placing the three patriarchs on the same plane. Philo too proceeds in a similar manner.

[99] A linear progression which follows the biblical text, with the opening of explicative parentheses, reference to other biblical passages and at times to preceding paragraphs by Philo himself, are found in *De Mutatione*, where linear progression is returned after such parentheses. See, for example, *Mut.* 151-175 referred to *Gen.* 17.17 (recalling of *Gen.* 18.12; *Is.* 48; *Gen.* 45.16; 45.18; 39.1; 45.18). Then , the text goes back to *Gen.* 17.17 and to themes treated in §154.

[100] Donini, *art. cit.* (n.89) 113-117. The procedure, in theory, is facilitated by the fact that the *Bible* of the time lacked punctuation; Philo' reference text, however, is the Greek text, and Philo at times strains the grammar. In reference to Alexander of Afrodisia, Donini speaks of a hyperbaton; that is, a shift in word order in a clause aimed at clarifying the meaning of the text. Concerning verse transposition in Rabbinical literature, cf. Lieberman, *op. cit.* (n.48) 41; H.L. Strack, G. Stemberger, *Introduction au Talmud at au Midrash* (Paris 1986; orig. edit. München 1982) 55, where it is recalled that for Rabbi Ishmael's school there is neither a before nor an after in the *Bible*.

[101] Cf. C. Colafemmina, 'Le regole ermeneutiche di Hillel' *Annali di Storia dell'esegesi* (8/2 1991) 450.

Donini dwells upon the problem of punctuation, showing the interpretative differences which derive from a different scansion of the passages.[102] Another significant element of the Philonic text is the reference to half-quoted verses.[103]

5.1. *Philo' s Exegetic Rules*

Can precise modalities be hypothesized in the transition from one biblical passage to another in Philonic exegesis? Is it possible, that is, to reconstruct the terms of utilization of the various biblical passages, given that - as we have seen - Philo often interrupts the continuity of the biblical text of reference, introducing digressions or even quite distant biblical passages into the original text?[104] Runia[105] speaks of

---

[102] *art. cit.* (n.89) 117-110. ἀναστροφή with reference to Sosibius and complete acceptance of the procedure in the Rabbinical schools of the II century. Cf. Lieberman, *op. cit.* (n.48) 65-67; Daube, *art. cit.* (n. 47) 27-34 discusses the *seres,* the rearranging of parts of a text, a method followed in the II century B.C. by Josiah, a disciple of Ishmael, and connects it with ἀναστροφή .

[103] Cf. Nikiprowetzky, *art. cit.* (n.26) 54: the terms of philonic commentary refer at times to parts of a *lemma* which are not cited, a procedure -as we have seen- which is amply followed in Rabbinical literature. Often the explanation of a text occurs regardless of the succession of the biblical passages used to support a thesis. Cf. Radice, *op. cit.* (n.75) 343 n.63. Philo would overlap the order of the text. Thus in *Mut.* 105. Also the subsequent paragraphs, present reversals in respect to the biblical text.

[104] See, for example, *Deus* 131 ff., where there is a continuous passing from one passage to another.

Once again, Nikiprowetzky's analysis is of fundamental importance (*art. cit.* (n.26) 54: 1) in Philo, the scriptural lemma is often broken down in secondary parts, each analyzed exegetically in a separate way. See, for example, *Deus* 20 ff.: analysis of " ἐνεθυμήθη ὁ θεὸς ὅτι ἐποίσῃ τὸν ἄνθρωπον ἐπὶ τῆς γῆς, καὶ διενοήθη " which is taken up again in *Deus* 33; 2) echo words that refer to other words in other passages thus giving rise to exegetic correspondences -a procedure which in some ways recalls *ghezerà shavà.* For example, in *Deus* 131-134 there are three key words: house, priest and pure, which recur, perhaps in inverted order, but always together. Especially in §134, there occurs a metaphorical transfer involving an analogy, which , however, is referred in that it is an analogy of the three terms taken as a whole. This would seem to be a metaphorical transfer by analogy with a significant whole, not of a single term, a term determined by its union with other terms. The same occurs in *Gig.* 1-5, where terms such as πολλοί e θυγατέρες recur and create correspondences. The terms do not recur, as the same argument is being discussed, but constitute an interpretative caesura. For example, in *Gig.* 1: to men were born daughters, in *Gig.* 4, generating females as opposed to generating virtue. Nikiprowetzky, however, appears more convincing when analyzing the passages in *Deus.* The simultaneous presence of some terms in the first passage means that, when in the second passage there appears one of the terms interpreted metaphorically, it is necessary to introduce

verbal transition, based mainly on the *ghezerà shavà* principle and of thematic transition. It can be hypothesized, as the aforementioned principle is widely utilized, that there are also other modalities of transition, partly based on the analogy principle, and partly on others. Many research studies have been undertaken to identify points of contact between Philonic exegesis and commentaries by other authors, to identify possible rules or interpretative forms present in Philo and in others. Such, for example, the studies by Daube,[106] Conley,[107] J. Leopold,[108] P. Boyancé,[109] Belkin,[110] Hamerton-Kelly,[111] Pepin,[112] Lieberman,[113] Borgen,[114] Winston and Dillon,[115] Christiansen,[116] and Alexandre.[117] There is no doubt of the presence in Philo of interpretative modes which can also be found in other authors. Thus, albeit with much prudence, I believe we can identify some regularities - if not rules - in Philonic exegesis which recall other exegetic ambits. In

---

also the other terms which appeared in the first passage. More than *ghezerà shavà* strictly speaking, applied, that is, to extant passages, here there seems to be an exegetic construction based on the same principle: the creation of the corresponding passage that does not exist; 3) the terms in philonic commentary at times refer to parts of a lemma that are not cited, and this procedure, as we have seen, is extensively used in Rabbinical literature.

[105] *art. cit.* (n.41) 236 ff., in particular 239-240, concerning the two types of transition (one verbal, the other thematic) from one biblical lemma to another, and than, back to the first passage. At p.255, n.150, Runia takes up again Hamerton-Kelly's observations on *ghezerà shavà* , although in *Further Observations* (*art. cit.* n.48) 120, he expresses a series of perplexities concerning the equivalence of *ghezerà shavà* to the "verbal mode of transition" in Philo. In other ways, conceptual transition somehow recalls (albeit here too, with the due caution called for by the situation) *ke-yotzé be-maqom aher*, that is the rule that refers to "something similar in another passage". For Daube, *art. cit.* (n.47) 252-254, however, said rule, which is in a way comparable to analogical reasoning, derives from συμβαίνειν , indicating a technical procedure.

[106] *art. cit.* (n.47); Id., 'Rabbinic Methods of Interpretation and Hellenistic Rhetoric', *Hebrew Union College Annual* 22 (1949) 239-264.

[107] *art. cit.* (n.58).

[108] 'Philo's Knowledge of Rhetorical Theory ' in D. Winston, J. Dillon, *op. cit.* (n.26).

[109] 'Echo des exégèses de la mythologie grecque chez Philon' in *Colloque du CNRS, Philon d'Alexandrie cit.* (n.24).

[110] *art. cit.* (n.43).

[111] *art. cit.* (n.48).

[112] *art. cit.* (n.24).

[113] *art. cit.* (n.48).

[114] *art. cit.* (n.24).

[115] *op. cit.* (n.26).

[116] *op. cit.* (n.82).

[117] *art. cit.* (n.54).

particular, it appears to me that a certain assonance with Rabbinic exegesis can be noticed. With due caution, however -as I said- and I do not refer so much to the fact that many of the hermeneutic rules handed down under the name of Hillel, and even more so, Rabbi Eliezer's thirty-two rules, were probably drawn up in a later age.[118] Caution concerns precisely the modes of exegesis which are however not immediately superimposable, even if they present affinities.

5.2. Rabbinic Hermeneutic Rules in Philo?

The clearest example of said hermeneutic rules traceable in Philo is that of *ghezerà shavà*, which various authors have already identified within Philo's text, and which, however, presents a characteristic that cannot be neglected. If in Rabbinic texts *ghezerà shavà* must always be substantiated by the authority of previous interpretations[119]such support is not always present in Philo's text, which seems to utilize verbal analogy with greater carefreeness.[120] Next to *ghezerà shavà*, there appear ,then, forms that are analogous to *klal ufrat*, to *qal vahomer*,[121] to *hekhreah*, to *seres*, and to other interpretative forms which are amply utilized also in Rabbinic literature, such as allegory or explanations based on homonymous roots. In the following paragraph I will attempt to identify such modes of interpretation within *De Mutatione* .

My having cited Rabbinic exegetic rules does not imply, however, a *pro-judaeis* stance on my part in the age-old *Philo graecus-Philo judaeus* controversy. On one hand, it is well known that Hillel's hermeneutic rules could trace their origins back to Greek rhetoric and to Roman juridical literature, and that exegetic forms could find references in the Stoic commentators on Homer and in Greek exegetic

---

[118] Cf. M. Mielziner, *Introduction to the Talmud* (New York 1968) 115-187; Strack, Stemberger, *op. cit.* (n.104) 37-55; Colafemmina, *art. cit.* (n.101) 443-54.

[119] See *Talmud Jerushalmi*,' Pesahim' VI.1.33a; concerning the caution and limits of using *ghezerà shavà*, see Talmud *Bavlì*, 'Keritot' 5a; 'Sanhedrin' 54a.

[120] In other ways, it is true that *ghezerà shavà* always relies on the authority of a tradition, which does not occur in Philo; this, however, does not mean that such was the case also initially, before codification. It is true that, perhaps, in the beginning, *ghezerà shavà* was simple analogy. Cf. Lieberman, *op. cit.* (n.48) 60, who believes that initially it was a case of simple analogy, comparable with σύγκρισις πρὸς ἴσον, although it always applied to equal terms (not conceptual analogy).

[121] Cf. Lieberman, *op. cit.* (n.48) 68.

literature.[122] The question of the origin and of the mutual influences of interpretative ambits is probably impossible to decide; at the present research stage it is well to accept the balance theory set forth by Hamerton-Kelly,[123] who, taking up Lieberman's theses on the rabbis' independence from Alexandrian culture, claims that

> "some cross-fertilisation is probable, although it is right that the rabbis probably did not "borrow" their methods from the Greeks".

Furthermore, what prevents us from thinking that certain modes of interpretation could by then have become common ground for both Rabbinic exegesis and Hellenistic literature and philology, and did not necessarily pertain to one ambit to the exclusion of the other?[124] Moreover, some references present in Philo seem to lead back more directly to Greek rhetoric.[125] Thus, for example, the custom of dividing by *species and genera*; arguments such as *a fortiori*, cause and effect relationships, definitions, etymological analyses, opposites, *a maiore ad minus, a minore ad maius*.[126] Christiansen analyses Philo's work in the light of διαίρεσις and establishes associations with Aristotle's categories and attributes; Alexandre[127]identifies a series of procedures

---

[122] Most authors and commentaries, be they Hebrew or Greek, wherein affinities, or at least elements of comparison, are to be found with Philo's exegesis, are subsequent to Philo. It could then be hypothesized that somehow they depend on him or on authors of Philo's period and milieu. In the Hellenistic period, the divergence between the Hebrew world and the Greek was much less marked then it was subsequently, and the circulation of ideas between the two spheres was an everyday occurence (Hillel, a disciple of Shemaiah and Abtalion who taught in Alexandria and, according to Hebrew tradition, were proselytes, underwent Alexandrian influence. Cf. Daube, *art. cit.* (n.47). Common to both ambits are critical interventions on texts, critical marks, annotations and exegetic procedures, cf. Lieberman, *op. cit.* (n.48) 38 ff. For example, *ghezerà shavà* could derive from Hellenistic exegesis. A comparison between Rabbinical literature and the Alexandrian school is developed by Lieberman, *op. cit.* (n.48) 78, who is rather wary of hypotheses of a reciprocal influence between the two ambits and sees some basic differences in the relationship with the biblical text on one hand, and with Homer on the other (pp.27-37). Daube, *art. cit.* (n.47) decidedly favours the thesis according to which the Rabbinical system of interpretation derives from Greek rhetoric. See also, Daube, *art. cit.* (n.106).

[123] *art. cit.* (n.48) 53.

[124] Cf. Lieberman, *art. cit.* (n.48) 57.

[125] Cf. Alexandre, *art. cit.* (n.54) 24-25; Leopold, *art. cit.* (n.108) 132 ff. on philonic terms about allegory and analogy, terms proper to rhetorical, poetic and grammar manuals and to literary criticism.

[126] Cf. Conley, *art. cit.* (n.58) 173.

[127] *art. cit.* (n.54) 16 n.24.

and *topoi* which, in his opinion, are to be found in Philo. These procedures are presented as rhetoric forms, but undoubtedly have an exegetic value.

From what we have said so far, I believe that the complexity of Philonic exegesis emerges quite clearly, together with the difficulty of identifying categories, modes of interpretation, rhetorical and dialectical *topoi*, and the author's reference points. Therefore, if, when analysing *De Mutatione*, I shall at times use categories such as *hekhreah, seres, ghezerà shavà* , or predication by *species and genera*, cause and effect relations, ἐκ ἐναντίων procedures,[128] this does not mean that I am taking a *pro judaeis* or a *pro graecis* position, or that I wish to support a direct derivation relation of Philo with Rabbinic exegesis or with Greek rhetoric. In those instances I am simply attempting to identify instruments whereby to break down and understand Philo's text, using available interpretative categories and rules.

To summarize: I tried to make some considerations about items listed at the beginning of this chapter. In particular I dwelled:

on the plurality of coexistent interpretations in Philo ,

on his considering the *Bible* as a text concealing a profound truth which must be investigated through exegesis,

on the formation of an exegetic tradition in which following interpreters stand at forerunners' side without opposing them,

on the sense of quotations with reference to a text which is considered sacred and ummodifiable

on the form of commentary to a certain extent comparable to commentaries on Plato and Homer.

Then I assumed that regularities in exegetic method are identifiable in Philo's text and that such regularities lead us, in a way, to Rabbinic exegetic forms.

In the second part of this chapter I'll try to examine such assumptions within a specific Philonic text and to see whether affinities can be grasped with Hillel's and Rabbi Eliezer's hermeneutic rules. The turn of Philonic text, albeit desegregated and fragmented, will hinder an analysis following the same order of the themes listed in the first part. Many items will converge on a same passage and some aspects

---

[128] A concept which can never be sufficiently stressed is that there is often an analogy between Rabbinical and Greek procedures, whereby ἐκ ἐναντίων recalls R. Ishmael's rule twenty- seven, ἐκ τὸ μᾶλλον καὶ ἧττον recalls *qal vahomer*, δὶς λεγόμενα σύγκρισις recalls *ghezerà shavà*, etc.

will be treated more than others. Nevertheless, I'll try to stress references to the assumptions of the first part of the paper.

6. *Examples of interpretative Modes in the 'De Mutatione'*

The following reading concerns some interpretative modes which, I believe, can be identified in *De Mutatione*. Therefore, neither an analysis of the treatise in its entirety, nor a discussion of the work's content in its totality will be attempted here. Mine is simply an attempt at grasping some aspects of Philo's relationship with the biblical text, together with some forms of his argumentation[129]. Thus, the fact that entire pages of *De Mutatione* will not even be cited, while instead I will dwell at length on extremely short individual passages, need not come as a surprise.

7.1. *Seeing God*

§1-10: the problem of the "vision" of God and his "appearing" to Abraham; a theme which is taken up again in §15, where verse 17.1 is recalled: "The Lord was seen by Abraham".
The theme of seeing God starts here, which I'll try to analyse in relation with the theme of listening God and the problem of God's unnameability.
Having clarified in the foregoing paragraphs that God cannot be seen in his essence (a thesis supported by §11-15, which therefore are not digressions, but which, in clarifying the concept of God as unnameable and that of his double denomination, introduce the Powers and stress the theme of divine unknowability), an attempt is made to clarify the meaning of the verse that refers to Abraham's "vision" of God. If the paragraphs following §15 explain that what is seen are the Powers, §18 introduces the function of the word as constituting a means whereby the relationship between God and his creatures is taught. In this way, what was anticipated in §8, which posited a distinction between knowledge through listening to the word and direct "vision", is again resumed. Through the word - that is, God's different denominations - there clearly emerges the different relationship between God and men, in respect to the positions of men themselves:

---

[129] Cf. Runia, *art. cit.* (n.41) 124: "Philo's structures are too fluid, too flexible to allow us to 'decode' them in a way that might render them 'accounted for' or in any way predictable. There is a method, but no fixed procedure or 'system' whose secret code we have to 'crack'.

depending, that is, on whether they are insensate, advanced, or perfect. Two terms, κύριος and θεός, indicate two realities, which however do not pertain to God, who is immutable, inalterable, self-sufficient, extraneous to what is relative, to whom everything belongs without Him belonging to anyone (§28). The two names connect with two different human attitudes.[130] Denomination, thus, has an explicative function; the word designates a different relationship which depends on man's degree of perfection. Again, however, it is the word that makes knowledge possible. Knowledge, therefore, not through vision, but through listening.[131] However, as we have seen,

"His word [of God] has no name of its own which we can speak"(§15).

There exists an unbridgeable hiatus between divine word and human word, and we are not allowed to pronounce the name of God, who is ἄρρητος, ἀπερινόητος καὶ ἀκατάληπτος. God speaks, but "is not spoken" properly. Man's forms of denomination, recognition and knowledge of God can only be indirect: his Powers, the created world, not God himself.

With apparent digressions Philo has thus built a forcible reasoning, which is however constructed upon interpretative shifts and terms variations: from vision to listening, to word, to name. In parallel, necessity is stated of grasping a reality which is concealed as divine and human word cannot intercommunicate. About these themes see the first part of this chapter.

7.2 Vision of God and sensible sight

Let us refer back to §1:

ὤφθε κύριος τῷ ᾿Αβραὰμ καὶ εἶπεν αὐτῷ ἐγώ εἰμι ὁ θεός σου

where God's double denomination appears which will be amply developed and explained in the following paragraphs. Here, however, I would like to linger upon the term ὤφθη, the theme, that is, of being seen, of God's appearing to Abraham, which, in the paragraphs immediately following, is clarified as a vision not perceived through the senses, but by the soul's eye. This concept is made clear immediately

---

[130] Cf. Nikiprowetzky, *art. cit.* (n.32) 123n.
[131] Cf. W. Michaelis, 'ὁράω' in G.Kittel, *Grande Lessico del Nuovo Testamento*, Brescia,1965; orig. edit. Stuttgart,1933) 5.316-381.

below where Philo speaks, *per differentiam*, of οἱ σώματος ὀφθαλμοί θεωροῦσι of ὁρωμένου καὶ τοῦ ὁρῶντος, whereas for the vision of God, terms such as δέχομαι, φαντασία, καταλαμβάνειν are used; terms, that is, which more than a vision, make us think of an immediate relation, not necessarily of a visual type. It is more a grasping with other faculties, than with the eyes, even though it is with the soul's eyes[132] In parallel, however, there are terms also for intellectual 'vision' that are proper to seeing: ὄμμαι, θεωρεῖν, θεατής. From this terminology, Philo's difficulty is immediately apparent. Said difficulty is characteristic of many exegetes of the biblical passages in question, and lies precisely in having to explain and interpret passages that speak of the 'vision' of God, while negating man 's possibility of seeing him. Even Moses, when he asks God:

> "Reveal Thyself to me that I may see Thee with knowledge" (*Ex.* 33.13),[133]

receives a negative reply:

> "Thou shalt see what is behind Me, but My face thou shalt not see".

In Philo' argumentation there is a shift from the impossibility of seeing God with the eyes of the senses, to the impossibility of 'seeing' God at all, with any organ or human faculty. "The conceptions of the mind are a light to themselves" (§4), in that "what the soul beholds it beholds by its own agency without the assistance of any other". Thus

> "when you hear that God was seen by man, you must think that this takes place without the light which the senses know, for what belongs to mind can be apprehended only by the mental Potencies. And God is the fountain of the purest radiance" (§ 6);

that is, God is himself a source of light and thus of 'vision' for the soul. This however does not enable man to "grasp" him, as man can neither portray him through the senses, nor visualize him through the intellect. Not even Moses could 'see' God.

---

[132] Cf. Runia, *art. cit.* (n.34) 75.

[133] Where the Greek translation, to which Philo refers in connection with Moses' request, presents a shift with respect to the Hebrew text, to which the answer is more appropriate: "בּיניך‎ חן-אמצא למען ואדעך ואדעך‎ את-דרכך‎ נא‎ הודיעני‎ : show me now Thy ways, that I may know Thee and find favour in Thy sight" (Revised Standard Version).

"All below the Existent, things material and immaterial alike, are available to apprehension even if they are not all actually apprehended as yet, but He alone by His very nature cannot be seen." (§9)

On one hand, human limits are stressed, man's impossibility of seeing a reality that is superior to his own cognitive faculties; on the other, the unknowability of God, whose nature cannot even be said (§11).[134] As man cannot know God, but only that which comes after him, a sort of second-level knowledge subvenes. Thus, in terms of naming God, there is a sort of indirect denomination, so

"that the human race should not totally lack a title to give to the supreme goodness."

Therefore, not the name κύριος was revealed to Abraham, Isaac and Jacob, but as θεός was he 'seen'. Not the 'vision' of God, but the 'vision' of the Power of the regality which previously man had not learned to recognize. Once having shown himself to man in his regality, God lets himself be known by he who listened and saw, as θεός. Again there is the mediation of the word, as interpreter, which teaches he who listens; a mediation taken up by Moses, as it is not God who declares himself as θεός and κύριος, but it is Moses who becomes Pharaoh's θεός. It is always through mediation of the word that God addresses Moses and, indirectly, Pharaoh. It is, therefore, not a direct 'vision', a visual-like revelation, but an experience of speaking and listening. The Ingenerate designates himself as κύριος of the wicked man, θεός of the man of progress, κύριος and θεός of the perfect (§ 23). We are dealing here with the plurality of names which we have spoken of in the first part of this chapter.

7.3. *The Word and the Name*

Our ambit is that of denomination, and in all the passages now cited, God speaks and reveals himself through the word. It is no longer a 'vision', as in Moses' case, but a 'listening' to divine words. A shift, therefore, from vision to saying.[135] The comparison between sight and listening is a frequent theme in Philo, who counterpoises Ishmael to Israel.[136] In terms analogous to those of the passages analyzed in *De*

---

[134] Cf. F. Calabi, 'Simbolo dell'assenza: le immagini nel giudaismo', *Quaderni di storia* 41(1995) 5-32.
[135] Cf. Cazeaux, *op. cit.* (n.21) 479.
[136] *Mut.* 201-204.

Mutatione, the theme is taken up again, for example, in *De Posteritate* (§166-9), even if, in fact, it centres completely on the knowledge of God and his Powers, without referring to divine denominations. The sight-listening comparison is presented through the image of the earrings which Aaron requests in order to construct the golden calf. It is a teaching bearing to the opposition between listening and prejudice with respect to idolatry, and between 'sight and intuition' with respect to the God of Israel.[137]

If, however, the first paragraphs deal essentially with the sight-hearing antithesis, the following paragraphs develop the theme of the differentiation between sensible sight and noetic sight, and clarify why it is impossible for man to see God. Man's ears, that is, are not negated as an organ for knowing God; they are simply insufficient (§167), as are the eyes of thought which, reflecting upon the Powers and things created, succeed in conceiving (κατανοεῖν) and knowing (γνωρίζειν) the existence of He who is, but not his essence. At any rate, it is an intuition, a clear 'vision' (ἐνάργεια), not a demonstration on discursive grounds: vision, therefore, an immediate contemplation of God's existence, which can also be grasped through ἀνθρώπου λογισμός. There is a confluence of human faculties, which can somehow reach a knowledge of God, but which are anyhow, inadequate: listening (God in fact speaks recalling vision (*Dt.* 32. 39)), immediate evidence (opposed to λογισμός), which becomes contemplation of existence.

> "πάνθ' ὅσα μετὰ τὸν θεὸν τῷ σπουδαίῳ καταληπτά, αὐτὸς δὲ μόνος ἀκατάληπτος. ἀκατάληπτός γε ἐκ τῆς ἀντικρύς καὶ κατ' εὐθυωρίαν προσβολῆς - διὰ γὰρ ταύτης οἷος ἦν ἐμηνύετ' ἄν- ἐκ δὲ τῶν ἐπομένων καὶ ἀκολούθων δυνάμεων (καταληπτός). αὗται γὰρ οὐ τὴν οὐσίαν, τὴν δ' ὕπαρξιν ἐκ τῶν ἀποτελουμένων αὐτῷ παριστᾶσι" (*Post.* 169).[138]

In connection with the Powers, God seems visible in a passage of *Q.G* (IV.1-2) which, in some ways, seems more inclined towards the possibility of intuitive 'vision' than other Philonic passages. However, it is stressed that

> "trinam apparitionem operatur intellectui humano. Is enim nequit tam acutum esse visu, ut illum qui superat virtutes sibi assistentes, velut distinctum Deum videre possit."

---

[137] Cf. Radice, *op. cit.* (n.43) 371-372 n.49. I thank P. Pozzi with whom I discussed these themes, for the help she gave me.

[138] Cf. *Deus* 62; *Praem.* 36-46; *Spec. Leg.* I.32-50; *Q.G* IV.1-2; *Post.* 13-16; *Fug.* 164-5, etc.

Vision, therefore, of the Powers of God; vision with the soul's eyes, and not with the body's. Contemplation, as we have seen, which parallels and goes beyond hearing, but -and this is the leap that occurs when the theme of God's unnameability is introduced in *De Mutatione*- knowledge comes through language. Giving names to things means knowing them, and God's real unknowability does not depend so much on the impossibility of 'seeing Him', as it does on the impossibility of giving him a name. Before and besides being ἀκατάληπτος, God is ἄρρητος.[139] The answer

> " I am He that is "is given for those who want to know God's name, which is tantamount to " My nature is to be, not to be spoken."[140]

There is - as we have seen - a shift from the impossibility of seeing God ("You shall see my back; but my face shall not be seen" (*Ex.* 32.23) (§9), to the impossibility of giving him a name.

> "It is a logical consequence that no personal name even can be properly assigned to the truly Existent." (§11)

The impossibility of denomination, that is, is the answer to the problem of God's knowability through name and through vision. The transition between the two cited passages in *Exodus* is justified in terms of the concept whereby to know is to give a name, and giving a name is to know; or, at least, the impossibility of giving a name coincides with unknowability:

> "καὶ μὲν εἰ ἄρρητον καὶ ἀπερινόητον καὶ ἀκατάληπτον "(§15).[141]

---

[139] Runia, *art. cit.* (n.34) 82-89.

[140] *Mut.* 11.

[141] Cf. *Somn.* II.67; *Leg.* 6. Cf. Dawson, *op. cit.* (n.55) 90-92. The consequentiality between God's unknowability and the absence of name is studied by Runia, *art. cit.*(n.34): "consequent upon Being's unknowability is the fact that He has no 'proper name' (ὄνομα κύριον)" (p.76). Runia upholds the inadequacy of those who, in Philo's discussion of God's names, see an intentional interplay between the two uses of the 'proper name' , with oscillations from one meaning to the other; or, instead, reference of the name κύριος to the Tetragrammaton. "Philo's thesis is straightforward: because God as he announces to Moses in *Ex*.3.14 is ὁ ὤν, he cannot be legitimately and properly named. Implicit at this point is the Platonist argument, derived from the theological reflection on the first and second hypotheses of the *Parmenides*, that any name or attribute adds to Being. A name entails predication, which necessarily involves a measure of plurality and -the aspect that Philo will later stress (§27)- a degree of relationality" (p.77). Runia then refers to the negative attributes which alone pertain to the Divinity.

However, to approach God and to yield to his will, a name, albeit
improper, is necessary (§13). Hence, the mediation of the name. His
true name was not revealed to anyone,

> "I appeared" -He says- "to Abraham, to Isaac and to Jacob as God Almighty,
> but my name the Lord I did not make myself known to them"(Ex. 6.3). If
> the terms of the hyperbaton were reversed, the order of discourse could be:
> "My proper (κύριος) name I did not reveal to Thee," but, He implies, only
> the substitute, and that for the reasons I have already mentioned. So
> impossible to name indeed is the Existent that not even the Potencies who
> serve Him tell us a proper name." (13-14)[142]

It can perhaps be hypothesized that, beside the Platonic echoes referred to by
Runia, a significant influence is exercised by the refusal to give a name, in the
sense of posing limits and measure, which runs through most Hebrew literature.
Beginning with Ex.3.14, but with reference also to other biblical passages, there is
an extension from the refusal of giving a name to God, to that of every excess in
terms of determinations and limiting attributions. Concerning these themes, see
F. Calabi, art. cit. (n.134).

As regards the power of names, in a perspective which clearly has nothing to
do with Philo's discourse, which, however, includes the theme of names as
symbols, and where knowledge of the name is the way to a superior reality,
whereby if one possesses the key to understand the world, and has the name of
the gods has access to the gods, cf. J. Dillon, 'The magical Power of Names in
Origen and Later Platonism' in The Golden Chain: Studies in the Development
of Platonism and Christianity (Aldershot Hampshire, 1990). On the nature of
God in Philo and in His being ἀκατονόμαστος ἄρρητος ε κατὰ πάσας ἰδέας
ἀκατάληπτος, cf. Dillon, 'The Nature of God in the Quod Deus" in Winston,
Dillon, op. cit. (n.26) 217 ff. where a comparison is drawn with Albinus' theses.
According to Dillon (p.219) Albinus claims that, for Plato, God is "all but
indescribable (μικροῦ δεῖν καὶ ἄρρητον), but, further on, God is said to be ἄρρητος
God is ineffable and comprehensible only through the intellect, as species and
genera are not predicable of Him. He is "above qualification". These are
Aristotelian principles; there is nothing, therefore, of non-Hellenic. Philo's
position is analogous: "Philo is able to draw on a tradition of scholastic
discussion as to the apprehensibility of God which Albinus is also reflecting. The
precise identity of this source is beyond our knowledge [...] the argument, at any
rate, is conducted entirely in terms of Greek philosophy (p.221). Cf. also Dillon,
'The Transcendence of God in Philo: some possible sources' in The Golden
Chain cit. 5-6.

[142] The κατάχρησις theme in these passages has been thoroughly gone into by
Runia, art. cit. (n.34) 75-91, who sees in it a notion drawn from rhetorical theory
applied in a theological sense. Runia extends his discussion to the use of
κατάχρησις in other treatises by Philo, identifying in them a hard line next to a
soft line. Next to the indication of a word's incorrect or generic use, of a bold
metaphor, there is a technical use of the term which is theorized for example by
Quintilian, so that "the term κατάχρησις " should only be used to describe the
deliberate misuse of a word in order to represent a meaning for which no correct

God is not knowable in his essence, and his name is not revealed to us even through his Powers. The true hiatus, which, owing to man's limitations, is insuperable, is therefore that of the name:

> " think it not then a hard saying that the Highest of all things should be unnamable when His word (λόγος) has no name (ὄνομα) of its own which we can speak. And indeed if He is unnamable He is also inconceivable and incomprehensible"(§15).

The reasoning is circular and concludes what is contained in paragraphs 9-10, where the impossibility of denomination stems from unknowability;[143] or better, man' s non-knowledge of God lies in the name:

> "I appeared [...] my proper name I did not reveal."

Here, the contrast is not so much between sight and listening, as it is between sight and name. True knowledge consists in naming, not in seeing or in listening .

7.4. *Symbols contained in Names*

Notwithstanding the impossibility of giving a name, yet, a name is necessary in order to follow the divine will (§13). In this connection, the name (improper) becomes a vehicle of listening, in the sense of yielding to the divine will.[144] That the capacity to know implies assigning names is also stressed in §63, where Adam is distinguished from other created beings precisely because of this capacity:

---

word is available"(p.84). Thus a technical use of the term which Runia analyzes in a series of philonic passages. The examples adduced by the author are in turn examined by J. Whitaker, 'Catachresis and Negative Theology: Philo of Alexandria and Basilides' in S. Gersh, Ch. Kannengiesser (edd.), *Platonism in Late Antiquity*, Christianity and Judaism in Antiquity, Ch. Kannengiesser Series Editor vol.8 (Notre Dame, 1992) 61-82, which is extremely critical of Runia's thesis.

[143] Cf. H.A.Wolfson, *Philo: Foundations of religious Philosophy in Judaism, Christianity and Islam*, (Cambridge Mass. 1947) 2.120. See also Runia, *art. cit.* (n.34) 78-79.

[144] On the consequentiality between listening to the divine word and yielding to his will, see *Mut.* 200. Conversely, some listen to divine words in a negative way, opposing them, such as Balaam. See *Mut.* 202-209.

"παρὰ Μωυσεῖ δὲ αἱ τῶν ὀνομάτων θέσεις ἐνέργειαι πραγμάτων εἰσὶν
ἐμφαντικώταται, ὡς αὐτὸ τὸ πρᾶγμα ἐξ ἀνάγκης εὐθὺς εἶναι τοὔνομα καὶ
(τοὔνομα καὶ) καθ' οὗτίθεται διαφέρειν μηδέν."[145]

In this light,

> "such changes of name are signs of moral values, the signs small, sensible,
> obvious, the values great, intelligible, hidden."[146]

The adding of a letter hides deep meanings, it indicates a change
in *status* and relationship with God, modifications in the way to God.
Even only one letter can conceal in itself a profound reality. Symbols
are contained in names (§69) and each letter encloses a profound
reality, the cipher of which can be given by its numeric value. The
function of letters is evidenced, for example, by "a" , the sister of unity,
whereby all things begin and end. One sole letter causes everything to
be modified, together with the positions of the soul (*Q. G.III.43*). In
parallel, the adding of a "r" to Sarah's name indicates a profound
reality, as

> "illud enim (elementum r) quod unius elementi additamentum putatur
> esse, totam armoniam genuit. [147]

The gift of God, therefore, does not consist in the changing of
names as such, but in improving the character to which the name
changes allude, beneath which truth is hidden. Herein lies the
foundation of those interpretations which seem

> "to fall short in property if taken literally, while really it is a symbol of the
> nature- truth which loves concealment."[148]

Names, therefore, indicate reality; but, in the case of God's name
and that of his Powers, man seeks in vain to know them properly (§14).
Given the correspondence between names and things, the proper name
indicates the essence of God that man cannot know. This is why God
did not reveal it.

Precisely those name changes which indicate reality introduce a
'vision of God' notion which is in apparent contrast with what has been
claimed so far. Paragraph 82, in fact, speaks of Israel, he who sees

---

[145] *Cher.* 56; cf. *Congr.* 44.
[146] *Mut.* 63-65
[147] *Q.G.* III.53; see *Mut.* 77 ff.
[148] *Mut.* 60; cf. *Cont.* 78.

God; even though, presumably, what Israel sees is a Power (see §15). Thus it is in §16:

"φαντασίαν ἔλαβε. Διὸ λέγεται "ὤφθης οὐ τὸ ὄν, ἀλλὰ κύριος οἷον ἐφάνη ὁ βασιλεύς, ἐξ ἀρχῆς μὲν ὤν, οὔπω δὲ τῇ ψυχῇ γνωριζόμενος."

Φαντασία is often spoken of, which certainly has the same root as φαίνω, but indicates something different from vision proper: an image, apparition, representation, also vision, but as in a dream, like a phantom.   Thus, Abraham's is not a vision of God, but a 'representation', 'image' of a Power (as in a mirror?).   However it is said that not Being 'was seen', but the Lord, and here the term used is "ὄφθη". Again, in §18 "φανείς, δ' ὁ ἄρχων" confers a still higher gift on him who sees and hears him (ἀκροατὴν καὶ θεατήν). He says (φάσκων) "I am Ty God"(θεός) . God appears to he who listens and sees, and speaks to him. Again, listening and sight are brought together by mediation of the word of God who presents himself as θεός. The word (λόγος) teaches that what is spoken of is not the world of which he is δημιουργός and θεός, but of human souls.

"His will is to be called the Lord and Master (κύριος καὶ δεσπότης) of the bad, the God (θεός) of those who are on the way to betterment, but of the best and most perfect both at once God and Lord (κύριος ὁμοῦς καὶ θεός)."

Once again, there appears the notion of 'being called'; that is, the designation whereby men call God, to whom different names will be attributed depending on the level of the interlocutor. Therefore, not God's "proper" name, but names that are improper, instrumental and, in a way, substitutive of the real name which cannot be said.

7.5. Examples of Haraz

Paragraph 19 indicates a series of lengthy quotations which are introduced as they contain the terms θεός, κύριος, δεσπότης; quotations, therefore, which are terminologically drawn together in a form recalling *haraz*. Such quotations aim at exemplifying Philo's thesis relative to the various forms by which God manifests himself to man, according to the latter's level of progress

"a man is God's as His possession (κτῆμα) , God is man 's to be his glory and assistance. If thou wouldst have God as thy heart's portion (κλῆρος), first become thyself a portion worthy for Him to take."(§26)

God, therefore, as man's possession, which would imply a
relationship of immediacy and of abandonment of transcendence;
man's "possessing" God, his "grasping" Him.[149]   However, it is
immediately made clear that even this wording is improper,

> "for the Existent, considered as existent is not relative [...] But the
> Potencies which He has projected into creation to benefit what He has
> framed are in some cases spoken of as in a sense relative."

Once again, what is improper in reference to God, can be said of
the Powers. If first the impossible relationship between God and man
was a relationship of vision-knowledge, it is now a relationship of
possession, albeit with due clarification as to the meaning of
possession.   On a different plane, reference is again made to the
relationship between God, the Powers, and man, which had been
touched upon with regard to vision and name.

7.6. *Terminological Analogies*

Beginning with §39, argumentation does not proceed by following
the same order as that of the biblical text, id est, context order; but by
pursuing analogies among different meanings. Looking at the different
types of transition used by Philo which we have mentioned in the first
part, we see that there follows a linking of passages referring one to the
other on the basis of conceptual, but also terminological, analogies. In
particular, passages are analyzed wherein the term εὐαρεστεῖν
appears; where, however, there is a distinction between being pleasing
to God and being pleasing before God.[150] Variation in the term θεῷ
with respect to ἐνώπιον αὐτοῦ modifies the meaning of the common
term: εὐαρεστεῖν, which appears in all the quoted passages. In this
process, the meaning of a common term is echoed by other terms, thus
undergoing modifications of its own, while the other terms themselves
become an essential part of the first.   This brings about an
interpretative shift of the passages, whereby *Gen.* 48.15 embraces both

---

[149] A lack of mediations which is stressed in §53 in respect to God's benefits and
to the covenant between God and man.

[150] Cazeaux, *op. cit.* (n.21) 498 explains the distinction between being "pleasing
to" and "pleasing before" in terms of the distinction between Lord and God.
God's transcendence and providentiality and , as regards man, the need to not
only orient himself towards elevation but also towards action (§39-46). In a way,
we could be dealing with parallel planes within a unitary exegesis.

concepts, therefore extending the notion present in the simple wording "to be pleasing to God."

> "Be well pleasing before Me" (*Gen*.17.1), that is, "be well pleasing not to Me only but to My works."(§40)

Thus, the expression

> "Thou shalt do what is well pleasing before the Lord thy God"(*Dt*. 12.28), meaning do such things as shall be worthy to appear before God, and when seen to be approved by Him, and such deeds are these commonly extended to our fellow-men." (§42)[151]

Paragraph 46 concludes the argumentation on God's work of creation as an act of His goodness. Passage 17.1 is taken up again, clarifying the following verse which is closely linked to the first in terms of its consequentiality: "after saying: "be well pleasing before Me", He adds further "and become blameless". There is a difference in validity between "positive well-doing and avoidance of sin". (§48). Going back to the claims in §36 in reference to human imperfection, two assumptions are posited: the impossibility of there being a perfectly good, just and wise man, and the need to content oneself with the absence of wickedness and vice. Paragraph 54 continues the analysis of *Gen*.17, analyzing the verse which immediately follows. Again, the accent is on God's immutability and inalterability as opposed to man's limits, of which Abraham becomes aware before the words of God. Abraham's falling before God, the voluntary falling of a man who is docile before divine guidance, represents the fall of every human faculty which is not sustained by the divine will. The " fall on his face", of which the biblical text speaks, is interpreted by Philo through an explanation which is absent in *Gen*.17.3: a falling on the sensations, on the word, on the mind. The face, that is, is broken down into its component elements so as to negate any human autonomy within the ambit of the sensorial, of expression and of intelligence. Every cognitive and verbal human form is strictly dependent on God and, once more, the impossibility for man to know and to speak, when God does not give him faculty to do so, is stressed. More than the human impossibility of knowing God - given the incommensurability between God and man, and given the character of unknowability which pertains to God - the theme here is that of the impossibility for man to autonomously activate any faculty; a theme which is amply developed

---

[151] Cf. Filone di Alessandria, *op. cit.* (n.75) 322 n.28.

in many other treatises, for example in *De Cherubin* and in *De Congressu eruditionis gratia*. With respect to the biblical text, Philo strains the concept of human limits, together with man's passivity before divine initiative. Again, it is claimed that God does not manifest himself directly, but through mediation, through the benefits which he dispenses and through the word (§59). What is again affirmed is God's non-designateability, invisibility and impossibility of being indicated (ἄδεικτον); God who manifests himself saying "And I", and adds: "Behold my covenant". Again, unknowability pertains to God, more than to man's limits, and God manifests himself through his benefits or through the word. The relationship is either mediated by the created world, or it is an immediate relationship, in which God reveals himself

"κλῆρον ἀποφήνας τῶν λαμβανόντων ἑαυτόν, οὓς εὐθέως καὶ προσρήσεως ἑτέρας ἠξίωσε."

7.7. The Name Changes

Here begins the treatise proper on name changes which stem from the verse in *Gen*.17.5: "Thy name shall not be called Abram," we read, "but Abraham", and by interpreting the names of Abraham, Sarah and Jacob, and through the etymological explanation of the names of Joseph, Benjamin, etc., the concept is reaffirmed whereby names contain symbols (§69). In the case of Abraham, for example, the addition of a letter indicates a change in status and in acquisitions: in place of the knowledge of astronomy, the science of divine and human things, and of their causes. An "a", that is, alludes to the acquisition of superior knowledge and of virtue.[152] The adding of a "r" to Sarah's name indicates a transition from specific to generic virtue.[153] If for Abraham and Sarah name changes consisted in the addition of a letter; in the case of Jacob and Israel, as for other figures who will be cited further on, change consists in the acquisition of a completely new name which is added to the first without excluding it, once and for all, in a continuous wavering between non definitely acquired states. Jacob becomes Israel=he who sees God, through exercise, through continuous

[152] See *Q.G.* III.43
[153] See *Q.G.* III.53, where it says that r equals 100. Further on, however, the text speaks of 200, since r is doubled. It is worth remembering that the Hebrew r equals 200. For the arithmological value of r and 100, see *Q.G* III.56. Cf. *Mut.* 77 ff. In the *LXX* Sara becomes Sarra. In the *massorah* שׂרי becomes שׂרה. See M. Harl (ed.), *La Bible d'Alexandrie, La Genèse* (Paris 1986) 171n.

and successive attempts which bring him to the vision of God; a state, however, which is neither continuous nor definitive.

In a way, the introduction of Jacob-Israel closes the matter, which was begun with God's appearing to Abraham. Reference is now to τοῦ τὸν θεόν ὁρῶντος (§81), to τὸν ὄντα δυνήσεται θεωρεῖν ὀξυδερκῶς, and to ἐννοματωθῆναι πρὸς τὴν τοῦ μόνου θέας ἀξίου τηλαυγῆ κατανόησιν (§82).[154]

As in the first paragraphs, there are terms indicating vision, and others that allude to noetic understanding. Certainly, it is not a question of antithetical terms, but of the use of an incomplete terminology in its individual constituents which, through the combining of various terms, succeeds in conveying an idea (albeit partial and improper) of the type of knowledge reached, each in a specific way, by Abraham and Jacob; the former through teaching, the latter through exercise (§83). Isaac's case is different. Being self-taught, he draws all instruction from within himself and

"goes on its way from the first equal and perfect like an even number" (§88).

Therefore, he does not undergo a name change.[155] Nor is there a name change for Benjamin indicating development. From the beginning, Benjamin has two names that co-exist and display two aspects; that is, two interpretations of a reality, without there being any progress, as with the Patriarchs, in whom there is moral progress, or with Joseph, in whom progress develops in terms of a before and after; that is, change linked to temporality. Benjamin shares an affinity with Joseph, in so far as in the two of them the two names indicate two aspects of one and the same nature.[156]

Exegesis, centred on the etymology of names, is also directed to other biblical figures. I refer in particular to explanations given of the names of Ruben and Simeon, for which the roots of seeing and listening - recurrent to such a large extent in the entire treatise - are recalled. Significant is the role of listening, in reference to Simeon and Levi (§200):

---

[154] Cf. *Fug.* 208.

[155] Unlike Abraham and Sarah, whose name changes indicate progress, Isaac has one name, Moses three. Cf. Runia, *art. cit.* (n.34) 82.

[156] Polynomia can indicate the different potentialities and characteristics of a personage, but also a different level of perfection, or of regression, or the sign of an imperfection, or positive and negative aspects of the same person. Cf. Nikiprowetzky, *art. cit.* (n.32) 122-123 n.

"blending the two natures he [Moses] makes them one, bearing the stamp of a single form, and unites hearing with action."[157]

7.8. Bringing together two or more passages

Etymological research, linked to the double name given to a single figure, such as Jethro and Raguel - albeit with the specificity of Philo's explanations - recall similar *midrash* exegeses. Equally present in Rabbinic research is the attempt to give explanations of a biblical figure's different attributes. The problem is addressed by Philo in reference to Moses, to whom various appellatives are attributed in various situations.[158] The non-fortuitous nature of names and the need to explain name changes which occur in the *Bible* are repeated and clearly expressed. Abraham's name comprises a symbolism bearing on articulated language (τὸν προφορικὸν λόγον), the intellect (νοῦς), the excellence of the sage's intellect.[159]

> "This is how we have learned to regard the story of Abraham. Literally (λόγῳ) his name was changed, actually (ἔργῳ) he changed over from nature-study to ethical philosophy and abandoned the study of the world to find a new home in the knowledge of its Maker, and from this he gained piety, the most splendid of possessions." (§76)

We have, then, a confluence of word, intellect and ἀρετή.

The close connection between word and intellect is also present in Moses and Aaron, in reference to whom - after a distinction is made between Israel and Ishmael, vision and listening, and between those who hear with honest mind and those others who do not (§204) - the word's function in expressing holy things grasped by the intellect (§207-208), and the wish that listening to God's word may continue for ever (§209) are clarified. Bringing together two passages, one from *Gen.* 17.18 (referred to Abraham), the other from *Dt.* 33.6 (referred to Jacob)[160] clarifies the complementary nature of education and predisposition in acquiring virtue. What justifies paralleling the aforementioned passages is the presence in both of them of a sole term: ζήτω which can institute comparison. Similarly, a chain of quotations, reciprocally clarifying one another, develop around the term οὗτος. In

---

[157] Filone di Alessandria, *op. cit.* (n.75) 376,n.134.
[158] See *Mut.* 125-129. Cf. Runia, *art. cit.* (n.34) 58-59; Nikiprowetzky, *art. cit.* (n. 32)
[159] See Filone di Alessandria, *op. cit.* (n.75) 331 n.40.
[160] In the biblical text it is Moses who speaks. The passage of Jacob's benediction in *Gen.* 49.3 sounds differently.

the following pages this concept will be examined in greater detail; what is of interest here is the theme of spontaneity, whereby a series of gifts are showered upon man. Said theme is taken up again in §252 and ff. in reference to spontaneous learning and the possession of faculties independent of any teaching: that is, natural faculties and virtues. Once more, there is the distinction between knowledge and virtue acquired through exercise or learning, beginning, that is, with the human will, and knowledge and virtue deriving directly from God by his will:

> "the earthly food is produced with the co-operation of husbandsmen, but the heavenly is sent like the snow by God the solely self-acting, with none to share his work."(258-259)

These, then, are spontaneous goods; produced not by a specifically applied art, but the fruit of a self-sufficient nature, deriving directly from

> "Him who sheds the gift of prudence in rich abundance,whose grace waters the universe" (§260).

De Mutatione concludes precisely on the theme of the spontaneity of virtue and the source of knowledge. The author restates the theme, which underpins his entire treatise, of the direct or mediated knowledge of God. However, as we have seen, divine gifts are so vast and boundless as to transcend man's capacity to receive them (§219).[161]

De Mutatione, which begins with the theme of God's apparition to Abraham, closes on Abraham's relationship with God at the moment in which "the Lord went up from Abraham." From the 'vision' of God to his unknowability and ineffability, and, concomitantly, to the knowability of the Powers and the possibility of naming them improperly, through a long process of exemplification, from the changing of names and the introduction of etymological explanations aimed at designating different forms of relationship with God, up to

---

[161] In Philon d' Alexandrie, *De Mutatione Nominum*, introduction, traduction et notes par R. Arnaldez (Paris 1964) 136 n.1, in these words Arnaldez identifies the description of mystical life. There remains to be demonstrated -in my opinion- that here reference is not made to superior beings, incorporeal entities. For Runia, *art. cit.* (n.34) 81 "Philo thinks here not only of angels and departed souls such as Enoch (§34) but especially of Moses who entered the 'darkness' of invisible and immaterial being (§7) and no doubt also of Isaac who is born 'in the other year' (*Gen.* 17.21), i.e. in the incorporeal and intelligible realm (§267)".

the moment in which the disciple detaches himself from his master in the act of perfection (§270).

Summing up

Before setting direct textual comparisons to introduce hermeneutic rules mentioned, I would like to summarize rapidly what I have said until now:
starting with the verse in *Gen.*17.1:

"Abraham became ninety-nine and the Lord was seen by Abraham and said to him, 'I am thy God' "

Philo has introduced the theme of God's 'vision'. From a distinction between sensible vision and vision with the soul's eyes, he goes on to discuss the impossibility of seeing God with whatever human faculty. Philo's argumentation, thus, shifts from the impossibility of seeing God through the eyes of the senses to that of seeing God in general; from man's impossibility of knowing God to God's unknowability and ineffability; from vision to saying; from the impossibility of seeing God to that of giving him a name and, contextually, to the possibility of 'seeing' and 'giving an improper name' to the Powers. Such shifts are partially due to "exegetic constraint": the need to explain the biblical text through a series of conceptual concatenations of even distant passages. It is true, in fact, that *De Mutatione* follows (except for the leap from *Gen.* 17.5 to 17.15) the development of the biblical text. It is also true that discussion is supported by passages from *Exodus* and other passages from *Genesis* that introduce the aforementioned shifts. There is certainly an ample use of quotations which are drawn together but not inglobed in the Philonic text; quotations, that is, of the first type with respect to the distinction introduced at pp. 94ff. An example of a veritable shower of quotations, which in their mutual approximation, constitute the framework of the discussion, appears in paragraphs 19 and following. They seem, moreover, to be quotations attributed to Moses, and therefore endowed with full authority, and as such presented in the text's intangibility as quotations "between inverted commas", non modifiable, that is, and seen in relation to the departure text. In parallel, literal and allegorical interpretations are co-present, together with shifts between various interpretations within the same argumentation. In respect to Runia's explanations relative to conceptual and terminological transitions, the ambit here seems to be that of conceptual transitions. However, there appear other argumentative forms which seem to rest on other types of interpretative rules. On one hand, there are references to forms of analogy which point to elements external to the biblical text, such as the sciences (§5); on the other, *a fortiori* argumentations which recall the rule of *qal vahomer* (§10-11;15);[162] on the other, reference to hyperbaton: the inversion of terms (§13), and yet on the other, interpretations relative to terms duplications which are to be explained (§19), in what appears to be - but is not - a redundancy. Given the quantity of interpretative forms employed, forms which recur throughout *De Mutatione*, and not only in the passages which I have analyzed so far, I will attempt to provide some pertinent examples. As already stated, great caution is required in identifying possible interpretative "rules", and often I merely suggest possible analogies with rules typical of Greek rhetoric or of Rabbinic exegesis.

8. Interpretative procedures

8.1. *Ghezerà shavà*

Analogies surface with *ghezerà shavà* (albeit with the limits I have mentioned)*:

§106-107 and then 110: an analogy based on the term Madian. *Ex.* 2.16, *Ex.* 18 and *Num.* 25.1-5 are drawn together. *Num.* 25.1-15 speaks of the daughters of Moab and Madian, with whom Israel commits acts that arouse the ire of God. *Ex.* 18 and *Ex.* 2.16 speak of Jethro, priest of Madian, who had seven daughters; a man, as can be evinced from his name, who honours judgement and justice. The two passages are drawn into close perspective: the daughters represent the forces of irrationality who are defeated by justice and intellect, and, as in the case of Beelfegor (Baal Peor) where the forces of irrationality are beaten and defeated, similarly Jethro's seven daughters, by means of the intellect, reach the divine word. Why is there a connection between the two cited passages? In both cases, the forces of irrationality, represented by a relationship with Madian, are vanquished. The episode referred in *Numbers* concerns, however, the Midianites, not Jethro. What element prompts selection of the passage in question? Can we think of an approximation based on the presence, in both

---

162 Cf. Runia, *art. cit.* (n.34) 78.
* I am most grateful to Giuseppe Laras, with whom I have discussed these passages, and who has given me both precious advice and precious doubts.

passages, of the name Madian? Interpretation of the name will continue in §110, where the reference is to *Ex.* 2.16. A slight interpretative shift occurs: Madian is no longer "elimination and selection consequent upon judgement", but "discernment and justice". The two interpretations refer to different passages, even if they are connected. Various interpretations bearing on a term, or on the various meanings of a term, are presented; a procedure recalling R. Eliezer's rule 32. However, here in Philo it is possible to think of the many interpretations which approach, without excluding one another. In the same way, there are various coexisting explanations of a term, or of a passage, in reference to the annunciation of Sarah's pregnancy (§141-142) or to Abraham's laughter and faith (§154-155; 175-180; 188-192) or to Leah (§254).

Going back to the analysis of Jethro and Madian: consequent upon a judgement, Raguel, the shepherd of the flock, eliminated the negative forces. Where do we learn this? By analogy with the passage in *Numbers*, where the Israelite and the woman of Madian are killed by Finees (Pinheas). As, in this case, Finees took the pointed spear and killed passion, similarly in the first case, to speak of Raguel,[163] Madian's shepherd, means defeating the forces of irrationality. In fact, *Ex.* 2.16 explains that the seven daughters (the forces of irrationality) are defeated by the divine word. The attempt, then is to explain *Ex.* 18 through *Numbers*, returning then to *Exodus* (2.16). In the interpretation of the passage in *Numbers*, men

> "initiated in the unholy rites of Baal Peor [...] flood the ruling mind and sink it to the lowest depths"

but then intellect is succoured by the "man of peace", Finees. The word "daughters" appears, which is also present in *Ex.* 2.16, where Jethro has seven "daughters". It is possible, then, that the comparison between the two passages, besides the term Madian, is constructed also in relation to θυγατέρες (בנות) ; a term present in both passages, even if Philo appears not to dwell on it.

Paragraphs 201-210 compare passages which can be linked through two terms which appear respectively in *Gen.* 17.18, in *Ex.* 6.26, in *Ex.* 6.27 (οὗτος), and in *Ex.* 17.18, in *Dt.* 33.6 (ζήτω). Thus, with its simultaneous presentation of the two terms, *Gen.* 17.18 could constitute

---

[163] As regards the many names that are attributed to Jethro, who in the *massorah* is also called Reuel and Ieter, also the *chachamim* question themselves and seek explanations.

an interpretative hinge with other passages that contain one or the other of the two terms. The basic role of the terms in question is stressed by Philo himself, who points to the non fortuitous use of the demonstrative pronoun:

> "In neither of these cases must we suppose that the words are used carelessly and that the demonstrative pronouns served no other purpose than to indicate the names" (§207).

It is interesting to note that comparison, on the basis of the demonstrative, originates from the use, in all the passages cited, of the term οὗτος in the *LXX*. In the *massorah*, instead, the demonstrative is missing in *Gen.*17.18, and, while זה appears in *Dt.* 21.20, *Ex.* 6.26 speaks of הוא, and *Ex.* 6.27 of הם.

8.2. *Other Procedures*

Another example of verbal-analogy procedure appears in §264-265 (καιρός). Analogies drawn from nature or from examples of daily life, and therefore non terminological, can be found in § 5; 106; 122; 161; 246.   Such analogies do not draw comparisons between biblical passages, but between procedural modes in Philo, in the *Bible*, and in other ambits.[164] A relationship based on proportion is in §229.   In other passages, Philo utilizes *a fortiori* reasoning - even though not always expressed in the *topos* form - which recall *qal vahomer* and, in parallel, *a minore ad maius* and *a maiore ad minus* procedures: §10-11; 15; 46; 165; 217; 243; 258,[165] while §13 contains an example of hyperbaton[166] explicitly recalled.   This is an inversion in word order, unlike the inversion in §110 which constitutes a shift in the order of the biblical passages.[167]   It is an inversion which is constructed beginning with the co-presence of two terms, or of two names, apparently referred to the same reality: God.   However, as we have seen, although the subject of the relationship (God) constitutes a sole reality, various are the realities which are alluded to (from the standpoint of the relationship between God and man).   In a way, therefore, it can be said that the two terms

---

[164] Such comparisons are amply present also in Greek philosophical literature, for example in Plato.

[165] Cfr. Conley, *art. cit.* (n.58) 173 who speaks of ἐκ τὸ μᾶλλον καὶ ἧττον , recalling Greek rhetoric.

[166] Cf. Runia, *art. cit.* (n.34) 76-77.

[167] Cf. Radice, *op. cit.* (n.75) 346 n.69.

(κύριος and θεος) indicate two realities. the double denomination thus is not redundant,[168] as is clarified in §19.

That two terms, or two expressions, indicate different realities, is attested to also in §41, where it is clarified that analogous expressions - "pleasing to God" and "pleasing before God" - have different meanings, as in §125, relative to the name of Moses. The use of two, even similar, expressions, or the use of various names for a character, are not fortuitous, but are always motivated. In parallel, an apparently strange expression is not fortuitous either, and is to be interpreted since it possesses a meaning that is not immediately evident.[169] Analysis of the particular use of an unusual expression; or, instead, drawing deductions from the repetition of a term in the same text, recall, respectively, R. Eliezer's rules 16 and 10.

The inversion procedure, not so much of terms, as of parts of passages,[170] is referred to by Daube,[171] who cites seres

"a verse, at first sight illogical, might be made logical be re-arrangement of its parts" (p. 27).

For Daube, albeit with differences, seres could derive from ἀναστροφή

"an alteration of the order of phrases and clauses in Homer with a view to arriving at the deeper meaning of the poet" (p. 31).

Closely linked to these procedures is the method whereby

"a word which should be referred both to what precedes and to what follows is "a word without a hekhreah" (p.36)

---

[168] Cf. Cazeaux, op. cit. (n.21) 484-487; 492.

[169] Cf. §177; 253, where Philo ponders a precise word which appear pleonastic. But nothing is pleonastic in the Bible (cf. Conf. 143). Concerning the verse in question, it may be noted that in the massorah there appears not a strengthening, but an adversative element: אבל. In the LXX there is val referred however, to the clause concerning Ishmael, after which there is a caesura. For an interpretation of the passage cf. Harl, op. cit. (n.153) 172. For explanations of apparent anomalies, contradictions and synonymies, see Daniélou, op. cit. (n.29) 124. Cf. also Runia, art. cit. (n.34) 80. The principle, according to which no word in a text is superfluous, and that therefore it is always necessary to seek the reason for words which apparently are read as useless repetitions, is typical of midrash literature. Cf.A. Ravenna, 'Introduzione' in Commento alla Genesi (Bereshit Rabbâ) (Torino 1978) 15.

[170] Cf. Donini, art. cit. (n.88) 114-116.

[171] art. cit. (n.47) 27-44.

a procedure in a way which can be traced back to σύνθεσις and διαίρεσις (p.39). Parallels among procedures, however, must not according to Daube - lead us to neglect distinctions:

> "in the first place, whereas in the Greek and Latin ones, from the formal point of view, the word in question readily goes with either what precedes it or what follows it, in the majority of the Rabbinic cases, only one division accords with good grammar (...). In the second place, with the probable exception of the sophists, a Greek or Latin grammarian would normally plump for one of the two alternatives (...) the Rabbis in the half a dozen cases without *hekhreah* connect the word both with the preceding and with the following clauses at the same time" (p.42).

The problem is addressed, with regard to Philo, by Pepin[172], who notices the procedure in *De Plantatione*. In *De Mutatione* (§166) we find reference to a passage in *Genesis* (18.12) where Philo, forcing the passage, applies κύριος both to the passage that precedes and to that which follows. Here, there is no reference of the term to both passages, but an assimilation of the first to the second.[173] It is not a question of undecidability (words without *hekhreah*), but of postponing, without however presenting itself strictly as *seres*, as the procedure does not consist, properly speaking, of rearranging parts of the passage. Philo here introduces an anticipation of the following passages; an anticipation making for concatenation among various passages.[174]

Other possible similarities exist between Philonic exegesis and Rabbinic hermeneutics: interpretation enlightened by context, a rule already present among those attributed to Hillel, of which an example can be found in *Mut.* 54, where *Gen.* 17.3 is interpreted in relation to *Gen.* 17.2, cited in §52; tracing a term back to all the places where it is present, and finding regularity in the explanation of a term in all the passages in the *Bible* where it appears;[175] playing with the roots of homonymous terms which, however, in Rabbinic exegesis applies generally to terms more than to names,[176] while in Philo it is rather an etymological approach to names, not necessarily linked to homonymous roots; the use itself of allegorical explanation, *mashal*, albeit with the

---

[172] *art. cit.* (n.24) 159.

[173] Cf. Radice, *op. cit.* (n.75) 364 n.109.

[174] Cf. Runia, *art. cit.* (n.34) 74-75. Anticipation as an interpretative procedure is examined extensively by Cazeaux, *op. cit.* (n.21), who sees it as one of the basic elements of Philonic exegesis.

[175] *Mut.* 267. Cf. Runia, *art. cit.* (n.34) 80.

[176] Cf. Lieberman, *op. cit.* (n.48) 68; Strack Stemberger, *op. cit.* (n.104) 53. Etymological explanations are also a constant *topos* of Greek rhetoric, which goes back to Aristotle. Cf. Conley, *art. cit.* (n.58) 173.

caution and diffidence with which it was applied by Rabbinic exegesis.[177]

Finally, as we have seen in the first part of this chapter, the very pace of discourse which often proceeds via concatenation of quotations, recalls here and there *haraz*. I would now simply like to give two possible, even if partial, examples present in the *De Mutatione*, in §19-21 and §107-109.[178] With regard to the different relationship with biblical quotations, compared with quotations by Greek philosophers, a theme which I developed in the first part of this chapter, I here refer to some passages in the *De Mutatione*: 152; 182; 187; 189; 179; 167; 243.

In the use of quotations and in the form of commentary, the second part of the *De Mutatione* seems to be different from the first. In the first, passage-by-passage commentary is predominant, and quotations are part of the text itself. The second part, more than a commentary strictly speaking, seems an exposition of theories (even if they originate from continuous *Bible* reading), and, to a greater extent than in the first part, quotations are mainly used in support of theses.

In the second part of this chapter I have attempted to give a reading of *De Mutatione* geared to highlighting some modes of Philonic exegesis. In particular, I have endeavored to identify possible analogies with the interpretative rules of the Greek commentators, or with those of Rabbinic interpretation. A more thorough approach would of course involve a much deeper analysis, one which, in all likelihood, is not even feasible with the data available to us. Here, I am merely suggesting a research approach aimed at investigating possible hermeneutic analogies. Such an approach follows an analytical trend which, besides examining the contents of Philo's texts, also focuses on their expositive dimension, the forms of commentary and quotation, and the modes of exegesis. The underlying tenet of such an approach is that Philo's work is, first and foremost, exegetic; that his works are primarily an interpretation of the *Bible*, an attempt to explain a text that is both inexhaustible and complex. For Philo, it is to this text that

---

[177] "L'interpretazione allegorica fiorì nell'ebraismo ellenistico ad Alessandria, tuttavia i rabbini palestinesi e babilonesi la ammisero solo per i libri sapienziali come i *Proverbi*. Venne proibita per il *Pentateuco*, mentre era richiesta per il *Cantico dei Cantici*" (J.J. Petuchowsky (ed.), *Come i nostri maestri spiegano la Scrittura* (Brescia, 1984; orig. edit. Freiburg-Basel-Wien 1982) 23. But, "pour la halakha Rabbi Ishmaél a interprété allégoriquement trois passages du *Pentateuque*" (Strack, Stemberger, *op. cit.* (n.100) 53.

[178] Another example of *haraz* is, perhaps, in *Heres* 20. Cazeaux, *op. cit.* (n.21) 570 mentions a list of analogous texts which provide proof by accumulation.

interpreters can and must refer - without however hoping to grasp it in its entirety. Furthermore, they must do so with the awareness that the *Bible* represents the text that God has given to men; the text that mirrors all reality.

BIBLIOGRAPHY

Philonic Texts:

Philonis Alexandrini opera quae supersunt, voll. I-VI, ediderunt Cohn L., Wendland P., Reiter S.; vol. VII, pars I-II, *Indices ad Philoni alexandrini opera* composuit I. Leisegang I., Berlino 1896-1930, 1962(2.ed.)

Philo in ten volumes (and two supplementary volumes), with an English translation by Colson F. H., Whitaker G. H. (and Marcus R.), London–Cambridge, Mass. (1929- 1962)

Les oeuvres de Philon d'Alexandrie, publiées sous le patronage de l'Université de Lyon, par Arnaldez R., Pouilloux J., Mondésert C., Paris (1961-)

Filone di Alessandria, *La creazione del mondo*, forward, transl. and notes by Calvetti G.. *Le allegorie delle leggi*, forward, transl. and notes by Bigatti R., Reale G. (ed.), Milano (1978)

Filone di Alessandria, *L'erede delle cose divine*, forward, transl. and notes by Radice R., introduction by Reale G., Milano (1981)

Filone di Alessandria, *Le origini del male. I Cherubini, I sacrifici di Abele e di Caino, Il malvagio tende a sopraffare il buono, La posterità di Caino, I Giganti, L'immutabilità di Dio*, transl. by Mazzarelli C., introd., transl. and notes by Radice R., Milano (1984)

Filone di Alessandria, *L'uomo e Dio. Il connubio con gli studi preliminari, La fuga e il ritrovamento, Il mutamento dei nomi, I sogni sono mandati da Dio*, introd., transl., forward. and notes by Kraus Reggiani C., presented by Reale G., Milano (1986)

Filone di Alessandria, *La filosofia Mosaica. La creazione del mondo secondo Mosè*, transl. by Kraus Reggiani C., *Le allegorie delle Leggi*, transl. by Radice R., forward, notes and commentaries by Radice R., introd. by Reale G. and Radice R., Milano (1987)

Filone di Alessandria, *La migrazione verso l'eterno. L'agricoltura, La piantagione di Noè, L'ebrietà, La sobrietà, La confusione delle lingue, La migrazione*, forward by Reale G., introd., forward, and notes by Radice R., Milano (1988)

Filone di Alessandria, *Tutti i trattati del Commentario allegorico alla Bibbia*, Radice R. (ed.), in collaboration with Reale G., Kraus Reggiani C., Mazzarelli C., forward by Reale G., Milano (1994)

Filone d'Alessandria, *La vita contemplativa*, Graffigna P. (ed.), Genova (1992)

Filone Alessandrino, *De opificio mundi, De Abrahamo, De Josepho*, Kraus Reggiani C. (ed.),Roma (1979)

BIBLIOGRAPHICAL TOOLS

Goodhart H. L., Goodenough E. R., 'A General Bibliography of Philo Judaeus', in Goodenough E. R., *The Politics of Philo Judaeus: Practice and Theory*, New Haven (1938), republish. Hildesheim (1967)

Hilgert E., 'A Bibliography of Philo Studies 1963-1970', *SPh* 1 (1972) 57-71

Hilgert E., 'A Bibliography of Philo Studies in 1971, with additions for 1965-1970', *SPh* 2 (1973) 51-54

Hilgert E., 'A Bibliography of Philo Studies 1972-1973' *SPh* 3 (1974-1975) 117-125

Hilgert E., 'A Bibliography of Philo Studies 1974-1975', *SPh* 4 (1976-1977) 78-85

Hilgert E., 'A Bibliography of Philo Studies 1976-1977', *SPh* 5 (1978) 113-120

Hilgert E., 'A Bibliography of Philo Studies 1977-1978', *SPh* 6 (1979-1980)

Radice R., *Filone di Alessandria: bibliografia generale 1937-1982*, Napoli (1983)

Radice R.,Runia D.T., *Philo of Alexandria. An Annotated Bibliography 1937-1986*, Leiden (1988)

'Philo of Alexandria. An Annotated Bibliography', *SPhA* 1-8 (1989-1996)

OTHER WORKS CITED

AA.VV.,*La figure de Moïse. Ecriture et relectures*, Genève (1978)

Aalders G. J. D., *Political Thought in Hellenistic Times*, Amsterdam (1975)

Amir Y., *Die hellenistische Gestalt des Judentums bei Philon von Alexandrien*, Neukirchen, Vluyn (1983)

Barraclough R., 'Philo's Politics. Roman Rule and Hellenistic Judaism',in *ANRW* II.21.1 (1984) 506-508

Belayche N., 'Les figures politiques des messies en Palestine de la première moitié du premier siècle de notre ère', in Tollet D. (ed.),*Politique et religion* 58-74

Belkin S., *Philo and the Oral Law: the Philonic Interpretation of Biblical Law in Relation to the Palestinian Halakah*. Cambridge, Mass. (1940)

Berchman R. M., *Arcana Mundi between Balaam and Hecate: Prophecy, Divination and Magic in Later Platonism*, *SBLSPS* 28 (1989), 107-185.

Bertelli L., *L'utopia greca*, in Firpo L. (ed.), *Storia delle Idee politiche, economiche e sociali* I (1982) 463-581

Bickerman E., 'The Septuagint as a Translation', *Proceedings of the American Academy for Jewish Research*, 28 (1959), republish. in *Studies in Jewish and Christian History*, part I, Leiden (1976)

Borgen P., 'Philo of Alexandria' in M. E. Stone (ed.), *Jewish Writings of the Second Temple Period*, Assen, Philadelphia (1984)

Borgen P., 'Heavenly Ascent in Philo: an Examination of Selected Passages' in J. H. Charlesworth and C. A. Evans, *The Pseudepigrapha and Early Biblical Interpretation*, Sheffield (1993) 243-268

Borgen P., *Philo of Alexandria. An Exegete for his Time*, Leiden (1997)

Bréhier E., *Les idées philosophiques et religieuses de Philon d'Alexandrie*, Paris (1925)

Brewer D. I., *Techniques and Assumptions in Jewish Exegesis before 70 C.E.*, Tübingen (1992)

Burkhardt H., 'Inspiration der Schrift durch weisheitliche Personal Inspiration: zur Inspirationslehre Philos von Alexandrien', *Theologische Zeitschrift* , 47 (1991) 214-225

Burkhardt H.,*Die Inspiration heiliger Schriften bei Philo von Alexandrien*, Basel (1992)

Calabi F., *La città dell'oikos. La 'politia' in Aristotele*, Lucca (1984)

Calabi F., Introduzione a Flavio Giuseppe, *In difesa degli Ebrei. Contro Apione*, Venezia (1993)

Calabi F. (ed.), *Lettera di Aristea a Filocrate*, Milano (1995)

Calabi F., 'Simbolo dell'assenza: le immagini nel giudaismo', *Quaderni di storia* 41 (1995) 5-32.

Calabi F., *Lingua di Dio, lingua degli uomini: Filone alessandrino e la traduzione della 'Bibbia'*, *I castelli di Yale* 2 (1997) 95-113

Campese S., 'Misthotiké', in M. Vegetti (ed.), Platone, *La Repubblica*, libro I, Pavia (1994) 193-201

Canfora L., *Il viaggio di Aristea*, Bari (1996) 95-113

Caquot A., Hadas-Lebel M., Riaud J. (edd.), *Hellenica et Judaica: Hommage a V. Nikiprowetzky* ל'ז,Paris (1986)

Cazeaux J., 'Nul n'est prophète en son pays. Contribution à l'étude de Joseph d'après Philon' in Kenney J. P. (ed.), *The School of Moses* 41-81

Cazeaux J., *La trame et la chaîne,ou les Structures littéraires et l'Exégèse dans cinq des Traités de Philon d'Alexandrie*, Leiden (1983)

Cervelli I., 'Dalla storiografia alla memoria. A proposito di Flavio Giuseppe e Yohanan ben Zakkai', *Studi Storici* 4 (1990) 919-982

Chambronne P., 'Loi et législateur chez Philon d'Alexandrie: remarques sur la formation d'un concept judéo-hellénistique', *Cahiers du*

Centre George-Radet, Talence, Université de Bordeaux III, 4 (1984)

Chesnut G. F.,'The Ruler and the Logos in Neopythagorean, MiddlePlatonic, and Late Stoic Political Philosophy', *ANRW* II.16.2 (1978) 1310-1320

Christansen I., *Die Technik der allegorischen Auslegungswissenschaft bei Philon von Alexandrien*, Tübingen (1969)

Colafemmina C., 'Le regole ermeneutiche di Hillel', *Annali di storia dell'esegesi* (8/2 1991) 443-454

Collins J. J., *Between Athens and Jerusalem: Jewish Identity in the Hellenistic Diaspora*, New York (1983)

Compagnon A., *La seconde main ou le travail de la citation*, Paris (1979)

Conley Th. M., 'Philo's Rhetoric: Argumentation and Style' in *ANRW*. II. 21.1. (1984) 343-371

Daniélou J., *Philon d'Alexandrie*, Paris (1958)

Daube D., 'Rabbinic Methods of Interpretation and Hellenistic Rhetoric', *Hebrew Union College Annual* 22 (1949) 239-264

Daube D., 'Alexandrian Methods of Interpretation and the Rabbis', in *Festschrift Hans Lewald*, Basel (1953)

Dawson D., *Allegorical Readers and Cultural Revision in Ancient Alexandria*, Berkeley Los Angeles (1992)

Dawson D., *Cities of the Gods*, Oxford (1992)

Decharneux B.,'Mantique et oracles dans l'oeuvre de Philon d'Alexandrie' in A. Motte (ed.), *Oracles et mantique en Grèce ancienne*, Actes du colloque de Liège (Mars 1989) = *Kernos* 3 (1990) 123-133

Decharneux B., *L'ange, le devin et le prophète: chemins de la parole dans l'oeuvre de Philon d'Alexandrie dit 'le Juif'*, Bruxelles (1994)

Delatte A., *Essai sur la politique pythagoricienne*, Liège (1922)

Delling G., 'The "One who sees God" in Philo' in Greenspahn F.E., Hilgert E., Mack B. L. (edd.), *Nourished with Peace* cit. 27-41

Dillon J.,*The Middle Platonists. 80 B.C. to A.D. 220*, Ithaca, New York (1977)

Dillon J., 'The Magical Power of Names in Origen and Later Platonism' in *The Golden Chain: Studies in the Development of Platonism and Christianity*, Aldershot Hampshire (1990)

D'Ippolito G., Gallo I. (edd.), *Strutture formali dei 'Moralia' di Plutarco, Atti del 3 Convegno Plutarcheo*, Palermo (1989), Napoli (1991)

Donini P., 'Alessandro di Afrodisia e i metodi dell'esegesi filosofica' in Moreschini C. (ed.), *Esegesi parafrasi e compilazione in età tardo antica*, Napoli (1995) 107-130

Dorival G., 'A propos de la Septante', in Tollet D. (ed.), *Politique et religion* cit.

Farias D., *Studi sul pensiero sociale di Filone di Alessandria*, Pubblicazioni degli Istituti di Scienze giuridiche, economiche, politiche e sociali della Facoltà di giurisprudenza dell'Università di Messina 180, Milano (1993)

Feldman L. H., 'Josephus' Portrait of Balaam', *SPhA* 5 (1993) 48-83

Firpo L. (ed.), *Storia delle Idee politiche economiche e sociali*, I e II, Torino (1982-1985)

Gastaldi S., *Le immagini delle virtù. Le strategie metaforiche nelle 'Etiche' di Aristotele*, Alessandria (1994)

Genot Bismuth J., *Le scenario de Damas. Jérusalem Hellenisée et les origines de l'Essénisme*, Paris (1992)

Giannantoni G., *Il pensiero politico greco dopo Alessandro Magno* in Firpo L. (ed.),*Storia delle idee politiche economiche e sociali*, I (1982) 357-362

Goodenough E. R., 'The Political Philosophy of Hellenistic Kingship', *Yale Classical Studies* 1 (1928) 55-102

Goodenough E.R.,*The Politics of Philo Judaeus: Practice andTheory*, New Haven (1938), ripubbl. Hildesheim (1967)

Goulet R., *La philosophie de Moïse: essai de reconstruction d'un commentaire philosophique préphilonien du Pentateuque*, Paris (1987)

Grabbe L. L., *Etimology in Early Jewish Interpretation: the Hebrew Names in Philo*, Atlanta Georgia (1988)

Graffigna P., 'Osservazioni sull'uso del termine φαντασία in Filone d'Alessandria', *Koinonia* 16 (1992) 5-19

Greene J.T., *Balaam: Prophet, Diviner and Priest in Selected Ancient Israelite and Hellenistic Jewish Sources*, SBLSPS 28 (1989)

Greene J.T., *Balaam and his Interpreters: a Hermeneutical History of the Balaam Traditions*, Atlanta Georgia (1992)

Greenspahn F.E., Hilgert E., Mack B.L. (edd.), *Nourished with Peace. Studies in Hellenistic Judaism in memory of Samuel Sandmel*, Scholars Press Homage Series 9 (Chico, California 1984)

Hadas- Lebel M., 'Le paganisme à travers les sources rabbiniques de II et III siècles. Contribution à l'étude du syncretisme dans l'empire romain', in *ANRW* II.19.2 (1979) 397-485

Hadas-Lebel M.,'A propos des révoltes juives contre Rome', in Tollet D., *Politique et religion cit.*

Hadas-Lebel M., *Jérusalem contre Rome*, Paris (1990)

Hadot P., 'Théologie, exégèse, révélation, écriture dans la philosophie grecque' in M. Tardieu (ed.), *Les règles de l'interpretation*, Paris (1987)

Hamerton-Kelly R., Scroggs R., *Jews, Greeks and Christians: Religious Cultures in Late Antiquity, Essays in Honor of W.D.Davies*, Leiden (1976)

Hamerton-Kelly R., 'Allegory, Typology and Sacred Violence: Sacrificial Representation and the Unity of the Bible in Paul and Philo', *SPhA3* (1991) 53-70

Harl M., (ed.), *La Bible d'Alexandrie, La Genèse*, Paris (1986)

Hay D.H., 'Philo's Treatise on the Logos-Cutter', *StPh.* 2 (1973) 9-22

Hay D.M., *Politics and Exegesis in Philo's Treatise on Dreams*, SBLSPS 26 (1987)

Hay D. M., 'Philo's View of Himself as an Exegete: inspired but not Authoritative', *SPhA* 3 (1991) 40-52

Hecht R.D., *Scripture and Commentary in Philo*, SBLSP 20 (1981) 129-164

Helleman W.E., 'Philo of Alexandria on Deification and Assimilation to God', *SPhA* 2 (1990) 51-71

Hilgert E., 'The Dual Image of Joseph in Hebrew and Early Jewish Literature', *Biblical Research* 30 (1985) 5-21

Isnardi Parente M. (ed.), *La filosofia dell'ellenismo*, Torino (1977)

Jastrow M., *A Dictionary of the Targumim, the Talmud Babli and Yerushalmi, and the Midrashic Literature*, Jerushalaim (1903)

Kenney J. P. (ed.), *The School of Moses: Studies in Philo and Hellenistic Religion*, Studia Philonica Monograph Series 1, Atlanta (1995)

Koester H., 'ΝΟΜΟΣ ΦΥΣΕΩΣ: the Concept of Natural Law in Greek Thought' in *Religions in Antiquity: Essays in memory of E.R. Goodenough*, Studies in the History of Religions. Supplements to Numen 14 (1968) 521-541

Kraus Reggiani C., *Introduzione* to *De Josepho* in Kraus Reggiani C. (ed.), *De Opificio, De Abrahamo, De Josepho*, Roma (1979)

Kraus Reggiani C., 'I rapporti tra l'impero romano e il mondo ebraico al tempo di Caligola secondo la "Legatio ad Gaium" di Filone alessandrino', in *ANRW* II.21.1 (1984) 554-586

Laporte J., *Introduction* in *De Josepho*, Paris (1964)

Levison J.R., 'Two Types of Ecstatic Prophecy according to Philo', *SPhA* 6 (1994) 83-89

Levy B., *Le logos et la lettre. Philon d'Alexandrie en regard des Pharisiens*, Lagrasse (1988)

Lieberman S., *Hellenism in Jewish Palestine: Studies in the Literary Transmission Beliefs and Manners of Palestine in the I Century B.C.E.-IV Century C.E.*, New York (1950)

Mack B.L., 'Exegetical Traditions in Alexandrian Judaism; a Program for the Analysis of the Philonic Corpus' in *SPh* 3 (1974-75) 71-112

Mack B.L.,*Under the Shadow of Moses: Authorship and Authority in Hellenistic Judaism*, SBLSP (1982)

Mack B.L., 'Philo Judaeus and Exegetical Traditions in Alexandria' in *ANRW* II. 21.1.(1984) 227-271

Mack B.L., 'Decoding the Scripture: Philo and the Rules of Rhetoric', in Greenspahn F.E., Hilgert E., Mack B.L.(edd.), *Nourished with Peace cit.*

Mack B.L., 'Moses on the Mountain Top: A Philonic View ' in Kenney J.P.(ed.), *The School of Moses cit.*

Mansfeld J., 'Heraclitus, Empedocles, and others in a Middle Platonist cento in Philo of Alexandria', *Vigiliae Christianae* 39 (1985) 131-156

Mansfeld J., *Heresiography in Context. Hippolytus' Elenchos as a Source for Greek Philosophy*, Leiden (1992)

Martin J.P., 'El texto y la interpretación: la exégesis según Filón de Alejandría', *Revista Biblica* 39 (1977) 211-222

Martin J.P., 'Philo and Augustine. De civitate Dei XIV 28 and XV: Some Preliminary Observations', *StPhA* 3 (1991) 283-294

Mayer G., 'Die herrscherliche Titular Gottes bei Philo von Alexandrien', in D.-A. Koch e H. Lichtenberger (ed.), *Begegnungen zwischen Christentum undJudentum in Antike und Mittelalter: Festschrift für Heinz Schreckenberg*, Schriften des Institutum Judaicum Delitzschianum 1, Göttingen (1993) 293- 302

Michaelis W., ' ὁράω' in Kittel, *Grande Lessico del Nuovo Testamento*, 5. 316-381

142 BIBLIOGRAPHY

Mielziner M., *Introduction to the Talmud*, New York (1968)

Montanari F., 'L'erudizione, la filologia, la grammatica' in *Lo spazio letterario della Grecia antica*,1. II (Roma 1993) 271ff.

Myre A., 'La loi dans l'ordre cosmique et politique selon Philon d'Alexandrie', *Science et Esprit* 24 (1972) 217-247

Myre A., 'Les caractéristiques de la loi mosa que selon Philon d'Alexandrie', *Science et ésprit* 27 (1975) 35-69

N.G. Cohen, 'The Greek Virtues and the Mosaic Law in Philo. An Elucidation of 'De Specialibus Legibus' IV 133-135', *StPhA* (1993) 9-19

Neusner J., *A Life of Yohanan ben Zakkai. Ca 1-80 C.E.*, Leiden (1970)

Neusner J., *Development of a Legend. Studies on the Tradition concerning Yohanan ben Zakkai*, Leiden (1970)

Neusner J., *The Rabbinic Tradition about the Pharisees before 70; I. The Masters*, Leiden (1971)

Neusner J., 'The Formation of Rabbinic Judaism: Yavenh(Jamnia) from A.D. 70 to 100', in *ANRW* II.19.2 (1979) 3-42

Niehoff M., *The Figure of Joseph in Post-Biblical Jexish Literature*, Leiden (1982)

Niehoff M.R., 'What's in a Name? Philo's Mystical Philosophy of Language', *Jewish Studies Quarterly* 2 (1995) 220-252

Nikiprowetzky V., *Le commentaire de l'Ecriture chez Philon d'Alexandrie*, Leiden (1977)

Nikiprowetzky V.,' "Moyses palpans vel liniens": On some Explanations of the Name of Moses in Philo of Alexandria', in Greenspahn F. E., Hilgert E., Mack B. L. (edd.), *Nourished with Peace cit.* (117- 142)

Otte K., *Das Sprachverständnis bei Philo von Alexandrien, Sprache als Mittel der Hermeneutik*, BGBE 7 Tübingen (1968)

Parente F.,'Il giudaismo alessandrino' in Firpo L. (ed.), *Storia delle Idee politiche economiche e sociali*, II.I 289-360

Pelletier A., *Introduction* in *Lettre d'Aristée à Philocrate*, Paris (1992)

Pepin J., 'Remarques sur la théorie de l'exégèse allégorique chez Philon', *Colloque du CNRS: Philon d'Alexandrie*, Lyon(1966), Paris (1967) 131-168

Petit M., 'L'homme politique: interprète de rêves selon Philon d'Alexandrie (*De Josepho* 125) ὁ πολιτικὸς πάντως ὀνειροκριτικός ἐστιν' in Tollet D., *Politique et religion* [...] 41-54

Petuchowski J. J. (ed.), *Come i nostri maestri spiegano la Scrittura*, Brescia (1984)

Radice R., *Platonismo e creazionismo in Filone d'Alessandria*, Milano (1989)

Radice R. (ed.), Filone di Alessandria, *Tutti i trattati del commentario allegorico alla Bibbia*, Milano (1994)

Ravenna A. , 'Introduzione' in *Commento alla Genesi (Bereshit Rabbâ)*, Torino (1978)

Riaud J., 'Quelques réflexions sur les Thérapeuts d'Alexandrie à la lumière de *De vita Mosis* II.67', *SPhA* 3 (1991) 184-191

Royse J. R., 'Philo, Κύριος and the Tetragrammaton', *SPhA* 3 (1991) 167-183

Runia D. T., *Philo of Alexandria and the Timaeus of Plato*, Leiden (1986)

Runia D. T., *Exegesis and Philosophy. Studies on Philo of Alexandria*, Aldershot, Hampshire (1990)

Runia D., *The Idea and the Reality of the City in the Thought of Philo of Alexandria*, unpublished

Sandmel S., 'Some Comments on Providence in Philo', in J. L. Crenshaw and S. Sandmel (edd.), *The divine Helmsman: Studies on God's Control of Human Events presented to Lou H. Silberman*, New York (1980)

Schäublin CH., 'Homerum ex Homero' in *Museum Helveticum* (34.1977) 224-227

Schofield M., *The Stoic Idea of the City*, Cambridge (1991)

Schofield M., *Zeno of Citium's anti-utopianism*, paper given at the Conference *Le Repubbliche antiche: Platone, i Critici, gli Imitatori*, Pavia 29-30 gennaio 1997.

Shuler P. L., 'Philo's Moses and Mattew's Jesus: A comparative Study in Ancient Literature', *SPhA* 2 (1990) 86-103

Sills D., *Vicious Rumours: Mosaic Narratives in First Century Alexandria*, SBLSP 31 (1992), 684-694

Stein E., 'Die Allegorische Exegese des Philo aus Alexandreia', *Beihefte zur Zeitschrift für die altest. Wissenschaft* 51 (1929)

Strack H. L., Stemberger G., *Introduction au Talmud et au Midrash*, Paris (1986; first pub. München1982)

Terian A., 'Inspiration and Originality: Philo's Distinctive Exclamations', *SPhA* 7 (1995) 59-62

Thiselton A. C.,'The «Interpretation» of Tongues: a New Suggestion in the Light of Greek Usage in Philo and Josephus', *The Journal of Theological Studies*, 30 (1979)

Tiede D. L., 'The Charismatic figure as miracle worker', *Society of Biblical Literature. Dissertation Series* 1, Missoula (1972)

Tobin T. H., *Tradition and Interpretation in Philo's Portrait of the Patriarch Joseph*, SBLSPS 25 (1986)

Tollet D. (ed.), *Politique et religion dans le judaïsme ancien et médiéval*, Paris (1989)

Troiani L., 'Il libro di Aristea ed il giudaismo ellenistico (Premesse per un'interpretazione)', in Virgilio B.(ed.), *Studi Ellenistici* II (1987) 31-61

Troiani L., 'Giudaismo ellenistico e cristianesimo', in B. Virgilio (ed.), "Aspetti e problemi dell'ellenismo", *Studi Ellenistici* IV (1994) 187-201

Umemoto N., 'Die Königherrschaft Gottes bei Philon' in M. Hengel e A. M. Schwemer (ed.), *Königsherrschaft Gottes und himmlischer Kult in Judentum, Christentum und in der hellenistischen Welt* , Tübingen (1991) 207-256

Vegetti M., *L' Etica degli antichi*, Bari (1989)

Virgilio B. (ed.), *Studi Ellenistici* II, Pisa (1987)

Wan S.-K., 'Charismatic Exegesis: Philo and Paul compared', *SPhA* 6 (1994) 54-82

Whittaker J., 'Catachresis and Negative Teology: Philo of Alexandria and Basilides' in S. Gersh, Ch. Kannengiesser (edd.), *Platonism in Late Antiquity*, Christianity and Judaism in Antiquity Ch. Kannengiesser Series Editor vol.8, Notre Dame (1992)

Winston D., Dillon J. (edd.), *Two Treatises of Philo of Alexandria: A Commentary on De Gigantibus and Quod Deus sit immutabilis*, Brown Judaic Series 25 (Chico, California 1983)

Winston D., *Two Types of Mosaic Prophecy according to Philo*, SBLSPS 27 (1988)

Winston D., 'Aspects of Philo Linguistic Theory', *SPhA* 3 (1991) *Heirs of the Septuagint. Philo, Hellenistic Judaism and Early Christianity*, 109-125

Wolfson H.A., *Philo. Foundations of Religious Philosophy in Judaism, Christianity and Islam*, Cambridge Mass. (1962)

INDEX OF PHILONIC PASSAGES

Spec. Leg.

Virt.

INDEX OF MODERN SCHOLARS

South Florida Studies in the History of Judaism

| 240187 | Jewish Law from Moses to the Mishnah | Neusner |
| 240188 | The Language and the Law of God | Calabi |

South Florida Academic Commentary Series

243001	The Talmud of Babylonia, An Academic Commentary, Volume XI, Bavli Tractate Moed Qatan	Neusner
243002	The Talmud of Babylonia, An Academic Commentary, Volume XXXIV, Bavli Tractate Keritot	Neusner
243003	The Talmud of Babylonia, An Academic Commentary, Volume XVII, Bavli Tractate Sotah	Neusner
243004	The Talmud of Babylonia, An Academic Commentary, Volume XXIV, Bavli Tractate Makkot	Neusner
243005	The Talmud of Babylonia, An Academic Commentary, Volume XXXII, Bavli Tractate Arakhin	Neusner
243006	The Talmud of Babylonia, An Academic Commentary, Volume VI, Bavli Tractate Sukkah	Neusner
243007	The Talmud of Babylonia, An Academic Commentary, Volume XII, Bavli Tractate Hagigah	Neusner
243008	The Talmud of Babylonia, An Academic Commentary, Volume XXVI, Bavli Tractate Horayot	Neusner
243009	The Talmud of Babylonia, An Academic Commentary, Volume XXVII, Bavli Tractate Shebuot	Neusner
243010	The Talmud of Babylonia, An Academic Commentary, Volume XXXIII, Bavli Tractate Temurah	Neusner
243011	The Talmud of Babylonia, An Academic Commentary, Volume XXXV, Bavli Tractates Meilah and Tamid	Neusner
243012	The Talmud of Babylonia, An Academic Commentary, Volume VIII, Bavli Tractate Rosh Hashanah	Neusner
243013	The Talmud of Babylonia, An Academic Commentary, Volume V, Bavli Tractate Yoma	Neusner
243014	The Talmud of Babylonia, An Academic Commentary, Volume XXXVI, Bavli Tractate Niddah	Neusner
243015	The Talmud of Babylonia, An Academic Commentary, Volume XX, Bavli Tractate Baba Qamma	Neusner
243016	The Talmud of Babylonia, An Academic Commentary, Volume XXXI, Bavli Tractate Bekhorot	Neusner
243017	The Talmud of Babylonia, An Academic Commentary, Volume XXX, Bavli Tractate Hullin	Neusner
243018	The Talmud of Babylonia, An Academic Commentary, Volume VII, Bavli Tractate Besah	Neusner
243019	The Talmud of Babylonia, An Academic Commentary, Volume X, Bavli Tractate Megillah	Neusner
243020	The Talmud of Babylonia, An Academic Commentary, Volume XXVIII, Bavli Tractate Zebahim A. Chapters I through VII	Neusner
243021	The Talmud of Babylonia, An Academic Commentary, Volume XXI, Bavli Tractate Baba Mesia, A. Chapters I through VI	Neusner

243041	The Talmud of Babylonia, A Complete Outline, Part II, The Division of Women; A: From Tractate Yebamot through Tractate Ketubot	Neusner
243042	The Talmud of Babylonia, A Complete Outline, Part II, The Division of Women; B: From Tractate Nedarim through Tractate Qiddushin	Neusner
243043	The Talmud of Babylonia, An Academic Commentary, Volume XIII, Bavli Tractate Yebamot, A. Chapters One through Eight	Neusner
243044	The Talmud of Babylonia, An Academic Commentary, XIII, Bavli Tractate Yebamot, B. Chapters Nine through Seventeen	Neusner
243045	The Talmud of the Land of Israel, A Complete Outline of the Second, Third and Fourth Divisions, Part II, The Division of Women, A. Yebamot to Nedarim	Neusner
243046	The Talmud of the Land of Israel, A Complete Outline of the Second, Third and Fourth Divisions, Part II, The Division of Women, B. Nazir to Sotah	Neusner
243047	The Talmud of the Land of Israel, A Complete Outline of the Second, Third and Fourth Divisions, Part I, The Division of Appointed Times, C. Pesahim and Sukkah	Neusner
243048	The Talmud of the Land of Israel, A Complete Outline of the Second, Third and Fourth Divisions, Part I, The Division of Appointed Times, A. Berakhot, Shabbat	Neusner
243049	The Talmud of the Land of Israel, A Complete Outline of the Second, Third and Fourth Divisions, Part I, The Division of Appointed Times, B. Erubin, Yoma and Besah	Neusner
243050	The Talmud of the Land of Israel, A Complete Outline of the Second, Third and Fourth Divisions, Part I, The Division of Appointed Times, D. Taanit, Megillah, Rosh Hashannah, Hagigah and Moed Qatan	Neusner
243051	The Talmud of the Land of Israel, A Complete Outline of the Second, Third and Fourth Divisions, Part III, The Division of Damages, A. Baba Qamma, Baba Mesia, Baba Batra, Horayot and Niddah	Neusner
243052	The Talmud of the Land of Israel, A Complete Outline of the Second, Third and Fourth Divisions, Part III, The Division of Damages, B. Sanhedrin, Makkot, Shebuot and Abldah Zarah	Neusner
243053	The Two Talmuds Compared, II. The Division of Women in the Talmud of the Land of Israel and the Talmud of Babylonia, Volume A, Tractates Yebamot and Ketubot	Neusner
243054	The Two Talmuds Compared, II. The Division of Women in the Talmud of the Land of Israel and the Talmud of Babylonia, Volume B, Tractates Nedarim, Nazir and Sotah	Neusner
243055	The Two Talmuds Compared, II. The Division of Women in the Talmud of the Land of Israel and the Talmud of Babylonia, Volume C, Tractates Qiddushin and Gittin	Neusner
243056	The Two Talmuds Compared, III. The Division of Damages in the Talmud of the Land of Israel and the Talmud of Babylonia, Volume A, Tractates Baba Qamma and Baba Mesia	Neusner

South Florida-Rochester-Saint Louis Studies on Religion and the Social Order

South Florida International Studies in Formative Christianity and Judaism

HIEBERT LIBRARY

3 6877 00161 8635

B
689
.Z7
C27
1998

DATE DUE

DE 09 '05			

DEMCO 38-297